LIARS

POET SUIGENERIS

Poet Suigeneris
LIARS

Liars is a work of fiction. Names, characters, places and incidents detailed are the product of the author's imagination or used fictitiously. Any resemblance to actual persons, living or dead, events or locales thereto, are entirely coincidental.

Book Design by Poet Suigeneris
Art & Graphics Design by Poet Suigeneris
For more information, please email Poet Suigeneris on his website
metapoetica.online
Visit Poet Suigeneris on his YouTube channel: poet suigeneris
Instagram: @poet._.suigeneris [or] @Poet Suigeneris
and on X: @Suigeneris77079 or @Poet Suigeneris

Published by Spines
ISBN: 979-8-89383-913-5

This work is dedicated to Andrea Sims.

ABOUT THE AUTHOR

Poet Suigeneris is a prolific vers librist foremost and a novelist secondarily, who joined the bohemian life of the Open Mic Poetry Circuit in the mid-to-late '90s. This writer of thrillers, science fiction, and non-fiction has, for 37 years, traveled from diners to speakeasies to community theaters, self-promoting his confrontational, emotional, sexual (sometimes political) poetry and prose from speakeasies to churches; from Harrisburg, Pennsylvania, to San Francisco, California. Yet, this native New Yorker from The Bronx has remained unpublished, practicing his craft throughout his entire career. He's begun to make his reputation on social media platforms such as Instagram, Twitter, and YouTube. His Instagram Reels, dubbed as Reel Thoughts, advertise this novel and others to his faithful following, which has been growing year-to-year since 2022. The poet currently lives in a small town in central Pennsylvania.

ALSO BY POET SUIGENERIS

-POETRY-

Well After Dark

Stirred by The Libra

~FICTION~

Beyond the Pale

THE NAMELESS FACELESS GIRL SERIES

Part 1: Gray Eminence

-NON-FICTION~

R.I.P.: Re-Humanized Introducing Poet

A Novel/Suspense-thriller

written by Poet Suigeneris

Theory of Mind

In psychology, theory of mind is the ability to infer and understand another's beliefs, thoughts, intentions, and feelings, and use this information to explain and predict human behavior.

Be advised that the foregoing series of events, either mundane or tragic, connected to this ghastly tragedy, scrutinizes two years a decade apart: 2013 and 2023. Flashbacks and present-day occurrences run parallel with incremental revelations, which circle back between both years until it becomes clear what the truth is amid the lies.

The liars started to expose themselves in the spring of 2013.

CHAPTER 1

MEET KIERNAN MONTGOMERY

Kiernan Montgomery used to be COO of AgriCare, a Fortune 500 Agricultural Software Corporation based out of Boston, Massachusetts. How she became a former COO exemplifies the ironic. She was raised to believe in and detest two kinds of people in life: liars and thieves. However, as it turned out, Kiernan was exposed for being both a liar and a thief at AgriCare.

Her boyfriend in college at the time, Jake, left behind a book at her apartment. It was called *The Art of the Deal*. Donald Trump was on the cover; it was about his worldview through the scope of business. A finance and business double major at Penn State, Kiernan couldn't put the book down. It was fascinating to her; in fact, its slogan "Truthful Hyperbole" stuck with her. As she climbed the corporate ladder of success, breaking glass ceiling after glass ceiling in tow, and looking dark-haired, sexy, and green-eyed, petite in stately pantsuits while doing it, she became the first female COO at AgriCare in 2009. Her top-floor, white-walled corner office didn't have framed pictures of her children and husband on her desk, nor of her three college degrees and other honors. Instead, Kiernan lined the foyer walls into her office with black-framed color glossies of other female tech leaders like Dana DiFerdinando, CIO of Arena Pharmaceutical; Jenni Flinders, Vice President of Microsoft; Cindy McKenzie, CIO of Fox Entertainment; and Martha Heller, President of Heller Search Associates. Just to name a few, because there were only a few women in these important roles.

Kiernan sensed a pressure, not only to do her best work but to be the best after work hours and make money doing it. Her being the best was achieved, and the best in her field without question. However, AgriCare paid Kiernan forty-five cents on the dollar compared to her male counterpart and CFO Robert Klenks, which infuriated her. From her perspective, Klenks' $4.2 million annual salary was a sexist form of *Truthful Hyperbole*, which she decided, starting in the fall of 2010 at AgriCare, to right a wrong by doing wrong.

For instance, when she told Klenks and CEO David Copple at a briefing that their Taiwanese vendor based in Kaohsiung City had purchased AgriCare's service and maintenance package of computer software that quarter for $3.1 million, but actually the vendor paid $2.1

million—the standard quarterly rate for the software—which Kiernan failed to report and refused to put in the Asia Tech account where the money transfer belonged. Kiernan pocketed the $1 million; a fact that didn't come to light because, when Klenks asked her about it—having noticed a discrepancy at tax-time audits—she explained (enter: *Truthful Hyperbole*), "... It's in the corporate account."

"Which one?" asked Klenks in her office. "The Asia Tech account or the Pacific 8?"

"The Pacific 8 since Taiwanetics Inc. is one of our 8 vendors."

"Kiernan..." he sighed, "You know better than that. It belongs deposited in the Asia Tech account, but how do you account for the $3.1 million? We only charge for that software $2.1 million."

Kiernan lowered her laptop screen while seated at her desk. She leaned back in her office chair, braided her fingers together, and rested her hands over her midsection—motions to buy time, surveying Klenks' demeanor, seeing he knew nothing concretely, just numbers that didn't add up. This bought her more time...to lie...to steal. She responded, "Jeff, it's the tariffs on this sale. You know that the Obama Administration imposed tariffs on imports and exports coming out of China. Given the One China policy, Taiwan gets hit with them too, and so do we. All U.S. companies. To circumvent the impact of that on our bottom line, I charged Taiwanetics $3.1 million to offset the cost of the tariffs."

Stern-faced, Klenks walked up to the front of Kiernan's glass slate of a desk—clean of all things but for her laptop half-closed and her cell phone off—and he stopped short of the edge when he asked, "So where's the $1.1 million you overcharged?"

Poker face intact, without skipping a beat, Kiernan answered, "It's in the Pacific 8 account, told you."

A Liar and a Thief.

She waited for his next question, the one that would inform her of how much he knew as AgriCare's CFO or how much he didn't know, which would only reinforce her belief that he was overpaid for having a penis, not a brain. Klenks asked, "Will you explain for auditing purposes that you managed the point of sale and transaction, which deposited the money in the wrong account for me?"

"Sure, I'll do that, Robert."

As he turned on his heels to walk away, Kiernan's sly grin broadened, because the question Klenks was supposed to ask—which would have compelled Kiernan to file her letter of resignation right there on the spot and hope to avoid prosecution—was: *Isn't your business-class expenditures account connected to the Pacific 8 account, because of our plans in place to build your overseas office in Singapore?*

But Klenks didn't ask that question, and that was the financial backdoor through which Kiernan found a loophole, receiving kickbacks and lining her pockets for the last three years at AgriCare; settling the score without regret, remuneration, or reversal.

But all good things or bad things must come to an end.

In 2012, acquisition plans had been developed by Klenks and Copple to sell AgriCare to a Quebecois tycoon for an estimated $18.6 billion (American). A month prior to the sale, however, due to antitrust laws in the U.S., the U.S. Chamber of Commerce, the Ways & Means Committee, and the U.S. Department of the Interior joined in a class action lawsuit against Red Maple Technologies and AgriCare. Kiernan was tapped by the CEO to manage the sale of AgriCare and the legal morass the sale was being burdened by since one of her degrees from Penn State University was in law. Kiernan wanted no part of this role, but she had no choice but to bend the knee.

Copple told her, "If you pull this off, get AgriCare sold at a profit, you can still have a position with the new company post-merger and keep that office on the horizon in Singapore."

"Yes, sir," said Kiernan. She knew that any corporate merger would trigger the most rigorous of audits, and Copple and Klenks would find out her dirty little secret in due course, and that was precisely what happened. Kiernan, Klenks, and Copple were called into a meeting with the Board of Red Maple Technologies and the tycoon who owned it; a conference call. Red Maple

Technologies' lawyers introduced a legal file titled *Initial Discovery*, which revealed that the plaintiffs in the antitrust lawsuit had discovered some accounting discrepancies in the millions of dollars, seemingly involving a corporate account known as Pacific 8. Kiernan swallowed hard as the men yelled, veins popping at their foreheads, at each other across the cherrywood conference table.

The meeting ended shortly thereafter.

Time was up for Kiernan to come clean, but the Quebecois hedge-fund tycoon and his lawyers beat her to the punch. After the courts sided with the plaintiffs and denied the defendants' motion to dismiss in the civil case, Red Maple Technologies and AgriCare board members decided to fault Kiernan not for the kickbacks, which they failed to pin on her, but for that law degree of hers which proved ineffective throughout negotiations with the Obama Administration lawyers. Red Maple Technologies, if it wanted to own AgriCare, would be forced into a settlement that required three things: hire American workers over Canadians at a 60/40 ratio across three states (Wisconsin, Vermont, and New York), relocate the corporate office from Windsor to Washington D.C., and end the contracts affiliated with the Pacific 8 account because illegality throughout its bookkeeping was visible while the culprit wasn't identifiable.

Copple tapped Klenks to give Kiernan the bad news

in her office, which he delighted in because he knew precisely who the liar and the thief was now.

Kiernan didn't hear Klenks enter her office initially. If he were a snake, he was well within venom-spewing distance before she flinched. He slapped down a sealed manila envelope upon Kiernan's glass desk and said, "This is for you!"

Kiernan lowered her laptop screen, which hid the open window displaying the Pacific 8 account and her half-entered access code. "What is that?" she asked.

"Your severance package. Take it or leave it. You have a week to decide to take it, but after seven days, should you not take it, the offer expires, and we will leave it; not fulfill its terms; not forward the cash as you leave us."

"Leave... us?" Kiernan sounded perplexed.

Klenks could barely suppress his smile as he confirmed, "Your halfway completed penthouse office in Singapore... mothballed. The cash-offer severance package, which I begged David and the Board not to afford you, is right there on your desk," he pointed, then pocketed his hands. Rocking on his heels, he said, "It's a soft landing you don't deserve. You're a liar. You stole from us! Now get out. I didn't tell the Board what you've done, but I will do so, and the police if necessary, if you continue to hurt this company through this merger phase or anytime thereafter. Do you understand?"

Kiernan snapped shut her laptop. She rose from her high-back black leather office chair, walked around it, pushed it in beneath her glass desk, fastened the top button of her navy blazer with long red-painted nails, and snatched up her cell phone and laptop, cradling them in the crooks of her arms. She glared at Klenks and said, "I don't need to see whatever is inside that envelope, but I'll go home and discuss the matter with my husband and..." She paused, choked up, but stiffened her spine, weeping-ripely, and added, "I'm not a liar."

"Even that's a lie," said Klenks. "You get no sympathy from me, woman. What do I call someone who refused to tell me what I should know as CFO, which you knew I should have known at the time, Kiernan? We're talking $1 million here back in July, and God knows what more you may have stolen out of that account over the years. An account that's been closed, by the way, so if you try to access it from home with your security access code, it won't let you enter. We trusted you. I TRUSTED YOU! You exploited my trust for your personal gain, right under our noses, the whole time you were here with us. Can you appreciate, AT LEAST, the damage you've caused? The sense of betrayal? The people you've hurt?"

Kiernan's lipstick-red lips parted, poised to answer his questions in two words, but Klenks, on the other side of things, placed his hands flat on her glass desk—

clawing the sheer surface as he leaned over the edge of it, sneering at her with squinty-eyed outrage—and interjected, "Don't you dare respond. You listen now! You sat in that Settlement Meeting between the parties and the lawyers, listening to the discovery and case against us that planned to destroy the merger if revealed in court; a merger that you were tasked with putting out the fires on. You just sat there and watched those government lawyers have us by the balls with their new set of rules going forward. The latest stipulations that would bind us to regulations which we tried to avoid all along; and all you had to do was stand up and say it was me. I took the kickbacks, and AgriCare didn't know anything about it. For sure, Red Maple didn't know anything about it; but, no, you just sat there. YOU JUST SAT THERE! And when the meeting was over, you—I mean, what the fuck—grabbed your coffee and left the room as if it were just another Board meeting." He sighed, stood up straight, swallowed hard, and said, "Looking at you, I see that you are incapable of legitimate remorse; and, quite frankly, the universe works, this will come back to you in some form, Kiernan. Believe that! There's nothing you can say to me. I wouldn't believe a single thing that comes out of that pretty little red mouth of yours. At this point, it's only good for a punch to it, or a dick in it. Now get out!"

A tear escaped her. She swiped at it before it could run down her cheek, then she bolted. Midway, she brushed past Klenks—nudging him, seeing that

Machiavellian grin. She really wanted to hit him, especially after he reminded her on the way out: "The severance package will be right here on this desk, Kiernan! Sign it! You have seven days!"

Kiernan felt leers of judgment aimed at her from all angles between the hanging pictures on the foyer walls, ostensibly closing in on her—the female tech leaders she admired, who would never have stolen from their companies, despite the insufferable sexism, unfair pay practices, or pressures to be better than their male counterparts. Kiernan armored herself with the belief that most women in the corporate world, at any level of expertise, know that their male counterparts only need to exhibit average work performance to be considered solid. The kind of solid that had been assured and reinforced by other average businessmen, and within this global testosterone-filled clique they occupied, an unspoken language existed between them, which was understood by osmosis—a talent not taught in any school, yet practiced like breathing.

These average businessmen have the gift of gab; just buying time to not be found out while breathing, and forever selling that greater vision to the detriment of true ambition. Meanwhile, to the exasperation of most workplace women—the exclusion of them from the golf courses of the world where business really gets done—what businessman's ego can take a woman leaning on her putter like a cane, just waiting for her turn on the green with a chip-in, listening to businessmen play the game, even outdoors, with so many handicaps between them while she had none?

Kiernan, being pushed out by the crumbling to her (no more tears), felt it was an honor, but at the end of the day, it was still a man's world. She had to go home and report to her husband, Jake, what had happened at work.

CHAPTER 2

WHO IS JAKE MONTGOMERY?

The Montgomery Family Condo
Newton, Mass (Suburb of Boston)
3:42 p.m.

I never attempted to know my wife, Kiernan. Why? She knows everything already, and it has been easier to believe her than challenge her. She knows herself from every angle under the sun; knows the direction we are headed as a family. I'll get briefed as the Stay-At-Home Dad here—a stooge. My perspective from the shade doesn't matter... The Inconsequential Husband, I am. If I'm not getting cut off mid-sentence or having her decisions trump mine or being led by the nose, it must be bedtime...

The wife being in control has been going on for a long time. Back in college, I recall Kiernan, while I was at rugby practice, completing my coursework. She got my books out of my locker and finished papers, assignments, and take-home quizzes. She claimed it was because I took too long, which put a damper on our social life off-campus...

Sure, the infringement made me feel like an idiot, especially when she tried to put it diplomatically: "It's just easier this way... Let me do it..." I learned to surrender my pride after a few drinks on her dime. I was the wallflower, the dumb jock that played Third Wheel on dates his best friend went on, so Kiernan coming along was a step up. Green-eyed, long brown hair, short in stature next to me... She stood as high as my nips... Petite... Sexy, an expensive dresser... Big boobs for a short chick—C-cup if she had worn a bra at all—and a lot of our classmates wanted her or wondered why she wanted me... My eyes, body, and kindness, she'd say... If she only knew, the kindness she perceived was my shyness... A shyness that couldn't tell her who I really was... But she was a fast-talker, smart, and she wanted us to experience college life together with friends, and since I hung out with Kevin and his girlfriend, it was just convenient to double-date with them...

Always behind academically, I'd study and study for hours just to maintain a C-minus average; well, that was until Kiernan came into my life... Her controlling ways made me a B-plus student in my last year. How could I say no to a chick that did my homework and me right afterward? No longer a virgin, she made me feel things I didn't think were possible for me, and I didn't have to wear a condom; she had that covered too. To a dumb jock like me, our budding relationship, its dynamic more than worked to my benefit—it salvaged my scholarship, and I was able to graduate in four years. Before I met Kiernan, I was on the six-year plan. Hell, my parents believed I'd flunk out, tuck tail, and come back home to Connecticut.

They thought I was lucky when I scored high on my SATs and then earned college offers, and I was lucky, because my parents didn't set money aside for me like normal parents. The full-ride rugby scholarship spared me embarrassment, not them. My parents would have relished using our working-class status as a cudgel to keep me down, keep me home, keep me like them working at the food processing plant down the road. That was their goal; that's why they called me a failure, in the hopes that I'd never become successful...

A failure instead. They called me that often throughout my childhood; a failure... They thought the characterization would stick, but Kiernan had come long post-childhood verbal abuse—making a liar out of them. I'll always be indebted to her for that, and the sex... Sex in college is important, especially when your peers are getting some and you're the odd man out and a jock. Jocks—rugby players are supposed to get laid... often! Kiernan taking my virginity was a relief, not a connection, not love-making, but a relief... to me, that is... I never told her that, of course...

I wanted to feel closer to Kiernan back then, and maybe if I had been, we'd have a stronger marriage today, but despite the emotional distance between us, the sense of service in every way, I feel very much connected to her like an arm is to the shoulder or a thumb is to the hand. But for a while now, it's numb; that connection... I can't say when things started to feel numb between us, but we've always been unalike; different... I lacked confidence, she didn't... I hated school, she didn't... I grew up poor, she didn't...

Kiernan was one of those rich upstate New York kids who got accepted to all the Ivy League schools, but her parents were the ones who made her enroll in a state university. Kiernan said they did it to humble her. Things always came easy to her, and her parents—religious zealots—thought her intelligence was worldly, not godly, and worthy of punishment. They put her in an all-girls Christian junior college in Pennsylvania for two years. Her purgatory, she called it. She was allowed to transfer to State then. And I met her in the spring of my junior year. Kevin talked her up to the frat. Said I got some hot church-chick coming to our rugby matches and cheering from the stands louder than the cheerleaders on the sidelines. He wasn't lying, but he had ulterior motives for trying to get me to be with Kiernan. He had his own girlfriend going on a year already, and it was getting awkward with my going out on dates with them without a girl of my own. His girl thought I was weird for going out with them; kind of like the Third Wheel, but I didn't mind it until I overheard her call me that once, coming back from the bathroom in the student pool hall. It was kind of common knowledge that I hadn't been with a girl before, so needless to say, when Kiernan came into the picture, everyone took a sigh of relief, including me...

Now all the attention was on Kiernan and me as The Couple; more ventriloquist-dummy in public but legitimately boyfriend and girlfriend in private. I was her best friend, but Kevin was mine, and I just never had the heart to tell her to stop trying to supplant him. Despite all she had done for me, she was two years too late on that front, but to know Kiernan is to appreciate her competitive side. She thought she'd catch up to Kevin in significance. Like a guy playing street basketball, she'd give Kevin that hard foul, and he'd give it right back to her. The verbal sparring between them was pure venom... They hated each other and loved showing it publicly, as if in my honor...

Waiters, bouncers, and other classmates in close proximity—if I had a dollar for every time we were asked to leave a place, I'd have at least $20—but I liked the feeling of being claimed by both of them. Fought for by both of them. Valued by both of them. It's why I love Kevin to this day, even though I haven't seen him in years...

It's why I married Kiernan after college, even though she has no idea who I am... then or since... I could tell her, of course, but I've conceded to being her possession for so long that I don't mind being possessed. When you are someone's possession, it only matters what you do for them, not how you feel about anything...

I've been her favorite glass that has held her water, and however I may feel about that is not something I would ever spill. That's why I'm her favorite glass. We're under no illusions about that, as she takes her drink... for going on sixteen years now. Serious-minded and pushy, but not stuck-up. Guys on campus wanted her at first sight, not me, however. The big green eyes, cherub face, no makeup, only pink lip gloss and a tart perfume; the kind of girl that wore a tracksuit that hugged her petite hourglass figure and zipped it down to show off her C-cup boobs—cleavage for days and a brash feminine swagger that made her shine. I was no moth to it, but she liked me, and that was enough; or should I say that was all that mattered. I had someone to come with me now whenever Kevin and Daliah called...

No earthquakes throughout our boyfriend-and-girlfriend days in college, nor later throughout marriage for sixteen years so far, but only because we rehearsed how to shift the dirt beneath our feet and bury things quickly, whether dead in the past or alive at present. We practiced avoidance with mutual interest and unspoken gratitude, especially after the kids were born. Our marriage could be summed up by that old common refrain, oftentimes said to our American soldiers back from several tours of duty: Thank you for your service...

Said enough times—Thank You For Your Service—just ask any service member, it can become a challenge not to question the sincerity of that statement. Now, Kiernan and I never said Thank You For Your Service literally, but over the course of our marriage, it has been implied; like when I don't ask her about what she had written in her diaries, nor where she hides them in the house after she's done with an entry, nor why she hides them from me at all. I should emphasize... I surrendered my mind to this woman early on as her boyfriend. I sacrificed my manhood later as her husband. I sold out massively being a stay-at-home Dad, maybe not in the eyes of our children, but to myself. What about my career? I dare not confess my thoughts to Kiernan. My thoughts, like her diary entries, I suppose, just not in written form but with mental reservations. Meanwhile, we exist inside the gilded cage of marriage, never a chirp...

Thank You For Your Service... A cold war, this...

And what this has done, saying things that we do not mean or not saying that which should be said directly, not causing that earthquake, still burying things—kills the romance along with the trust. Even the truth dies piecemeal because keeping secrets, whether in a book or in the mind, makes face-to-face conversation either ceremonial and superficial. It makes one hard or disaffected. The next thing you notice, wife and husband no longer talk at all; not intimately or willingly but rather reflexively and defensively; and no longer as one voice, as it pertains to the children, which eventually creates a Daddy's Girl and a Momma's Boy with unabashed acclaim... Yeah, I never attempted to know Kiernan or the children, but with that said: they have never cared to ask who am I... Who is Jake Montgomery?

Movement.

A chill ran down Jake's spine. Blinking, he smelled his son—a mix of Big Red chewing gum and a strong olivaceous body odor—before he heard Chase's presence at his back. Jake's sights narrowed past his own reflection over his shoulder and saw his son, waist-high, framed by the wooden bathroom doorway. Jake swallowed hard. He took a beat, and with both of his hands, he parted the length of his silky black hair in front of his blue eyes. He swept it back. He hooked it behind his ears with hooked fingers. He stared down Chase through the bathroom mirror and asked, "What do you want, son?"

Chase, a dark scruffy-haired, rail-thin ten-year-old boy, recovered his calm from having been startled. Whenever his father addressed him, it made his stomach trundle like thunder before the storm. A storm of indefatigable judgment. Though Chase had done nothing wrong—having emerged unlooked-for at the opened bathroom door to find his father staring at himself with intense scrutiny created the sense that he had. He knew his father felt spied upon, though not Chase's intent or action, misperception dwarfed reality.

...Every time I turn around, this kid is behind me or watching me or annoying me...

Chase self-deprecatingly apologized for his intrusion

before he said, "Mom's home early. She wants to know if you mind chicken."

"Chicken? Your mother is planning to cook? Hmm... Something's wrong," answered Jake through the bathroom mirror's reflection of his son at his back. "Tell her chicken is fine."

"Okay."

Jake turned on the faucet and dropped his sights.

Chase stood still.

Jake looked up while rubbing his hands together under the hot water; peripherally, there was Chase unmoved behind him. "Anything else? I'm about to shave, son."

"Are you and Mom fighting?"

"No. Why?"

"Just asking."

"Everything's fine, son."

"Then why is Mom home so early from work?"

Jake stepped back, repelled the bathroom mirror like a door, reached for his disposable razor from the bottom shelf, and said, "While I'm shaving, go ask Mom why she's home early. She'll tell you." Jake's right brow hiked up as he said sarcastically, "You're her little buddy. She tells you everything."

Chase wasn't amused; a serious boy toward his father. They rarely joked, but he knew why his father said that. Chase oftentimes accused Summer of being Daddy's favorite, and Jake never let an opportunity pass to remind Chase—in his tone, he was accurate. Jake reached for his face cloth hanging from the towel rod over the commode. He said, "Let me know what your mother says..."

...Hmmph!... Jake muttered. "Oh well."

No reflection in the bathroom mirror of Chase at Jake's back. On sock feet, he had gone.

CHAPTER 3

THE GILDED CAGE OF MARRIAGE

Dinner with Jake and the kids at home (a first for Kiernan in three years); check! Put the kids to bed and take a long bath to unwind (she'd let her tears out there alone); check! Pillow talk with Jake about Agri-Care's offer and the future (she'd communicate but no confessions); check! Kiernan's thought process, acutely goal-oriented, calculating, and deceitful, refused to let Jake see her defeated—not one more man would get the better of her for what remained of this day—which she had decided in her car on the way home, along with taking Agri-Care's severance package and retiring at 42 years old.

For as long as he had withstood it, Kiernan patronized Jake—feigned to beseech his advice, though an hour ago had a revamped outlook for her next Five Year Plan (the family not excluded)—when she turned to Jake and asked, "What should I do?"

Since when does my opinion matter? thought Jake.

He cleared his throat and sat upright in bed against plump pillows. A quick jerk of his head to sideswipe his hair away from his face since his hands gripped the hardcover of an open novel; right at an intriguing scene too. His bright cobalt blue eyes honed in on Kiernan's mien like flashlights in search of a child lost in the woods. Her inner child, perhaps lost or playing a game. The poker face on her; stern, he couldn't discern whichever. He took a beat. He tried to recall a time Kiernan showed weakness or expressed indecision; their wedding day, maybe. He heard rumors at the reception which Kiernan called lies. Nonetheless, his wife asked him for advice, which caught him off guard, so he proffered a cliché: "A bird in the hand is worth more than two in the bush."

"So should I take it, even though I don't know the amount of this offer sheet?"

"What did you say happened at Agri-Care? What did you do?"

Jake looked over at his wife seated upright like himself, glaring at him, as she said sharply, "Why do you presume automatically that I've done something wrong?"

"Never mind. I don't want to argue tonight, dear. I wanted to help with my little two cents I have. I don't know the first thing you do at Agri-Care." Jake returned his attention to his novel split open by both of his hands. Half-concerned, half-confused, he added, "I know you're a big wig over there; that's it."

Kiernan turned from Jake, reached over on her side of things for her nightstand, opened partway its lithe black painted drawer, extracted from it a small petite bottle of hand lotion, and she squirted white lotion; a tart earthy fragrance emanated from the dollop into her palms as she rubbed them together vigorously; almost angrily, she tossed the bottle of lotion back into her nightstand drawer and slammed it shut.

"What did I say wrong now?"

"NOTHING!" answered Kiernan, who rose from the bed. Staring back at him, she said, “I have to go pee."

Jake looked up at her exasperatedly, rolled his eyes, then returned to his book and muttered, "Uh-huh."

Kiernan didn't have to matriculate; she had to escape.

Jake knew as much, but he didn't care anymore, having overheard her sigh, "...A bird in the hand is worth more than two in the bush...that's it?"

The bathroom door slammed down the hall.

Jake didn't flinch. His husky right brow hiked quizzically downward at the verso page of his novel. Distractedly reading by lamplight on his side of things, he knew Kiernan aspired to an altercation with him at home, because at work they had taken something from her more significant than her job: her self-worth, apparently.

"I don't want to argue," said Jake as he placed his novel down—split open on his nightstand. "Fuck this."

Jake moved quickly to disrobe. He peeled off his blue jeans, removed his white t-shirt overhead, and plopped down on the bed in sock feet over the white comforter, supine; his head propped up highly by pillows. He retrieved his novel from his nightstand and kept it split open to his page, repositioned over his shaven chest. He closed his eyes; a feigned sleep.

Better to avoid Kiernan than acknowledge her while her mood sought out casualties. Kiernan stepped into the bedroom; lamplights aglow, Jake asleep and unaware of her seething. She walked to the foot of the bed and told herself, "Jake?" she barked. "Jake!"

He groaned and turned his head away from the soft white hue of the lamplight.

"Jake, I know you're awake... We're moving."

Jake's eyes opened immediately. "We're what?"

"We're moving. You should be happy. My publicist found a family townhome for sale in Burlington, Vermont—where Kevin and his wife live. A place called the—"

"The Links," Jake interjected, "Townhomes and Estates. It's where the Top 1% live, dear."

Jake masked his enthusiasm with bland intonations and a flat affect. He rubbed his eyes, yawned though he didn't have to, while his wife stared at him pensively from the foot of the bed. Her arms crossed limply. He knew why she wanted to move house all of a sudden; Agri-Care, in a single boardroom meeting, ruined

Boston for her and escape was necessary. She hated losing, even if it happened over a family board game like Scrabble or Monopoly with Jake and the kids; if she didn't come in first place by night's end, it necessitated the silent treatment for days after.

He dared not fight her on the matter of moving.

"Vermont, huh?" said Jake. "Are you sure about Vermont? You won't know anyone. It would be like starting over, even for Summer and Chase. New schools again. They are not going to like that. They loved New York before we brought them here. So, I'm telling you now, I am not giving them the news. You are."

"Fine."

"Hun, Kevin and Daliah are more my friends than yours; even in college it was that way, and you can barely tolerate Kevin. Now you're saying we might be neighbors? Honey, why don't we just stick it out here? Let this all blow over. Find a new job doing the same thing for a competitor around here, I mean—we..."

"No!" she said sharply. "I already paid for the townhome. We have a viewing with the realtor within the week. We're not staying here. I'm done with this condo. I want a house. I'm done with Boston. It's too cramped. I want wide-open spaces for the children, and the winters can't be any worse in Vermont."

"No arguments from me, dear. Besides, I can't wait to call Kevin and tell him that the gang is back together again circa 2013, baby!"

Kiernan shook her head dismissively as she walked off toward her side of the bed. She kicked off her flip-flop slippers below and peeled back the comforter to get into bed. "The gang is not back together," she whined, "but you and Kevin will be."

Jake smiled at that.

Kiernan rolled her eyes with pursed lips and before turning on her side, she said, "And no more quick-get-rich schemes between you two. I'm not lending him any more money, and don't you ask me for any on his behalf either."

"He's rich now, dear."

"Oh really?"

"So I heard from Cassidy at the Alumni Association a few years back. Kevin is a major car dealer in the area up there. A millionaire, they tell me. Daliah's a—"

"A grade school teacher, still. I know. I just didn't know about Kevin. Well, good for him. Good for him. He finally made something of himself. A philosophy major in college; all too much infatuated with quoting Rumi, sells cars now. What a waste of a degree."

"Or... what a way to follow your dreams and succeed, right?"

Husband and wife locked glares—seeing the other beyond their eyes—until Kiernan broke scrutiny, scoffed in Jake's face, and chortled, saying, "You're incurable."

She turned her back, ducked under the covers shoulder-high on her side, and seethed.

"Good night, I guess?" remarked Jake at her back.

Kiernan refused to respond or fall asleep. Jake returned to the dog-eared verso page of his novel, which he angled toward his lamplight on his side of things. A good night indeed, he thought.

CHAPTER 4

DISTRUST

CFO Robert Klenks and CEO David Copple, at the behest of Red Maple Technologies owner and Quebecois hedge-fund tycoon Jean-Marcel Jodoin, who listened in on speakerphone, met with Kiernan in her old corner office at Agri-Care. Clashing colognes and perfumes, steely-eyed glares, and strategic silent treatments aside, the tension-packed milieu and near-wordless impromptu meeting was so quiet Jodoin overheard scarcely two things: the faint shuffling of papers *(...Klenks and Copple scrutinizing Kiernan's two-page letter of resignation...)* and something akin to the sound of a mouse scurrying behind a floorboard *(...Kiernan signing the final page of her severance package, which included an NDA...)*.

"She signed it?" asked Jodoin.

"Yes, sir," answered Klenks.

Kiernan placed the black ballpoint pen down atop

the paperwork on the desk by her old speakerphone, a tinge and mix of remorse, guilt, and anger in tow.

CEO Copple said, "Can't say it was nice doing business with you because you stole from us, but we appreciate your discretion going forward. The sale of this company won't be completed for another year, so if you—"

"I won't say a word, David," said Kiernan. "No charges filed, right?"

Klenks interrupted, "That was the concession afforded you if you came in before the expiration date and accepted the terms of the severance package. We could've screwed you over like you did us, but—"

"Klenks! Stop it!" shouted Jodoin. "This is not a press conference for prize fighters, here!"

Klenks rolled his eyes at Kiernan, within arm's reach, nodded at the speakerphone blinking a micro-dot of a green light below the keypad. Its receiver was off to the side on the desk. David Copple was not amused.

"Of course, sir. Sorry," replied Klenks. "Do we have your key badge?"

"I gave it to my secretary when I left here the day before yesterday," answered Kiernan. "I'm sorry about all of this."

Jodoin said, "Are you, Kiernan?"

She looked at the landline phone like a newborn child in a cradle and answered dolefully, "Yes, I am."

"I have just one question, then. Will you keep the

number quiet, even from family? You signed the NDA, I presume, right?"

"Yes, sir."

"Good. Copple read it over the phone, so I know the terms, but it does not stress 'family members' not knowing the amount and amenities of the package."

"I understand, sir. And I don't even care about the money, sir."

"Oh really!" blurted Klenks as he fiddled with his red tie nervously and stepped forward, which compelled Kiernan to step back. The front extension of her own desk stopped her. She felt cornered.

Copple interjected, "Klenks? Do we have to kick you out?"

"If the money doesn't matter," shouted Klenks, "then why did she steal from us!"

It was a valid question, and the protracted pause from Copple and Jodoin led Kiernan to believe that she had to offer an explanation that didn't insult their collective intelligence. She asked, "Honestly? You all want to know?"

"Yes," said Jodoin quietly over the speakerphone; a curiosity to his tone, a hurt, a longing, which Kiernan eviscerated with a single word: "Vengeance." She said, "I stole from you all out of vengeance."

"We were good to you, Kiernan. Vengeance, really? We loved you," said Copple.

Kiernan's mouth opened to respond as she turned to

Copple, but Jodoin's hurt came through searingly over the speakerphone, "Get out!"

Copple shut down; whatever Kiernan was about to say no longer mattered. The sale of the company trumped everything, even their seven-year relationship as friends. Klenks smirked. The boss was on his side, and that felt like a kiss from God.

Kiernan nodded, scooped up from the desk Agri-Care's severance package in a large manila envelope, and said, "I wish I were as strong as your trust was in me." She bolted out of the office, weeping-ripe.

Copple and Klenks looked at each other, shaking their heads and wringing their hands. A piercing, loud din of a dial tone sounded behind her back. Shaken to his core, Jodoin had hung up.

In the settlement two weeks later, Jodoin would acquire Agri-Care for $247 billion, and though he had to hire more Americans than Canadians to evade profit-killing state taxation and tariffs, he sacked Copple and Klenks and the entire Human Resources and PR Departments at Agri-Care. Because in a wordy but thorough email Kiernan sent to him later that afternoon, Jodoin had been made to understand how Agri-Care disvalued women at every level of employment for years. So her vengeance—he reviewed attachments of legitimate invoices from her personal archive and the missing link to any government auditor—wasn't your disgruntled employee payback-kickback but your quintessential Robin Hood-type paying it forward to other women, herself included, at the company in the form of 1,237 under-the-table, year-end bonuses; none lower than $39,000 but none higher than $2.5 million.

...So, yes, I lied, Kiernan wrote, *yes, I stole from Agri-Care, not quite Red Maple Technologies, sir.* She argued: *Do what you will with the evidence in this email. I'm at your mercy, but with a vengeance, I'd do it again because the women there deserved more...*

Her email concluded: *Distrust that, never!*

†

After Kiernan accepted the severance package, she had been assured in an email that her message to Jodoin was read, appreciated, and deleted. Eager to get on with the next phase of her life and marriage, she withdrew $4.8 million from her savings account and properly retired at 41. The breadwinner-turned-housewife called her realtor, and the following week the family packed up their Boston condo, overloaded their U-Haul, and moved to North Burlington, Vermont, as promised. A lavish ranch-style tutor townhome awaited at The CourseLinks Estates and Townhomes, set upon a decommissioned PGA golf course whose centerpiece was a gazebo. In all, the sale set her back $3.4 million. In a bucolic upper-class gated community of cul-de-sacs and winding grey concrete sidewalks, which bracketed unpainted black asphalt streets named after pro golfers, their townhome on Veejay Singh Lane had white painted walls and ceiling with few rooms but lots of echoey open floorplan space. A sunken living room floor. A dark wood back deck. A townhome sandwiched by others in a cul-de-sac of ten. Through the cottage-style windows, Summer inhaled petrichor like that of a rosebud unplucked. Chase stood with his back up against the wall in the foyer; hands in his sweatpants pockets with a moue. Chase whined about missing Boston and his friends there.

"We'll be fine here," Mom assured her son, "You'll make friends."

Immediately, Kevin and Jake hit it off as though fifteen years apart was but a noisome blip in time. They went everywhere together: to the grocery store, to the clubhouse, to the gym, jogging after dinner... you name it. However, on the wives' end of things, Daliah and Kiernan felt the pressure to bond, though they didn't trust each other as women ever since college. Daliah knew she loved Kevin and why Kevin and Jake loved each other, but Kiernan always looked at the three of them as oddballs. A stuck-up rich college girl turned successful, uppity businesswoman. It wasn't until Kiernan confided in Daliah that she was fired from Agri-Care and needed help with the kids while her foremost job must be the role of wife to Jake. Daliah earned Kiernan's trust with a gift every overwhelmed mother needs: a babysitter. Neesha McGovern, a high schooler, watched over Summer and Chase whenever Kiernan had errands to complete, a spa day to enjoy, or a married couple's dinner date to attend. A godsend—Neesha—if only to Kiernan, because the stay-at-home mom role thrust upon her now had more time to rediscover her husband Jake. No longer a passerby nor an obligatory, disembodied kiss on the cheek before going to the office, he was a gorgeous, broodingly tall man with full-bodied black hair, Serbian good looks, even better since college, and an all-year-round tan, swarthy complexion, with pensive cobalt-blue eyes which said more than his mouth ever did. Secrets? Regrets? Dreams? She didn't understand the language Jake's eyes communicated, but she sensed behind his one hundred yard stares a longing which had nothing to do with her or their children; that much she understood, and it was enough to spark... distrust.

The year was 1999.

The wedding was scheduled within the hour. 215 guests and family members were already seated and awaiting the ceremony to commence. Meanwhile, inside a windowless banquet hall anteroom, converted into a dressing room, 20-something Kiernan sat cross-legged before a lighted oval-shaped vanity mirror in her wedding gown. She had just been crowned by her ghostly-white veil, placed upon her by her older sister Gracey, who stood at her back with a comb in her left hand and bobby pins in her right fist. They argued about Jake once again, and Gracey rebutted,

"Vilifying a man for being a man, a Walter Mitty, is as tragic as any man who has been preconditioned to believe that a woman's intellectual prowess is narrowly confined to her way around the kitchen. It's not fair to impugn your soon-to-be husband because you think you see something in his eyes that wants more. If you're accurate, by the way, I fear you think his wanting more is really wanting something other; other than you. Kiernan? C'mon, give the man a break, or just ask him if what you see in his eyes is actually that."

"NO! I can't!"

"Then let the matter die, Kiernan."

"No, I can't."

"Do you hear yourself right now? You are about to marry this man you don't trust, and—"

"I didn't say that," her voice raised a pitch. "I didn't say that I didn't trust him."

"You implied it."

"Did I?" She turned from her reflection in the mirror to look up at her sister. She paused, swallowed hard, but Gracey interjected, "What? Just say it."

"My instincts are never wrong, Gracey."

"What is it that you fear, Kiernan?"

"I don't know exactly. I can't put it into words, but I just... I just know..."

"Know what?"

"He isn't true, but it's true love."

"One-sided true love?"

"I hope not... I mean."

"And you get that all from his stares off into

nowhere? Can a man be tired? Can a man daydream without being deceitful?"

"I know, right. But it's a gut feeling."

"Then I'll call Mom and Dad in here right now, get them out of their seats, and we'll end this thing."

Kiernan grabbed her sister's wrist pleadingly and said, "Tell me I'm being silly; that this is just pre-marital jitters; that all is going to be okay; tell me that, Gracey."

Gracey obliged her sister, but seeing Kiernan in this moment of sheer terror, she inherited doubts about Jake of her own. She turned Kiernan's head around by the point of the comb. Gracey leaned down to become cheek-to-cheek with Kiernan, who was now weeping, and neither sister said anything for a minute. They stared at each other's reflection in the mirror. Gracey stole a deep breath and said, "If you don't trust him, don't marry him."

Easy to say when the wedding gown that the parents bought cost $280,567, and it was a perfect fit. Not to short-thrift attention to cost regarding the Queen Anne's Lace-patterned veil-and-train combo, which set their parents back $54,200 alone. Kiernan's white Italian satin open-toe stilettos, a mere $2,000. The something borrowed, not from Mom or Grandma Kluger (God rest her soul), but from the jewelers Roskins & Shein, who knew Mother Kluger since grade school, and so as long as The Klugers insured the Egyptian-style Mother-of-Pearl choker—with a $15,000 deductible—and returned it intact to the jewelers after the reception, Kiernan could wear it at her wedding, but it wasn't for sale. Kiernan couldn't turn back now. The wedding and its reception accommodated 215 guests and family members, some of whom came in from out of town, so Mom and Dad Kluger paid for their round-trip plane tickets to secure a robust audience at a sum of $85,464. The banquet hall itself, for a June wedding, cost, with the security deposit, $5,670. Gracey's plane ticket—being one of those out-of-towners, coming in from Fairbanks, Alaska—and her hotel room stay for 3 days and 2 nights, bridesmaid gown, and accessories neared $34,000 for everything. Mom and Dad Kluger made certain that their middle child knew the cost of her wedding down to the dollar, which implied, "This Jake Better Be The One," and Kiernan's second thoughts, whether spot-on or outlandish, didn't matter at all because she told her parents that Jake was The One, and any second thoughts after so much spending for a mere two-hour gathering would become just one more expenditure—one that the family couldn't afford. She had to go through with it because Dad Kluger didn't leak these costs and rates to Gracey just because; he used money as a vehicle to demonstrate acts of kindness, but his children were always in debt to those acts of kindness. He kept the receipts too. "Kluger money doesn't grow on trees," he would remind his daughters. "I married your mother because I wanted children, not ingrates. Make certain that I see you girls always as the former and not the latter, so help you God."

At risk of being an ingrate, Kiernan had to marry Jake, so she broke her stare from Gracey's in the mirror and said, "I'm just being silly. Typical bride; wedding jitters."

Gracey stood up and worked on Kiernan's curly brown tendrils down the sides of her face—not saying a word—until she asked, "Are you ready, Mrs. Kluger-Montgomery?"

"I'm so ready," said Kiernan. "I've changed my mind. I won't hyphenate my surname. I'll be simply Kiernan Montgomery."

Gracey nodded wistfully; something died that morning before the wedding, and neither sister could confirm what the sense had been leaving that dressing room—even if it said hello to their faces, they'd still fail to call it by name. "Here Comes The Bride" played by a string quartet meanwhile up ahead, but the thing that died that morning was... trust.

Sixteen years later, two children with the stretch marks as proof later, out of Boston, sidelined from the globetrotting, corporate rat race that almost made her a stranger to her own family, now in the dark—Kiernan lay on her side in her new house, in her almost-done warm master bedroom with Jake couchant; his book split open across his shaven midsection in white boxer briefs.

She studied him under moonlight; a stray beam hit him just right from behind her, which reminded her: *tomorrow... curtains.*

Jake still had his rugby player physique; just grizzled instead of corded in dad-bod form; its brooding strength at rest; vulnerable. Three years older than she, Kiernan envied that Jake—after all these years while she was making millions around the world, he was stationed at home with the kids, waiting at school bus stops, helping with their homework, making dinners, and packing bag lunches for the next school day—this man seemed to age in reverse. Keeping his gym membership and stealing two hours a day for himself while the kids were in school made forty-four look thirty-three. How dare he be sexy?

The motherfucker didn't even snore.

She surveilled his physique touched by a gauzy, stray moonbeam that shot through their uncurtained bedroom window, over her shoulder and onto him—from his bulging Adam's apple down to the front of his boxer brief also bulging. The crumpled white bedsheets, knee-high, covered both of them. Her sights circled over him; up and down him. She inhaled him. His musk was a mixture of Irish Spring soap and a hint of tonight's dinner in his five o'clock shadow; chicken parm. The long and even planes of his shaven, greying chest hairs—such large pecs—inflating and deflating with his every inhalation and exhalation. A rhythmic and erotic manly sibilance to his breathing in and out. She gorgonized him but recognized in that moment, with a chill in tow, why the distrust...

Distrust...

It convinces you that the apple he gave you may have a worm in it; that the glass of water he poured you for dinner might be tainted; that whatever he says or does conceals an ulterior motive at best; or at worst, he prescribed for your delusions zero ruth, because your suffering fuels his guilt trips, both espoused with righteous indignation. Subsequently, you notice that your penchant for making positive outcomes out of negative results has been an over-stressed power, finding strength down rabbit holes of conspiracies to fill a void that seemed to materialize out of nowhere and with the pull of a black hole. A black hole that speaks to you, and it opines that your husband's advice to accept that severance package, permanently stripping you out of couture tailored pantsuits and re-packaging you in sweatpants bought from a clearance rack in Target, was perhaps the husband's master plan—to dethrone his wife as the breadwinner of the household. This made you toss out that apple, pretend to drink that glass of water, and see your husband going to work now as him leaving you alone in a new house, his old duties now yours, feeling tricked—reduced to mindlessly signing Parent-Teacher Consent Forms on the kitchen countertop as opposed to strategically evaluating multi-million dollar contracts at her office desk...

Distrust...

It will make a new stay-at-home mom rush to a Walmart and purchase a lady-friendly pistol, a .22 caliber, and keep it loaded beneath the bed on her side of things; starting a diary but hiding it better than the pistol...

Distrust...

It made Kiernan re-evaluate Jake's penis inside of her over the years, more so since losing the job and leaving Boston for Burlington—feeling it not as passionately penetrating but poorly penitent; not sensed as rock-hard but as hardly into it, and it all being irrefutable proof of infidelity, though as quiet as it is being suffocated, reason still muffles that it's proof of only one's...

Distrust...

†

She snuggled closer to Jake. She maneuvered his right hand that lay limply over his book cover and intertwined their fingers. In dreamland, Jake sensed nothing. Kiernan used her free hand to hike up the white lacey hem of her wine-colored negligee, exposing her nates and Brazilian wax to moonlight. Piecemeal, she inched closer to Jake. Now the tip of her nose touched his shoulder. She scooted up higher so that her chin could perch over the round of his shoulder and nestle alongside his throat below his scruffy jawline. A tender region on him; an erogenous zone. He stopped breathing for a second and groaned lowly—indelicate sexual advances aside, Jake could sleep through a thrash metal concert, and with family history as a reminder, she knew not to take offense or permit distrust to warp her perceptions; sleep had not been more important than sex. He was simply tired. She brought his inactive hand, intertwined with hers, down toward the pungent heat that egressed from between her legs. She breathed fire, lustfully; wordlessly. She wanted her husband more than ever before. Retired now, she longed for more sex, not less or the status quo—Jake better get used to that; she thought. It had been almost a year since they had full-on sex; three years, maybe four, if quickies and side-by-side masturbation didn't count as sex. Despite Jake's imperfections, to Kiernan, he was still the best-worst kind of dessert: too decadent to devour every day, yet not enough once you've had a taste.

It occurred to her in that instant—while snuggling with her husband, whose dream-state made it impossible for him to snuggle back—perhaps it wasn't distrust of Jake but an overall jealousy. Jealousy that men aged better than women. Jealousy over the family dynamic that honors a man's sacrifices over the woman's, as if the incubation of the fetus for nine months doesn't count, nor breastfeeding for six months thereafter, nor the sleepless nights to recover from both; a wrecked body and sore boobs. That's a sacrifice no man has ever sensed, yet it's uniquely fundamental to motherhood; thus, jealousy evidenced by the fact that the man's parental sacrifices never came with genital restoration surgeries or postpartum depression or stretch marks. Jealousy over the high probability of infidelity during pregnancy—while the wife feels fat and gross, the husband feels the pending doom of monogamous fatherhood (his penis not his own but feeling owned) and that forever fear of The Other Woman swooping in like a licentious bird of prey, taking up the susceptible married man whose vulnerabilities she could smell a mile away while on the job or in the supermarket or at the gym. Kiernan recognized while staring at Jake breathing that her latest perspective—jealousy over him rather than distrust of him—nagged with the same intensity at her. She'd pick the lesser of the two evils, as if either-or wouldn't doom her marriage. Whether it had been jealousy or distrust, both emotions brought their self-imposed wounds with idiosyncrasies that bled out happiness and confidence from a couple. It's worse when the jealousy and distrust existed unjustifiably.

I'm being silly, she thought.

And as self-fulfilling prophecy would have it—Fate's incorrigible little brother—Jake, a sleep-talker, stirred and groggily said something Kiernan couldn't make out coherently at first. Jake clenched her hand. Breathing out of his mouth now, he turned his head to face Kiernan. Still asleep, Jake lowly muttered, "May... Luf Ta Meh (...*moaning*...) Kevin..."

Shocked! Wide-eyed... A sinking feeling in her stomach...

Kiernan lurched back from Jake, flailing. She fell out of bed on her backside but soon gathered some composure; sweating with bated breath, stricken and appalled. She stood up on bare feet. She cinched closed her negligee, standing in front of splintered moonlight that shone on her back. A silhouette abed with a nimbus, through the uncurtained window—shaking her head in disgust—she said, "What the fuck!"

CHAPTER 5

FAMILY LIFE WITH A FINGERTIP'S GRIP ON THE EDGE

Later that morning, 3:18 a.m.
The Montgomery Townhome
Burlington, VT

Jake had been stirred awake, glassy-eyed, poked by an alien sense that he had slept alone without Kiernan in bed most of the night. He had reached back behind himself to get a sense of where his wife was but touched a pit in the mattress—a rude absence where her body should've been. He shot up and got out of bed. Save for the forgiving creaky wood flooring after Jake's every third or fourth step forward, all had sustained quiet at home. Turtle wax wood polish and potpourri tainted the air that he shifted.

Jake, on sock-feet and bare-chested, adjusted himself in tight white boxer briefs as he made his way down the dusky white-walled hallway of shut doors. An archway, his endpoint, framed pale moonlight eerily. He walked through it and met the rounded ledge to the sunken living room floor below. There, he dropped his gaze where a stray beam of moonlight through an adjacent window exposed her asleep in the fetal position on the pillowy L-shaped sectional at the center of the space. Not knowing why Kiernan had chosen the sectional over their bed, he decided to let that Q&A sleep too. He scooped up his wife, cradled her like an infant in his arms—seemingly just as light—and returned her to their bedroom.

He placed her gently in their bed, kissed her once upon the forehead through chestnut brown hair before her head drooped left-to-right away from him on her pillow. He ran around the foot of the bed to get to his side of things and got in bed. He reached down at their feet for the comforter and raised it to their necks, covering them—never waking her. On his side, facing a white mound of comforter that was Kiernan cocooned by it, eventually he caught up with his wife in dreamland, feeling like a man secured by fatherhood, repurposed since married with children, and disguising family life with a fingertip's grip on the edge by never addressing it.

From having dreamt deeply of a distant other-world

and their alien distrust of her earthly ambitions, Kiernan winced at shards of stray sunlight that hit her at just the right angle as she peeked from beneath the comforter around her head and pillow. *How did I get here?* she thought. On her side of things in bed, the digital clock on her nightstand showed the time to be seven-thirty-five. She ducked her head back beneath the comforter; too bright the morning, but it smelled like someone in the distance had already celebrated first light. Bacon and eggs sizzled, and something sweet—perhaps pancakes or French toast with syrup—was the aroma of Jake's cooking calling her from the kitchen to get out of bed, or was it her empty stomach starved for such a breakfast?

A breakfast she was supposed to cook.

Summer's birthday breakfast and church after; totally forgotten by her.

Kiernan decided to get up; meanwhile, Jake crept up the hallway, wincing each time the wood floors creaked under his weight as he approached the threshold, the open door to their bedroom. With an irrepressible grin on his face and seeing that Kiernan didn't sense him in the room as she separated herself from the comforter into the morning light, Jake pounced. He tackled Kiernan from behind, shocking her.

"Weren't you supposed to get up and make Summer's birthday breakfast? Huh?" charged Jake, laughing.

"NO!" she screeched, giggling, "I FORGOT! I FORGOT!"

"Church too! Sleepyhead!" said Jake, tickling Kiernan under her arms. He said, "Now what?! Huh?"

Jake and Kiernan giggled; she writhed as he straddled her while beet-red, laughing in bed. "No, Jake, stop! No—Jake! STOP! (...*giggling*...) JAKE! (...*screeching*...) Okay! (...*screeching*...) Okay!" cried Kiernan with bated breath.

Jake glanced back behind himself as he straddled Kiernan and said, "Come and get your mom for sleeping in! Get her!"

Summer and Chase, appearing out of nowhere to Kiernan, climbed over Jake's back to get to her below—laughter was contagious and breath-taking in the mosh pit of flapping arms and kicking legs and a strewn comforter; clumsy horseplay in bed that felt minutes-long but lasted only seconds. Kiernan struggled to catch her breath, receiving kisses in rapid-fire succession. Sixteen years of marriage had equipped Jake well with the most accurate map of his wife; he knew her every weak spot, the go-to areas for conjuring her languor, desire, or humor.

Then, an ominous thud against the bedroom wood flooring. A second's silence stilled everyone in the room before a bone-chilling caterwaul roused hairs at the pitch of a bullhorn's siren, but from which child? Kiernan and Jake stopped cold, rubber-necking from the headboard toward the unmade foot of the bed because the children weren't immediately visible.

"Chase, honey?" worried Kiernan. "Chase!"

"Summer! Are you okay?" shouted Jake. "Shit!"

Suddenly, Summer popped up from the floor at the foot of the bed and ran out of the bedroom; not a tear. The process of elimination left no doubt it was Chase who cried. Crouching, Kiernan looked up at Jake and said, "Get off me! It's Chase!"

Exasperatedly, Jake swiped at his black hair that curtained his face, pulling it back behind his ear as he dismounted Kiernan. She bolted from the bed on her side. As she rounded the bedpost at the foot of the bed, Chase appeared on his knees in black sweatpants and a white t-shirt, rubbing the back of his head. Kiernan scooped him up in her embrace, giving him a tight, long-lasting hug. Quiet now, Chase sniffled and rubbed his bloodshot eyes clear of fallen tears. Crouched down at eye level with Chase, Kiernan dried the rest of his tears with the hem of her negligee. She asked, "Son, are you okay?"

Chase nodded meekly before he stopped self-soothing the back of his head. He whined, "Summer hates me."

Jake, sitting on his legs in bed, dismissively shook his head in the background.

Kiernan answered, "Summer doesn't hate you, Chase."

She patted Chase on his bum, reared up to kiss him on his forehead, and explained, "You know Mommy has an older sister, right?"

"Yeah," answered Chase, "Aunt Gracey."

"Yep, Aunt Gracey," said Kiernan. "Well, when I was six, Aunt Gracey was ten, but tall, and she whacked me with a broomstick handle. I cried just like you are now. Fast-forward ten years later, I'm sixteen, Aunt Gracey was twenty, away at college, and she got into a car accident..."

"A crash?" asked Chase with astonishment, making and gesturing explosion sounds.

"Yep! A car crash in college. Her right arm got broken; set in a cast and all that. Now, who do you think she wanted to spend Spring Break with while stuck in her dorm room?"

Chase pointed at his mom.

"Yep!" Kiernan smiled, "All her friends left her behind, and after our mom, your grandma, warned her not to sneak off and go to the shore anyway for Spring Break, then I knew, eventually, I'd get a bus ticket to spend some quality time with my sister. The point I'm trying to make, Chase, is that Summer sees you merely as an extra right now. No one important in this movie where she has the leading role as Big Sister. But when you get a little older, and her focus is no longer about stealing childhood scenes in the house, but real-life consequences out there, she will seek you out because you will become the most trusted man in her life as her only brother. You mark my words.

You may be expendable right now to her, but know later on in life, you will mean the world to her."

Chase shook his head.

"You'll see, okay?"

Chase nodded, his blue eyes flooded with tears of hurt and disappointment.

"Okay," said Kiernan. "Now you wait right here beside me."

Kiernan turned from Chase to Jake, still perched on his knees in bed, listening and observing. Her expression had changed from compassionate to contemptuous, and Jake read the shift as clearly as his unspoken marching orders to call their daughter to the bedroom.

OPERATION: *Deal With Your Daughter* was in effect. Immediately, Jake cupped his hands around his mouth and shouted, "SUMMER KRISTINA TERESA MONTGOMERY! FRONT AND CENTER, YOUNG LADY!"

All eyes turned toward the open bedroom door, awaiting Summer's arrival from wherever she was hiding. It took a minute; meanwhile, Kiernan, crouched down, hugging Chase with one arm, whispered, "Jake?"

"Yes, dear?"

"Don't you fall for her bullshit. Hold firm!"

Jake nodded just as Summer slipped into the bedroom. She stopped just past the threshold, leaning against the door with her hands behind her back. Her long, limp blonde hair cascaded over her shoulders. She had changed her clothes and now wore a yellow flowing sundress with brown sandals. Her expression was unreadable but polite—her poker face on. Everyone in the room anticipated Summer would deny being Chase's assailant and then brim with emotions to project victimhood as a strategy. An avid chess player since she was five years old, Summer thought five moves ahead. A reader of Greek tragedies and plays, she had developed a gift for gab, which won Jake over every time. A precocious 13-year-old who was definitely a Daddy's Girl, she often treated Jake's favor for her like pawns at her disposal and for her own personal gain. Kiernan waited for Jake to say something, and so he started, "Summer, you can't—"

"Daddy?" Summer interrupted. "Your phone is on vibrate."

"What?"

"Your phone..." She brought her hands forward, revealing Jake's cell phone in her right hand, holding it out toward him. The glowing screen caught his attention. Summer said, "You got a call." She averted her gaze to see her mother crouched, holding Chase around his waist, both perplexed. Coyly, she announced, "Daddy, I think it's Kevin."

"What?"

"Look," said Summer, smirking; she knew her pawn would block the queen's will to punish her.

Jake turned toward Kiernan and Chase at the foot of the bed and said, "I gotta take this. I'm sorry."

Jake snatched his cell phone from Summer's outstretched hand. He hopped out of the unmade bed and bolted from the room. Kiernan noticed the slow-forging of Summer's devilish grin at her, brimming with satisfaction. Summer knew her parents well; she knew her mom would pressure her dad to enforce discipline after the fight with Chase went horribly wrong. So, she had found her dad's phone on the kitchen counter, perused his contacts until she found Kevin's number, and called it. After several rings, she hung up, knowing Kevin would call back. Kevin called her dad daily, sometimes four times a day, and Jake never ignored him. Knowing her dad had been appointed as the enforcer and that he would never want that role against his daughter, Summer knew he would take that call from Kevin to avoid punishing her.

Kiernan's glare chilled Summer. The girl's grin faded as she started to back away, fear creeping in. Kiernan, unlike Jake, had no qualms about spanking Summer. Chase grabbed the sides of Kiernan's face, drawing her fuming attention toward him alone, and Summer took the opportunity to escape her mother's gaze. Chase whined, "Mommy, Summer gets away with everything."

Kiernan scoffed and said, "And so does your father."

10 Years Later

CHAPTER 6

VISIT #124

PRESENT-DAY: January 6th
SE State Correctional Facility
Windsor, VT
[10:05 a.m.]

Jake sensed a rude presence. It reeked of a tart men's cologne which, he presumed correctly, had been strategically applied earlier that morning like a body wash to mask the egress of liquor consumed overindulgently the night before. From the corrections officer's well-lit vantage point on the tier, seeing Jake through the interstices of his beige-chipped-painted cell bars—alone in a cement-walled, windowless dusky cell; couchant upon the top bunk already made with his hands folded behind his shaven head; topless with his state-issued inmate jumpsuit hiked up waist-high and cinched by its sleeves; his ankles crossed, brown pleather state-issued boots donned—he was surprised to see Jake asleep.

Not every closed eye is a sleeping eye.

Inmates almost always knew when a visitor planned to see them; in fact, inmates were the last to know since their incoming and outgoing letters were screened and their phone calls recorded by prison personnel, per norm.

The corrections officer, a young Latino, balding already, in his twenties, short-statured, and thewy in his dark blue uniform with shoulder patches of an American flag and a badge of the Vermont Department of Corrections, was institutionally stone-faced upon approach toward the cell bars. The corrections officer peered in, squinty-eyed, between the interstices of the cell bars: a bunk bed, a desk, a stainless steel toilet-sink combo, stale urine in the toilet. At the back of the cell, the window appeared covered by torn-out pages of the Bible, which shaded the morning light on the other side to a dusky complexion within the confines of the cell.

At first glance, the cell appeared unoccupied. The empty bottom bunk drew the corrections officer's focus up to the top bunk. There was Jake, supine. The corrections officer poked his nose between the cell bars and sniffed. Jake smelled like a wet dog to him. A slight snore; he heard Jake breathing evenly, healthily. His bare chest appeared to rise and fall normally. The infamous inmate wasn't dead, in other words, to his discernment. Not every closed eye is a sleeping eye, however.

Jake was playing opossum—he couldn't let The System know that visits meant everything to him, lest the powers that be might curtail them or outright deny the institutional privilege for sport; just to hurt him or any other inmate at SE State Correctional Facility. The powers that be practiced pettiness, indifference, and retaliation; agendas of unwritten policy. In his decade down, Jake had seen it all behind bars, and he believed he had been merely fortunate to avoid the prison staff's punitive prescriptions. They hadn't singled him out yet; perhaps it was the visits (*once a month, never a month missed, for ten years and four months straight so far*) that compelled the powers that be to restrain themselves, Jake believed. And he was right.

The corrections officer barked through the cell bars, "Montgomery!"

Jake cracked a wry smile on the top bunk and answered quietly, "Yes."

His tone signaled to the corrections officer that Jake wasn't asleep at all, and that didn't go over too well. "Get your stink-ass down from that bunk, murderer!" yelled the corrections officer, "VISIT!"

Jake uncrossed his ankles, swept his legs over the edge of his top bunk—letting his legs dangle a bit as he sat upright. He looked down at the corrections officer on the other side of things. The corrections officer glanced behind himself, just slightly, in a swift motion, and came forward, closer to the cell bars, with an inmate-familiar skin notepad of sorts. He then plucked a pen from his breast pocket.

A booklet of passes.

Jake hopped down out of his bunk and headed toward his sink to wash, as the corrections officer proceeded to authenticate a pass with a time, date, and his signature. Inmates at SE State Correctional Facility were not allowed to roam freely from one cellblock or unit to another; thus, the pass. A corrections officer's authenticated pass granted inmates permission to leave a cellblock or unit for another. Likened in concept to a grade schooler's hall pass system, whereby the teacher afforded the student an engraved wooden slate or signed paper, and as long as the student held onto their pass, they were excused from any referrals for discipline from the hall monitor on the lurk. The prisoner's pass system was comparable to that one. Uniformed corrections officers stood post at various areas within the labyrinth of corridors throughout the prison.

"Stick a hand out and wave once when you're ready, and an officer will pop open your door," ordered the corrections officer with a flat tone and angry disposition. The corrections officer walked off. Jake finished washing his shaven bald head, face, and hands; then retrieved a towel and took notice of the pass. The size of an index card, propped up on its side between the cell bars at Jake's shoulder height; meanwhile, he dried his head, hands, and face with the white state-issued terrycloth towel and returned it to the grey-painted nail that protruded from the concrete wall alongside his mirror.

Akin to looking into a Mac Truck's metal hubcap smeared and ghostly, Jake's reflection in his mirror was unrecognizable, insofar as what he had become. An inmate. His appearance notwithstanding. He remembered his long black hair that used to curtain his face; his polished, jock style. The flip of his hair every five seconds was part of his sex appeal.

No more.

His head was now shaved. Haircuts cost money in state prison, which he lost, so he had given up his locks a long time ago. A state-issued Bic disposable razor every Thursday. Longish hair with euro-style flair in prison made him either the butt of jokes or the target of gay inmates. No more trimmed goatee with a five o'clock shadow precision; instead, he let his facial hair grow out into a full black coarse beard with flecks of gray through it.

Physically, Jake appeared gaunt, especially so at 6'3". No more that bull-of-a-man Adonis others viewed him as. He rivaled in appearance a meth addict, but he hadn't lost his teeth yet. Dark patches anchored his blue eyes, making them appear sunken and soulless. Those effervescent blue eyes, once as bright as headlights, were now bloodshot and tired after ten years of incarceration. He saw a future confined by the past, with no freedom in sight in-between. His permanently tanned skin, a decade later, appeared ashen and blotchy all over his body.

Think: clothes, but the colors in the washer accidentally mixed in with the whites drenched with bleach.

Jake looked ruined.

Now 54 years old, but looking ten years older, Jake snatched up his pass, waved his left hand out from between his cell bars, and got noticed by corrections officers stationed in a crow's-nest module situated at the front of the cellblock. A buzz sounded—odd over his shaven head—then his cell door clicked ajar.

He pushed it open, vacating the cell. It locked behind him electronically.

The shape of a horseshoe, the elevated gated tier Jake walked across—all eyes on him—before he reached the staircase, which led him to the first level of the well-peopled and boisterous cellblock. Over the handrail, Jake gazed outward and counted some 20 to 40 state inmates in jumpsuits like his, labeled D.O.C. upon their backs and surnames on their breast pockets. No secrets in prison. Most of the state inmates Jake spied were Black, only because they always tracked his steps, so he learned over the decade to eyeball them likewise; so far, an unspoken tension. Given a very White Vermont, Jake wondered how the state was able to arrest and incarcerate so many Black individuals; in all, it seemed disproportionately wacky and obscenely unreal to him.

Where'd they all come from?

Nonetheless, he noticed that the Blacks and Whites got on well in the cellblock. They played chess and cards together, seated at the dayroom tables, sharing food, drink, smokes, and laughs. They watched the same TV shows. Musical tastes split the races, but they were considerate of one another...on this cellblock of 30 and over...to turn the music down somewhat or not play it too long, but only the dayroom TV played in the background as Jake made his way around the other inmates to get to the cellblock exit.

"Jake! Jake!"

Jake stopped, turned, and saw that it was his only friend on the cellblock—an inmate his age nicknamed Sticks. He was a lifer at SE State Correctional Facility and known for his arts and crafts penchant. It was how he bought his smokes, commissary, and protection. A scrawny White guy with a steep receding hairline. Bald at the top but brown hair greying. Missing all of his front teeth. His left cheek was always puffed out with chew, but never a spittoon in his hand. He was a swaller. He smelled like glue and wet newspaper if you got too close. A mere 5'8" stature that walked hunched over. Somehow he managed to convince a cellblock of mean-eyed inmates to give him their popsicle sticks from their lunch trays; not throw them in the trash, and they agreed.

Every lunch tray, the other inmates on the cellblock would save their popsicle sticks for inmate Stanley Mosokowitz, going on 20 years. One day, a corrections officer—a religious type—performing one of his bed-check rounds peeked into inmate Mosokowitz's cell and spotted, on the concrete floor, hundreds, if not just shy of a thousand, popsicle sticks. Instead of uttering "Oh, shit," the Bible-thumper said, "Oh, Sticks!"

A nickname was born. No one called Sticks Stan or Stanley or Stanley Mosokowitz ever again, not even the corrections officers or their higher-ups, and Jake wouldn't buck The System nor who it selected to denigrate.

"What's up, Sticks!" answered Jake (the two fist-bump). "I was just heading out to..."

"Your visit, right?"

"Yes, sir. My daughter. Why? What's up?"

"Sorry to hold you up, then. I just wanted to know if you'd be up for playing chess later. I could use a break from... you know."

"What are you building now?"

"A Catholic cathedral with a courtyard. I've been working on it for two weeks."

"For you or someone else?"

"Someone else," said Sticks. He leaned into Jake, looked up at him with a wry smile, and muttered, “Five smut mags and three vapes, I'm getting for it."

Jake nodded. "Cool."

"Alright, I'm gonna go," said Sticks, backing away. Jake turned to walk away. Behind him, Sticks shouted, "Don't look up, though!"

Inside joke.

"Shit!" muttered Jake on the way out. He looked up. Out perched his middle finger... to the mural overhead and Sticks behind him. What Jake noticed was that which he hated, and Sticks knew it. Cellblock G's massive, ostensibly scandalous entranceway/exit mural.

The blue-green dominant eyesore of a mural—tile floor to ceiling around the entranceway/exit sliding steel door—had been painted by some ass-wipe state inmate from another cellblock, in good with corrections officers and the administration; probably a C.I. rat also best described as a bootlicker; most likely an inmate-trustee whom block corrections officers relied on to help them not do a thing on their shift. A kiss-ass, the muralist, because the largeness of the mural alluded to the time and access granted him to paint such a thing. And, boy, did The System, the jailers, exploit the talents of this inmate-muralist; this kiss-ass; this bootlicker who more than obliged them. The mural proved he had been let loose, and his quasi-Picasso-Surrealist bend did not sign his work. C.I. rat, he was smart, Jake thought.

Anonymous, this inmate-muralist painted countless different colored human eyeballs floating in a blue-green iridescent morass. A backdrop that bubbled and swirled ceilingward down a drain counterclockwise, along with handcuffs, shackles, gavels, *The Black's Law Dictionary*, white prison jumpsuits without bodies in them, crosses (the Crucifixion, to be precise), in the hundreds, a lighted menorah, the *Quran*, and, for some reason, a bloodied fetus contained within a glass box cracked. Across the mural's field of expression—what Jake and other inmates always raised their middle finger toward—front and center over the entranceway/exit sliding steel door, bright-yellow whimsical lettering plastered clarion this maxim:

"If [**you don't**] know who you are before you enter The System,
it will change you;
but if [**you do**] know who you are before you enter The System,
you will never change."

Off the cellblock, pass in hand validated after an officer's checkpoint, down the well-lit vacant corridor of white-painted shut doors with silvery push-handle crossbars, seeing the visiting room door at the endpoint, that mural's maxim stuck with Jake every time; every visit. Fathom reading those words unavoidably so every day for a decade: the only thing Jake wanted to know as proof of love from his two children, but only one of them showed up to oblige him... Summer.

Back to the Start of Lies...
Spring, 2013

CHAPTER 7

Meet Kevin Moran

(FLASHBACK) April 10th
Moran Motors New & Used Cars
Downtown Burlington, VT
1:10 p.m.

Generous but a taker. Gregarious but a faker. Kevin Moran appeared to be fun-loving until he wasn't. He only made eye contact with folks if the swindle or swearing called for it. A winker at the ladies. A backslapper with the guys. A liar to himself and to others while only fooling his wife. Kevin regarded people as mere opportunities to exploit for his personal gain, but he had yet to meet a man or woman who played people for sport like himself, so he sincerely believed he was unique, not lucky; invincible, not incorrigible.

A sexy woman—a busty blonde in red high heels and tight blue jeans—walked into the sunny showroom: *click-*

clack! click-clack!—an echoey glass cube indoors. Kevin had in his hands a post-marked parcel from Europe, which he stuffed quickly in the top drawer and rose to his feet. Like a scanner, he could see through her skimpy clothing, or so he imagined he could. He vacated the desk and followed her, her tart-smelling fragrance leading him toward the grey Saab on sale, parked in the far corner of the showroom space. The middle-aged woman, who looked 20 years younger, was dressed provocatively in her tight, strategically placed denim blue jeans, which appeared liquefied like leggings in their grip on her ass, thighs, and calves. They didn't reach her ankles. Her red high-heeled shoes were open-toed, her toenails painted black (sexy and trashy), making this short-statured woman, outwardly sassy just by her stance, appear confident. She donned a red crop top (braless) underneath a man's crisp white collared shirt, which she had rolled at the crooks of her arms and unbuttoned. Clearly, she had the buttoned shirt open to expose her pierced navel with a thin golden hoop in it. No earrings or wristwatch. No visible tattoos, though she carried a biker-chick air about her. Nice apple-bottom ass. Upon first entry, he recalled seeing smoky-eye eyeliner around her sultry green eyes, which glinted like shimmery basins. He gorgonized her, especially the hair flipping. She did it six times while standing by the passenger side door of the shiny new Saab. Kevin stood behind her, waiting for her to face him at some point. He could smell her tart perfume masking her womanly scent. He noticed at her pate, not a true blonde, because her roots gave her away. She motioned suddenly toward the trunk of the Saab, inspecting its features.

"A grey leather interior," she remarked.

"Yes. Heated seats too, even the backseats."

A Michelle Pfeiffer look-alike as *Catwoman in Batman*, Kevin deduced.

Coolly, the woman walked back to the passenger side door where Kevin stood, but she turned her back while she stood in front of him, clutching her purse's shoulder strap at breast height. Peacocking the roundness of her ass in those blue jeans, she turned her head slightly over her left shoulder, caught a glimpse of Kevin peripherally, paused for effect, then asked, "Are you alone here?"

"Yes."

The woman turned, faced Kevin with a snarky upturned gaze—hiding her grin packed with ulterior motives—pretending to be interested in the grey Saab at her back. She asked, "There's no price tag. How much?"

"For the Saab?"

"No, for you."

"What?"

"Do I intimidate you?"

"No."

"How much for the Saab?"

"$37,540 with all the bells and whistles. $32,000 flat without. But can we start over? Ma'am! I'm Kevin Moran, the owner here at Moran Motors... Welcome—Where You Take The Wheel. Sorry! If that sounds like something between motto-schtick and salesmanship, I really do mean to help. Are you really interested in this Saab here? Were there other vehicles, maybe out on the lot? Some pickups, or I'm guessing, here, Ma'am..."

"Shhh..." said the woman, cringing at being called Ma'am without turning around to face Kevin.

The woman, a stand-alone customer—which Kevin identified right away by the lack of a wedding band on her ring finger and no boyfriend in tow after her—was arguably single, he thought, and all his to manipulate. No other customers had entered the showroom. With Kevin's secretary Miranda out getting lunch, the moment ripened for scandal, rivaled only by the sexy woman who triggered it. It never occurred to Kevin that the moment could be a ploy any more than he could discern that she could have stayed outside on the lot and looked at the numerous low-priced tagged cars parked; clearly a woman of modest means—much in stock half-off, labeled as clearance sale vehicles out there. Instead, she entered the high-price showroom with just three cars on display, which attracted businessmen in suits. The woman staked out the dealership; she spied from the lot where Kevin's secretary had left Moran Motors 20 minutes ago. So, with small talk aside, the time was now to make her move.

"What's your name again?" asked the woman.

"I'm Kevin Moran; nice to meet you."

Kevin Moran extended his hand to shake hers, and she obliged, pressing his hand a bit longer than the courteous norm. Hands parted, but not their glares; eye-to-eye contact appeared damn near coitus itself. The chemistry between them was instantaneous.

Now! she told herself (*...a quick lick of her red-painted lips...*) Now!

Kevin said, "I can show you the—" (*cell phone ringtone of the Penn State Nittany Lions Fight Song sounded off in his back pocket*)—"Excuse me. I have to take this," he added with a raised finger as he reached behind himself for his cell phone. Kevin turned his back to the woman and said into his cell phone, "Jake... Jake, you hung up on me! Summer gave you the phone. I heard it, then click!"

"Thanks!"

"It was an accident. I know. I know, but, man, you got me out of a pickle this morning."

"What pickle?"

"Never mind; household politics."

"Queen Kiernan has your nuts in a vice again? What for now? Did you forget it's Summer's birthday?"

"No! Hell no, but Kiernan did. She slept in this morning; now they're about to go to the spa."

"Then what's the pickle?"

"Never mind, Kevin. Never mind. Why'd you call? I'm returning your call."

Kevin felt a pointed tap on his shoulder from behind him. He turned to the woman, saying, "Excuse me, Jake... yes Ma'am? One min—"

"Call me Ma'am again, and I'll walk!"

Stunned, Kevin pulled the cell phone from his right

ear and firmly said, "Sorry, you won't have to tell me twice" (*he winked at her with a milquetoast grin*).

"My name," she paused while strangling her purse strap with both hands—a swift bleached blonde hair-flip tossed in quite peeved—she announced, "...is Shannoah. Shannoah Blakely."

"Nice to meet you, Shannoah Blakely. I'm sorry. This call will only be a minute, I promise. I'm all yours then."

Kevin turned his back before Shannoah could respond. "Jake?" he fretted. "Hello? Can you hear me?"

"Um, yeah? Who in the hell was that? An employee?"

"No. A customer."

"Yikes, dude!"

"Yeah, don't worry, I'll win her over. (Shannoah overheard him...) But listen—real quick—I gotta tell you why I called. I got it, dude! I got it!"

"Got what, Kev?"

"Do you remember that show on the History Channel called Vikings?"

"Hell yeah!"

"Well, I just received the shipment of something I bought for you; that Norse-inspired dagger I got from some props guy who used to work on the set. He lives in Norway. He got it to me in the mail. It's in my secretary's desk. Well, I got it engraved and everything. It has a kick-ass slogan in Latin. I came up with it. I can't wait for you to see it, Jake."

"Sounds cool. But listen, don't tell Kiernan about

what you bought me, dude. It will be a thing. She'll tell Daliah on you, and it will be a thing."

"I can't buy you stuff? Dude, I knew you before Kiernan did (*...Shannoah hurried toward Kevin from behind him...*) You're back with me! The old crew is back! I should (*...click-clack, click-clack; Shannoah's heels on tile flooring...*) uh-huh... That might really do it!"

Suddenly Kevin sensed what he initially believed to be a hug from behind around his waist. His gaze dropped. Wide-eyed, he noticed a woman's two hands, red-painted nails like talons, reach down and unzip his zipper.

"WHOA!" he exclaimed. "Stop!"

"What? What? Me?" asked Jake in Kevin's ear. Kevin pulled his cell phone from his ear, looking down. He swallowed hard. Shannoah Blakely had swung herself around Kevin's torso, using it like the pole of a go-go dancer working for tips. Crouched down, she reached inside the mouth of Kevin's unzipped dark slacks and pulled out his nearly fully engorged penis. She licked the tip of his head once, then she engulfed it, greedily.

"MY GAWD!" exclaimed Kevin as he raised his cell phone to his ear. He hissed, then said, "Jake! I gotta go!"

(*...Click...*)

CHAPTER 8

THE MONTGOMERY GIRLS' SPA DAY & HEARSAY

Meanwhile...
Tai-Beauty Hair & Nails Salon
Uptown Burlington, VT
[1:25 p.m.]

Kiernan was hard-pressed to dismiss a scheduled spa appointment, Summer being a brat on her birthday notwithstanding. She and Summer reclined nicely in their overly cushy vinyl swivel salon chairs, all relaxed. Another woman, dressed rather provocatively and keenly aware of The Montgomery Girls, touched Kiernan's armrest with hers, leering at them with a grin.

Kiernan had been smeared with an avocado mud mask twenty minutes ago, cucumber slices over her eyes. Summer, seated next to her, leaned back with cucumber slices over her closed eyes too—but no mud mask. Kiernan didn't mind her daughter enjoying the posh perks of adulthood like her, but she had drawn the line on Summer wearing makeup or a mud mask. Summer had a fresh, clear complexion, not even a pimple, and Kiernan didn't want to jinx her daughter's natural beauty.

Glaring white fluorescent lighting was a slight din overhead. Another mother and daughter team, the Wangnis, owner and future-owner, worked The Montgomery Girls' pedicures next, starting with a warm, lavender Epsom salt foot bath and sole scrub. Soapy water flecked with purple petals; violets. Mother Wangni, with her long straight black hair styled pulled back harshly by a large silvery barrette and in a long ponytail with a brown denim apron on, sat on a red plastic footstool and worked on Kiernan's feet, holding them up, one by one, between her legs. Daughter Wangni worked on Summer almost in sync.

Ambient sounds of seagulls squawking behind ocean waves crashing played through The Montgomery Girls' speakers inlaid within the red vinyl headrests. The audio was supposed to aid in washing away stressors from outside the spa, but it wouldn't. Summer, the birthday girl, learned before coming to the spa with her mother that their Mother-Daughter Birthday Spa appointment, reserved last year, was nearly canceled by Mom, if not for Dad's interference; a delicious matter worthwhile airing out publicly to the Wangnis, the woman that sat next to them, and whoever was in earshot.

Teenagers.

Kiernan confirmed that the cancellation move in a phone call was true, which compelled Mother Wangni—working on Kiernan's foot scrub—to look up and ask quizzically, "Wah hah-pen 'ta Shace at 'ta hoss?"

"Well," answered Kiernan, plucking off her cucumber slices from her eyes before rolling them at Summer, adding, "Funny, you should ask, Ms. Wangni. Our birthday girl here—"

"Thirteen years old, by the way, yay!" quipped Summer snarkily.

"Wow! Thirteen," said the Wangni daughter at Summer's feet, rinsing them off with lavender water.

Kiernan continued, "...After being provided a lovely French toast breakfast—"

"That she slept through, by the way. Don't leave that out, Mom."

Kiernan, shaking her head at Summer, said, "Her Dad made her Canadian bacon with this French toast breakfast on her day. Her choice. Her favorite, right? Girly here comes into my bedroom, pounces on her little brother, and tries to crack his skull at the foot of the bed. My son, Chase; you know?"

"Yah! Yah!" agreed Mrs. Wangni, "Shace, yah. Blood? He bleed?"

"No, no blood. Thank God."

Summer chirped, "All of this is hearsay."

The woman at Kiernan's side appeared to turn her head toward The Montgomery Girls and listen intently to this story, just getting started. Kiernan said, "...So when Summer here refused to apologize to her little brother who could've ended up in the emergency room —again, refusing to apologize—I picked up the phone and called the spa. That's when your lovely daughter picked up."

Daughter Wangni, Zhioxue, glanced over at her mother beside her seated on her footstool and said, "Mrs. Montgomery wanted to cancel."

Mother Wangni gasped. She turned to look up at Kiernan and asked, "Wha? Why you cancel on me? No-no, not good."

"I didn't want to, you see, but—"

"But she likes to punish me," interjected Summer.

"Not true," said Kiernan. "My daughter seems to have an accountability problem, which her father has made worse while I was at work all these years. Now that I'm home again—"

"She plans to ruin everything."

"No, Summer!" said Kiernan, a pitch too high. "I plan to bring some discipline back to the home that has been slouching in my absence. I've worked hard all my life. My children enjoy a lifestyle of privilege with none of the accountability that earns such privileges. It has been handed to them without asking or assistance or appreciation. I'm going to change all that."

"I bet you are," chirped Summer.

Kiernan laughed smugly and glanced down at her bare feet in Mrs. Wangni's hands and whined, "See what I have to deal with?"

Mrs. Wangni nodded sympathetically.

Zhioxue, her daughter, chortled.

Kiernan said, "So, I stayed committed to the appointment because your lovely daughter over there gave me a call-back. She offered me half-off on the facial treatment and a free pedicure if I kept the appointment, (*...Mrs. Wangni nodding proudly at her daughter...*) but it was Summer's dad who pushed me to keep the appointment with Summer. That's if I'd agree to go out on a double-date with him later tonight. A fancy dinner downtown at The Vine, you know? With The Morans." (... *The woman seated next to Kiernan tilts her head curiously at the mention of that surname...*) "I couldn't turn that dinner-date down, and besides, I hadn't seen our friends from college in years. I'm retired now, and I haven't dressed nicely in a while. So, I said to myself, 'Self? Why should I be punished for somebody else's sins? I ain't Jesus!'"

"Amen!" mocked Summer.

The Wangni Girls giggled tearfully.

After a long pause and a roll of the eyes at Summer, Kiernan sighed, saying, "As you can see, a mother's work is rarely done."

"Ew say da' MO-RAWNS, yes?" asked Mrs. Wangni while towel-drying Kiernan's feet.

"Yes, why?"

"Oh, da' MO-RAWNS! Da-lee-ah come-ear at 'en month. All time. She, sweet lady."

"Yes, she is," confirmed Zhioxue quietly.

Summer sighed out of boredom... loudly.

Kiernan struggled to ignore Summer but added, "Yes, um... Daliah is a teacher. We all went to college together. Jake, her husband, and me. We just moved out here recently and found out they were already here. Totally by accident, I just bought a house in the same neighborhood, just a block away from them. I guess that's fate, huh?"

"Fate, indeed," said Mrs. Wangni as she rubbed a mint-woodsy spice oil into Kiernan's soles, massaging them. Kiernan cooed, meanwhile. Summer looked on, and so had the lady seated next to Kiernan amid her foot-soak just about done; needing attention too, but not getting it. She didn't care about that, though. The lady had more controversial interests unbeknownst to The Montgomery Girls.

"Yeah!" said Kiernan. "Those Morans... Can't get away from them, I guess. He owns... I mean by he, Kevin Moran. He owns all the dealerships in this town, basically."

"Yah-yah, I know. Good money. Good people," answered Mrs. Wangni.

Zhioxue said to Summer, "I'm done. If you want to take a walk or get a water?"

"No, I'm fine. Thank you."

Mrs. Wangni said to Kiernan, "Yes, you just about done too—"

Kiernan's cell phone rang.

"Hold on a sec," said Kiernan as she scrambled through her purse at her side to pull out her cell phone.

She saw on her caller ID that it was Jake, and she tapped the screen once. "Hello, dear. You're on speaker. What's up?"

"Hi, honey. You and my birthday girl having a good time?"

"Sure, I guess. What's up?"

Summer craned over Kiernan's armrest and yelled, "Hi, Daddy!"

"Hi, sweetheart!" Then his attention turned to Kiernan, "Reservations made for four. Kevin and Daliah will meet us there, separate cars, then. Violets On The Vine is a go."

"What time, exactly?"

"Eight."

Summer interrupted, "Daddy, tell Chase to remember my birthday present. We'll be home within the hour."

Jake chortled. "Sweetheart? After bashing his head in, you got some kahunas, birthday girl."

"I know, right!" said Summer, laughing.

Kiernan shot Summer a glare. She sat back in her salon chair. The lady seated beside Kiernan grimaced devilishly, listening in. Kiernan told Jake, "We're almost done here. I'll be home soon."

"Okay, bye."

Kiernan pressed the screen on her cell phone, which she held out in front of her like a plate, then put it away in her purse. The Wangni Girls finished The Montgomery Girls' feet and proceeded to work on the mud mask Kiernan donned and had long since cracked by talking so much from her chair. Mrs. Wangni closed in with a blue handheld plastic basin half-filled with hot water and a white facecloth floating inside of it. She placed the basin off to the side on a granite-top parlor table behind Kiernan's salon chair, grabbed the hot facecloth, wrung it out, and applied it to Kiernan's face repeatedly until the mud mask was swiped clear from her face.

A youthful face, clean of all things, emerged with just a few streaks of mud mask, but Mrs. Wangni would attend to that. Meanwhile, Kiernan, lost in her thoughts, looked mean to Mrs. Wangni who, between swipes of the facecloth, felt compelled to ask, "Wa es it, Kiernan?"

"Am I pretty?"

"AWWW!" exclaimed Mrs. Wangni, who reached down for the salon chair seat-adjustment lever and yanked it up toward herself, which straightened the back of the chair and launched Kiernan upright. Mrs. Wangni swung the chair around so it would face forward and toward the mirror on the wall.

"Look at yo'self!" said Mrs. Wangni. Summer swiveled in her chair to look at her mother looking back at herself in the mirror. Mrs. Wangni assured Kiernan, "You are gorgeous. NO mid-life cry-sis. No-no, here! So young, you are!"

While Kiernan started to smile, Summer chirped, "That's hearsay."

CHAPTER 9

VISIT #125

PRESENT-DAY: April 29th
SE State Correctional Facility
Windsor, VT
[10:35 a.m.]

Last month's visit didn't end well between Summer and her father.

Prison officials on duty had to intervene because their visiting room dispute got a little too boisterous. Jake, having stood up from his seat next to Summer, had to be restrained. He was lording over Summer, wagging his finger at her, shouting obscenities. Only the two of them knew the subject matter that made the visit devolve in such a way. Later, it was decided by the deputy warden that Jake's contact visits with his daughter would be suspended for ninety days. The warden approved the disciplinary sanction.

Now father and daughter were forced to visit each other face-to-face with a smudged plexiglass window between them in a smelly booth. It was more private than a visiting room setting, but not ideal because of what certain inmates do in the booths when with their wives or lovers on the other side, with no prison guard watching their every move and no janitorial crew to clean up afterward.

Jake was happy nevertheless to see Summer. She looked well-put-together, her light blonde hair pulled back strictly into a bun, arching her thin brows even more so. Pink lip gloss with hints of glitter glazed her pouty mouth, forming a morose line. She sat down, having pulled her blouse cuffs past her blazer's cuffs. She donned a single-breasted, navy-colored pantsuit, a silky white blouse open and frilly in the front showing a little cleavage. He could smell her apple-tart perfume on his side of things. No longer his little girl, he thought.

A woman now.

A working mother and wife too. Busy as a result. He didn't think she'd show up and admitted as much, and she was quick to remind him that she never missed a monthly visit; an exchange said before hello or how are you.

Father and daughter each held a chintzy black landline phone to their ear as they peered through the plexiglass, saccadic gazes each reading something behind the other's eyes that wasn't there and keeping it to themselves. But Jake decided before going in, on this visit, he would listen more than talk. He couldn't lose Summer. She was the only one in the family that would visit him, and eye contact between them never wavered.

To Jake, Summer's eyes appeared to flash more green and suspicious of him than her mother's ever did, and to Summer, Jake's blue-eyedness appeared less loving and even less transparent than Chase's. Her little brother was now a young man in college. That's where the conversation turned last month for the worse; talk of Chase being in college and too busy to see his old man. At least that was the excuse he told Summer to tell him. Jake, not letting the dispute die with dignity, ever pugnacious, started in again about Chase.

"There has to be an underlying reason that you are not telling me. College students get weekends off, Summer. Did you tell him what I said?"

"Yes, Daddy."

"What'd he say?"

"Nothing. He doesn't want to visit you nor talk to you. I'll see it. There! You happy?"

"Did he tell you that, though?"

"He doesn't have to say it, Daddy. I can see it in his eyes. Chase's eyes don't conceal or mislead or lie."

"I know it. He's like his mother in that way."

Jake dropped his glance toward the countertop on his side of things. He struggled to find a next topic that wasn't triggering between them, non-confrontational. He hated the fact that his son hated him, outright disowned him, not because he had been coached into it or lied to for some time, but earnestly gained was his inconsolableness. Chase hated his father knowingly and willingly. Jake made one last-ditch effort on the subject of Chase. He looked up and through the plexiglass, and also through Summer, when he admitted, "I just haven't seen him since..."

Summer's eyes widened. She sensed, perhaps, that her father was on the precipice of admitting something about the past; what got him incarcerated. The booth, she thought, made him vulnerable, she hoped. She waited with bated breath until Jake sighed and said, "Nevermind."

Just like that, the mystery behind the whereabouts of her mother lived on, and she appeared deflated seated there, but she held onto that shallow receiver with its mechanized filtering of the human voice, as her father changed topics to lighten her mood. "Sticks, you remember him, right?"

It wasn't the first time Jake wasted precious visitation time talking about Sticks, the fellow inmate who made knick-knacks out of popsicle sticks for other inmates and their families, selling them to get cigarettes for himself. Summer replied, "Yes, Dad, I know about Sticks. Figurines or something he makes?"

"Yeah, like lighthouses, churches, skyscrapers sometimes—ones like in real life or ones that he imagines in the future. They look real futuristic, like. He—"

"Dad?"

"What?"

"Stop."

"So, what do you want to talk about, then? You really seem serious today. Moody. Problems at home? How's my granddaughter?"

He couldn't remember her name, and Summer sensed as much.

"No problems at home, Dad."

"Problems at work?"

"There's always a problem at a courthouse, Daddy. They're just not my problems. It's where people go to resolve them."

"I'm well aware of that, dear."

"So, no problems at work where I clerk. No problems at home. I'm in love, and I love being a mother. I want to talk about something meaningful involving you, Daddy. I want to talk about..."

"Your mother."

"That's right," she said, leaning forward on her elbows, clutching the receiver to her ear like the handle of a hammer. "Mom," she vexed. "I want to talk about Mom."

"I don't."

"You don't? Why?"

"Sticks says—"

"Fuck Sticks, Daddy! Fuck him!"

"My word, Summer... that mouth."

"Sorry, Dad. I don't want to talk about some inmate who makes figures or crafts or whatever he does. I will never meet this man. He doesn't get you out of prison, so I don't care about him. I want to talk about Mom. I need answers. Maybe there's something you missed... something in your defense not raised before. Like, I was thinking about it; why was Mom's gas card found in that grey Saab, that lady's car? What's her name? Um, Blakely? I know all of this is a decade old, but who was this woman to you, Daddy? Who was she to Kevin? We can probably get the county investigators to review those aspects of the case while your case is on this post-conviction relief appeal, Daddy. I don't believe Mom is dead anymore than I am being told that she has vanished. People aren't magic tricks! She has to be somewhere, Dad. Maybe—"

"I don't care where she is, Summer."

Summer gasped, "Daddy?"

"No, Summer. She left me. She tore this family apart! She bickered at me constantly. She was distrustful. Disloyal! She wouldn't just talk to me. Then, she'd write shit down all the time... that frickin' diary of hers! I'm fucking sick of going over this... re-living this!"

"Where is it, though?"

"Where is what?"

"Mom's diary. And what does Neesha have to do with them? How long did Mom say that she kept a diary going?"

"Summer, Neesha... I don't know. Stop! I don't want to talk about this. I don't know where she is or where she hid her diary."

"Hid? Where? Wait—why did she hide them?"

"She'd hide them from me... from y'all when you were little."

"Dad, I never thought to ask you about this until now. It just came to me, but..." (*sitting upright rigidly in her metal folding chair with her hands flat on her lap*) "...what were you and Mom fighting about that night? Remember? I had just turned thirteen. You were pretty angry about something. The yelling between you two, it woke me and Chase up, and I saw you in the hallway with Mom. You picked her up, smashed her head, the back of it, like, into the wall, remember? You ran out of the house..."

"Summer, enough. I'm still your father, even if behind bars."

His glare was cold, still, and Summer felt the chill of it through the plexiglass.

"Fine!" she erupted, standing up from her seat. "I'm going then!"

"Fine! Don't let the door hit your ass on the way out!"

"Fine!"

"FINE!"

Both father and daughter bolted from the booth on their side of things, both concealing their tears on the way out. A door on her end slammed, and cell bars on his end screeched ajar, then clanked closed.

CHAPTER 10

VIOLETS ON THE VINE

(FLASHBACK) April 10th Violets On The Vine
Fine Dining & Cuisine
Downtown Burlington, VT
[8:15]

Donning black tie suits and black-and-white print dresses with black blazers, the Morans and the Montgomerys entered the restaurant and waited the customary ten minutes. The myth: the wait times were orchestrated to make patrons of the restaurant absorb the garden ambiance like no other. Nevertheless, not first-timers to the pricey establishment, the couples made reservations for seating with a city view.

The dining area's far wall was entirely a window. From the high, verdant ceiling-to-floor window with a panoramic view of Downtown Burlington and beyond, it twinkled like a vast, spooky cosmos in the distance, being some twenty stories high. Indoors, a hushed, mellifluous setting prevailed. The restaurant was well-patronized and polite, with more suits and dresses than everyman's jeans and T-shirts (*or college sweatshirts*), despite no dress code. Piped in through hidden speakers was classical music. Most times it was classical music, and tonight played lowly was Rachmaninoff's "Rhapsody on a Theme of Paganini," the 10th variation to be precise. As themes go, the restaurant's famed vines dripped from the ceiling, budding with purple African violets, leaving a head clearance from them of about a foot or less.

Think: a garden, not aground but a ceiling.

How dirt never rained down on patrons' eating experiences was an inexplicable marvel. Unblinking white string lights intermingled with the pendant verdant vines and throughout the ceiling-garden entire. This presented a starry effect indoors, and wedded with that classical music, it was captivating. Meals starting at $70.00 a plate, it better not be like an Olive Garden.

Their dinner table by the window gleamed, dressed with golden-plated utensils which bracketed bone-white china atop a blood-red tablecloth hemmed by tassels. As they assumed their red-cushioned seats with polished wooden armrests, wives and husbands situated across from their equal, Kiernan couldn't restrain herself. Side-eyeing slyly that whom her distrust cast as her rival: Kevin Moran.

He was a smidge taller than Jake; thinner than Jake; smarter than Jake; a year younger than Jake; by far more successful than Jake, and he came across as kinder than Jake. But his likewise blue eyes, not at all like Jake's, had a hue marine. To Kiernan, they flashed hardened depths where nothing swam. A middle-aged frat boy type with crow's feet, ostensibly trapped in the gilded cage of marriage, as she imagined Kevin might describe matrimony. His clean-shaven appearance, Kiernan recognized, was a mask upon a man who was dirty. He smelled good and expensive. He was handsome, indeed. If the actor Jason Bateman from that TV show The Ozarks needed a look-alike to perform his stunts, Kevin Moran would fit the bill.

This family friend, whom Kiernan's distrust (or jealousy) signaled with a chill down her spine tonight (*and for the first time in sixteen years*), meant that Kevin was no friend at all, but something else. Two fallacious assumptions, Jake would argue if he knew Kiernan's thoughts, and undoubtedly in support of his college buddy Kevin, which by proxy would discredit his wife, and therein lies the rub.

Two waiters worked their table, filling their water wine glasses and their actual wine glasses with a New England brand Pinot Noir called Sailor's Peace. "Try it!" shouted Kevin, who glanced at Kiernan, who appeared skeptical. She cleared her mind about Kevin to play well with others but asked, "Vermont? New Hampshire? Maine? Where is this brand from?"

They all shared a chuckle.

"Southern Maine, I believe," asserted Daliah. "It's

stock wine. Ask the waiters when they come back with the menus to take our orders."

"Now that's a teacher, smart, honey," blurted Kevin. Instantly, Kiernan detected his patronizing microaggression, an attempt to shrink and shame Daliah's place at the table before he could get a foothold at it.

"I'll be the guinea pig. I'll take the first swig," offered Jake.

"Hear, hear!" cheered Kevin sarcastically.

"Oh my god, this is hilarious!" said Daliah.

The waiters could be seen advancing their way, slinking past other tables in the dining area.

"To friends!" cheered Jake and Kiernan together as they raised their wine glasses, half-filled with the dark, sparkling Sailor's Peace. The Morans joined in. Displays of improvisatory energy produced a clang from their wine glasses. The waiters proceeded to lay menus down upon their bone-white china. But about that stock wine, Kiernan reacted, "Wait, mmm! This is good. Sweet!"

"Very sweet!" smacked Jake.

"Where was this brand made?" asked Kevin of one of the waiters standing by closest to his side of things. The waiter responded quietly, "Maine, sir." The other waiter, standing by the wives, nodded once to concur.

"Well, look at that!" rallied Kevin mockingly. "My wife was correct. Maine it is."

Kiernan reacted, "Aren't you lucky to have such a knowledgeable woman to inform you?"

Daliah grinned self-deprecatingly.

"I guess I should be, huh?" remarked Kevin, squinting at Kiernan, irked. He added, "I am grateful, yes." He took a swig of that stock wine only to hide his displeasure. He hated being shown up by anyone, man or woman.

Kiernan's retort: "Yes, you should be." These responses were spoken through strained smiles, but the barbs still made it through their teeth. For the first time in some sixteen years as family friends, Kevin sensed that Kiernan had tired of him and wasn't a fan, and Jake discerned the same sentiments.

Daliah's kind, high-pitched voice warmed the chill at the table. She announced, "Waiters, I think we're ready to order."

The two waiters stepped up and hunched over the couples, activated their pens and notepads, and scribbled away in shorthand that which the couples favored. Jake and Kiernan ordered their meals individually without consultation. Kevin ordered for Daliah and himself, as he always had done when the couples had dinners like these. Kiernan, every time, rolled her eyes, not at Kevin, but at Daliah for her sense that she surrendered her power to him in these instances at the micro level, and at the macro level, Kiernan believed she had set women's liberation rights back a century out of mere acquiescence.

The restaurant's milieu, as it pertained to the music piped in, switched abruptly from classical to jazz.

"Oh, I love this composition," remarked Daliah.

Kiernan asked, "Who is this?"

"John Coltrane's *'Jupiter.'* It's from his last album called *Interstellar Space*. He recorded it five months before he died in 1967."

"I never really sat down and listened to jazz."

"Oh, I love it." Daliah whispered the beginning part of the next response: "I had... a Black boyfriend... (Kevin missed that part) in high school who got me hip to it."

Kiernan and Daliah shared a brief laugh between them.

Kiernan said, "I think it's amazing that you hold such a wide breadth of diverse knowledge and facts right off the top of your brain. I could never—"

...Lady-talk, Kevin surmised. He turned his attention to Jake seated in front of him, which compelled Jake to shift his gaze from the wives, who bored him anyway (...who wants to talk about jazz?), to Kevin in wait. This sparked the table's dissolution into halves with an ease into collusion and exclusion, as husbands and wives clung to their separate vines of conversation, dangling stretches both epiphanic and myopic...

~Husbands~

Kevin: (Grinning devilishly) "So, I sold a car."
Jake: "Yeah... that's kinda what you do, so..."
Kevin: "Husband-talk, now. Follow me."
Jake: "Okay? (...quick glance at Kiernan...) Go!"

Kevin: (*...Hand gesture a buxom woman...*) "
Grabbed it in the showroom today."
Jake: "You gotta give me more than that.
Grabbed what?"
Kevin: (*Glances down at his crotch...*)
"Grabbed it."
"Grabbed it."
Jake: (*...thinking...*) "Get out of here! Where?"
Kevin: "In the showroom!"
Jake: "You mean, when you cut me off on
The phone earlier? (*...excitedly giggling...*)
I knew something was up!"
Kevin: (*...nodding emphatically...*) "Yep!
I couldn't believe what was happening! I
saw the heavens... and other things. I realiz-
ed there is a god."

~Wives~

Daliah: "Every time I see Chase at school, I
want one of my own."
Kiernan: "What? A son?"
Daliah: "Or girl."

Kiernan: "Boy or girl, they are work."
Daliah: "I had a very traumatic experience
in my early teens which rendered me in-
fertile, possibly."
Kiernan: "Possibly? You don't know?"
Daliah: "Well, I haven't gone for a second
Daliah: "Well, I haven't gone for a second
opinion since the first one, and the way
I've been intimate with Kevin, it just has
not happened for us, so..."
Kiernan: "Maybe it could be him (*side
eye in Kevin's direction...*) instead of you
that's infertile?"
Daliah: (*...giggles...*) "Oh, no, never. I'm
certain it's me."
Kiernan: (*Shaking her head...)*

~Husbands~

Jake: "Name?"
Kevin: "Shannoah Blakely."
Jake: "So, you fired her?" (*...Jake peeped
Kiernan eavesdropping...*)
Kevin: (*...He gets the unspoken warning...*) "Yep!
We got her working in Sales."
(*...Kiernan loses interest with Husband's vine...*)

Jake: "You finished... there, um... Showroom?"
Kevin: (*...giggling...*) "Hell no! Lookout Point."
Jake: (*...frowning...*) "Wasn't it crowded at midday?
I called around 1 or 2 o'clock, right?"
Kevin: "Teens ain't going to Lookout Point at
1 o'clock in the afternoon."
Jake: "Yeah, that's right. Only hikers, bikers, joggers,
Wedding planners, photographers, bird-watchers,
Rock climbers, and the occasional pilot of a drone."
(*meal arrives for Kevin: Sea scallops with a butter
squash puree and grilled asparagus spears.)*
Jake: "Thank you" (...he says to the waiter...)
(*meal arrives for Jake: Baked lobster tail with a
bowl of smoked clam chowder and a roll.)*

~Wives~

Daliah: (*...shrugs her shoulders...*)
Kiernan: "Surely Kevin... *(...Kiernan has
overheard the name Shannoah Blakely...)* he
can pay for any reproductive procedure?"
Daliah: "Yes, but would I make a good
mom, you think?"
Kiernan: "Aww!... Daliah, of course!"

Daliah: "I do, sorely, want children."
Kiernan: "And you will have a brood for
sure. But one of my greatest challenges
is raising Summer."
Daliah: "In what way?"
Kiernan: "I've been blessed and cursed
by a mini-version of myself."
Daliah: "Independent? Smart?"
Kiernan: "Chase is a breeze next to her."
(*Meal arrives for Kiernan: Orange roughy
fillets sautéed in a Cajun roué and smeared
with a sesame glaze atop grits.)*
(*Meal arrives for Daliah: Deep-fried catfish
on a bed of jasmine rice with navy beans.)*

~Husbands~

Kevin: "Umm... This looks good! (*...he forked an entire sea scallop and ate it in one bite...*) Let me sum up life for ya, buddy... We've been at this thing for 23 years now... 'If you ain't getting what you should get, you're getting Got!'"
Jake: (*...nodding... sipping wine... He has heard Kevin, over the years, reconstitute this refrain from a wise-ass Black kid from a Psych 101 class at Penn State.)*

The Reality: Opportunities are neutral vehicles, but it is man who is fallible or cynical or immoral with drive.
The Result: Infidelity was victory.

~Wives~

Daliah: "I'm hungry, but I need to say this: You are the gold standard, Kiernan. You're a mother, truly golden. A woman's purpose is to mine her gold—her fertilization; not as much as her silver—her acumen; not as much as her copper—her intuition. Of course, there's worth in silver, even in copper; but to be golden is to bear children."
Kiernan: (*...chewing...*) "Uh-huh."

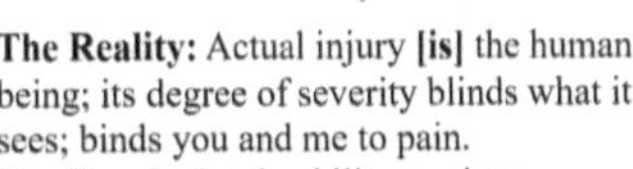

The Reality: Actual injury **[is]** the human being; its degree of severity blinds what it sees; binds you and me to pain.
The Result: Intolerability as virtue.

After their meals were eaten, the last of the stock-wine imbibed, and their crosstalk exhausted, Kevin paid the enormous bill and left a tip to rival it. The married couples went home in the same direction—The Links Estates & Townhomes—but in separate vehicles. In Kevin and Daliah's sedan, the talk was jovial and loving...

"(...laughing...) No, honey, it's true. Violets don't naturally grow on vines. What they got going on there at the restaurant is called hybridization."

"Hybrid-did-what?!" (...laughing...) blurted Kevin. "Oh, honey."

Kevin reached for his wife's hand over the middle console, raised it up to his pursed lips, and kissed the back of Daliah's left hand, which donned his 18-karat pear-shaped diamond engagement ring and gold wedding band. They said their "I Love You's" seconds apart. In Kiernan and Jake's SUV, there was less talk and more suspicion between them:

"Who is Shannoah Blakely?"

"What? I don't know. Some new hire of Kevin's, I guess, at the dealership."

"Is that what we're going with, Jake?"

"Kiernan, I don't know wha—"

"Turn here."

"I will. Damn, Kiernan. What did I do?"

CHAPTER II

WHERE YOU TAKE THE WHEEL, SHANNOAH BLAKELY

Meanwhile... [11:37 a.m.]
(Two Days After the Violets On The Vine Dinner)

Motto as sexual innuendo hails male ego...

(Receptionist's landline phone rings...)

"Hello, Moran Motor's—*Where You Take The Wheel*—how may I help you? Mr. Moran's not available in the showroom at the moment, but if... Well, he's currently at lunch, Ma'am... (*screaming ensues through the earpiece...*) Sorry, sorry, I apologize for calling you... Yes, 'Miss'... 'Miss.' Okay, please hold."

Miranda lowers the phone and says, "Yikes!"

Kevin's indispensable secretary, stationed in the corner of the showroom, seated just outside the Manager's Office—a roofless pre-fab 40-by-60 boxed enclosure whose three sides were corrugated opaque fiberglass walls, which made animated people through them on the inside appear like phantoms to those on the outside, but its fourth side (...*facing Miranda's desk*...) was a wood-framed door (...*shut at the moment*...)—its clear window labeled *Manager's Office* topped by a partially opened transom. Miranda's view through it showed Kevin otherwise preoccupied.

In other words, he appeared mid-chomp upon a shredded lettuce and tomato, drenched in olive oil, stuffed with smoked turkey slices, Genoa salami, and Swiss cheese hoagie, which she had gotten for him ten minutes ago. But Miranda hated dealing with Hot Ones: customers who bought a vehicle from a particular dealer and now have displeasure for whatever reason post-sale. Furthermore, it was a fallacy that Kevin couldn't be disturbed at lunch. He's taken myriad calls from franchisees, his wife and kids, and even close friends. Miranda had transferred several in a single day of what she's dubbed as "Jake-calls"—too many to count.

This irate woman, who was a customer, asked for Kevin, and the Boss's lunchtime No-calls Rule wasn't definitive but discretionary! Lunchtime be damned! The lady on the other end of the line, who reviled being called "Ma'am" in whatever context, was reduced to a blinking red light—a button in a row of them at the base of the landline phone's panel—ostensibly needing no one other than Kevin to voice her problem. Without further deliberation or delay, Miranda decided Kevin should take the call.

His call, not her problem.

She pushed the blinking red button, which reconnected her to the lady. Miranda spoke swiftly: "I'm going to transfer you; please hold!"

(*Kevin's Office landline phone rings...*)

With one hand squeezing a drippy hoagie and the other clutching a store-bought bottle of cold sweet tea with the straw jutting out of the bottle's mouth, Kevin placed his drink down upon his cluttered desk, decided not to screen the incoming call because he believed it to be Jake on the other side of things. He picked up the receiver and answered, "Hello?" (*...no immediate response...*)

"Hello?" asked Kevin. "Is anybody there?"

The lady's voice replied, "Is this Kevin? Kevin Moran?"

"Not Jake," he realized, a customer (*...Damn you, Miranda...*), and responded, "Ah, yes?"

"Are we on speaker?"

"Why? Who is this?"

"Are we on speaker?"

"No."

"We went to Lookout Point."

"(...Shit!...) Um, yep! I recall, Shannoah... Shannoah Blakely. Nice of you to call—um, Ma'am!—(...ripe with sarcasm...) but I'm kinda busy—Ma'am!—at the moment. So, what's up? If you can make it quick?"

"I'm pregnant."

CHAPTER 12

FROM LOVE-MAKING TO LIAR

(Later that evening…)
The Montgomery Townhome
[8:46 p.m.]

Jake's cell phone appeared rested in the upright position in its charging base atop the frosted glass-top credenza by the front door down the dusky foyer. Kevin's incoming texts mounted unanswered, but Jake's cell phone, like Summer and Chase in their beds, was down for the night. (*…giggling…shhh!… in the background…*)

Also down were the lights throughout the townhome. The sparsely furnished décor of the minimalist Scandinavian flair—contrasting cedar wood framing with coarse bone-white fabrics; black glazed clay lamps capped by rust-colored pleated shades situated upon the end tables clean of all things that bracketed the L-configured white sectional. No runners. No throw rugs.

No houseplants. No pets of any kind. No religious iconography. No hanging pictures on the walls made of white stucco. Clean lines only. (...a running chase across creaking wood flooring... shhh!...)

Skinny cottage-style windows, whose nine windowpanes were costume-designed to block out all but sunlight and moonlight until it was a low opaque hue at the push of a button on a cell phone, appeared transparent tonight. They let in the moonlight upon Jake and Kiernan at play, unbridled passions, upon the white sectional. Kiernan backed away in retreat until its left-side armrest barricaded her in. She appeared out of breath. Jake appeared famished. This, apparently, was foreplay...

Jake crawled, not like a toddler but like a panther in pursuit of prey. He snatched off her left sock after she had kicked at him once, and when she kicked a second time, he snatched her right sock from her foot. She tried to shoe him away barefooted to no avail. Coming forward, he would not be denied tonight. This made her giggle, which made him smile wryly. He lunged at her, and he had her now... *finally*. She relented in his grasp. With his left hand, he cradled the back of her head to brace her for his long, hungry kisses. They groaned in each other's mouths. To the other, they tasted like food. With his right hand, he ripped her sheer white pajamas.

Its front buttons popped off!

Click-clacks, similar to the sound of bouncing marbles and their roll down wood flooring, echoed slightly throughout the space. Her sheer pajama top split apart, exposing her breasts and erect nipples entirely; a map to him of where he must explore. Ghostly lines of the earliest marital embraces upon her bare, lithe upper body, he retraced those lines; coloring within them with his broad tongue's length; traveling slick warm tracks of saliva against trembling parts of her: between her breasts, around her waistline, from the small of her back northward toward the nape of her neck. Stopping at her hairline. The heat of these laid tracks cooled in the central air suddenly, then she goose-pimpled.

She orgasmed for the first time in her panties.

He peeled back her remaining shell to the good flesh, both vulnerable and volatile. Their clothes were tossed aside upon the wood flooring. He pounced. Straddled her. A large man. Erect. Thankfully, Kiernan thought, erect. She marveled at his hairless tumescence, lunate and throbbing, upturned to the left and lording. He snatched her up by the neck again with both hands. This chokehold made her head limp and crane backward. Her mouth agape with thirst. Whipping her tongue at him like a snake after the hiss or the demon in *The Exorcist*—passion, this!

He had to bring himself down to her. His mouth onto hers... longing. Incubus versus Succubus, but a mutual must at play for the other's life-force, not just for each other's sex. Floating upon the cloud that was their sectional—their limbs, their torsos, their hands, their hair, their pheromones, their desires twisted them into positions likened to knotted ropes lying flat. Their writhing was tied to the obscenity of lust and the intensity to bust too soon...

"Jake?" Kiernan whispered so as not to wake the children, "I want you inside of me." He obeyed her.

Jake lifted himself from Kiernan from the knees upwards; clutched his engorged penis to harness a direct downward aim. He parted Kiernan's legs wider with his thighs. He lowered himself into her carefully, and at first plunge, she orgasmed a second time. Kiernan wailed as Jake groaned. A lover's symphony, which kept pace by the clapping collisions of their pelvic thrusts into each other... *its own applause.*

She reached up and swiped backward Jake's black curtain of hair away from his face to see his eyes. Those beautiful, penetrating cobalt-blue eyes; to connect with him, as he plunged deeper than his previous plunges inside of her, as though only now he sought her pain more than her passion. He wriggled free his face from her grasp. His eyes closed. A closed sky. They shut her out. And Kiernan, likened to a beggar pounding upon a door that just wouldn't open, was forced to accept that Jake had refused to allow her inside of him as he had been inside of her, poised to ejaculate. Each of Jake's thrusts in and out more erratic, in and out more curved, and in and out more piercing. Like jagged strikes of lightning in her rainstorm, he felt more dangerous.

Jake quaked convulsively.

His arms, as thick as crossbeams, crumbled beneath

the weight of himself. He crash-landed upon Kiernan below, and she sensed inside of herself, along with greater girth, the commencement of a life-giving lamination. Warm squirts from him, of the kind which helped make Summer and Chase their children. Jake shivered after that, as if too cold though sweaty and hot; now relieved. Kiernan calmly cradled him like a child while hoping they didn't just conceive a third.

He raised up slightly... *only slightly*.

Planking Kiernan; his elbows stabbed down into the plump cushions; breast-to-chest, and face-to-face in the semi-dark upon the sectional. Finally, Jake revealed flashes of his eye color to his wife. The sky opened up to her, it felt like... The gas-lit fireplace repelled the darkness from their staring at each other. No hiding. The quiet of the house amplified their breaths winding down from heights of ecstasy back to the ambient echoes of a humbled family life... Earth.

Jake kissed Kiernan... just a peck on the lips.

He looked down into her green eyes, unblinking. He smiled. She didn't smile back. She waited. She needed to hear it. The thing that husbands say to their wives as customarily as handshakes are shared between business partners after the deal was done. Things felt awkward between them suddenly. Kiernan's gaze became pleading, then he admitted it: "I love you, Kiernan."

(...she gasped...)

"Wait a second!" whispered Kiernan. "Let me up."

Jake, surprised, asked, "What?"

Kiernan didn't ask for permission nor forgiveness; she slithered from under the weight of Jake, quickly snatched up her torn sheer pajamas, covered her privates, and darted out of the living room space. Quickly, Jake sat up, found his sweatpants, and tracked the flight of his wife. It appeared she was heading back to their bedroom, but the hallway swallowed her. He couldn't be too sure. He fled the sofa to investigate the turn of events; the love joy she killed. At the end of the hall, Jake noticed their bedroom lights were a loud beacon. He walked toward it. He passed their bedroom's threshold, curiously. He noticed Kiernan seated on her side of the bed, her back to him. She was hunched over. As he walked around the foot of the bed, Jake glanced down, and he noticed Kiernan had her diary split open to a page tabled by her bare lap... *gripping a pen... writing something?*

"What are you doing?"

Kiernan didn't look up. Still writing. Her pen moved swiftly from left to right as though she had inhabited the mind of a self-possessed author desperate to convert visions into written word before the vision vanished; never to be fully depicted again if not captured right then. Jake, having none of this, blasted, "Are you fucking kidding me right now?!"

Kiernan glanced up and whispered, "Shhh! The kids are sleeping!" She placed her pen back to paper to finish coloring in her depictions of Jake with those precise words and long sentences in her diary full of them.

"I don't give a fuck!" blasted Jake.

He lunged for Kiernan's diary. Her quick reflexes executed four maneuvers in one swift motion: she dropped her pen between the pages, making it a placeholder for her interrupted thoughts; shut the diary; fastened its lock; and squirreled it away behind herself, away from Jake. "No! Jake. Stop!" she demanded. Jake never crossed her under the acute projection of that maternal outraged tone. The kids never would either. It was her Red Line.

"I mean, what are you writing?"

"Just what you said," replied Kiernan, but she sensed herself too vulnerable; albeit half-naked for a discussion where Jake, clearly angry, wanted to debate the issue. So she scurried for her sweatpants and a t-shirt that lay upon a chair all night by the bed.

Jake watched her get dressed. He found a t-shirt of his own. Continuing the discussion, he asked, "What did I say?" Truly at a loss.

"You said: 'I love you, Kiernan.' It's been 8 years, 7 months, and 23 days. Chase was only two when you last said it."

Jake appeared dumbfounded.

"You've been counting it?"

"Yes," answered Kiernan, but she was embarrassed. He really looked hurt.

"Oh my God, woman! What's wrong with you?"

"Jake, shhh! The children," she blurted, but she despised it when Jake reversed and reconstituted his shortcomings as her delusions, and she pointed at him, warning, "Don't you do that!"

"For one, don't tell me to shhh! in my own house, (*...her house, she thought, but she let that slide...*) and don't do what, sweetie? Show you how much of a neurotic nutcase you can be? No, how about—YOU DON'T DO THAT!—stop love-making to write about me!" Jake asked sincerely, "I mean, don't you want to talk to me? In the moment? No secrets, Kiernan! No secrets at all!" Kiernan scoffed and asked coldly... rhetorically, "No secrets at all, huh?"

Jake nodded emphatically and blurted, "That's right! No secrets at all. What are you implying?"

"You're a fucking liar! That's what I'm implying!"

"That's slander, dear, not an implication. What am I lying about, Kiernan?"

Her mien quaked with outrage triggered by vivid recollections of that night when she had sidled up next to Jake in bed and heard him talk in his sleep. Jake wanted answers. Kiernan was conflicted: Should she sate his questions? Full disclosure, though a delicious truth, was fattening. The repercussions would unseal Pandora's Box and introduce a slew of problems for their marriage going forward. Killing his sanctimonious tone was a pyrrhic victory indeed. Conversely, Kiernan was still that business-minded woman, though a stay-at-home mom, because in the business sphere a woman had to appear twice as brave, thrice as strong-willed, and quadruple the risk-taker as her male counterpart just to cut it. A woman with such former training had displayed these very traits alongside Summer selling Girl Scout cookies.

Of course, in her mind, she said, "Fuck it!"

As though dynamite had exploded in Jake's face, Kiernan advanced toward him, stood upon her tipped toes, now at eye level with her husband, and she screamed, "MAKE LOVE TO ME... (*...pausing for emphasis...*) KEVIN! That's what you said in your sleep, asshole!"

Flummoxed and beyond shocked, Jake's face lost all expressiveness instantly. Something of a Poker Face arrived upon him, because he'd recognized Kiernan had concealed for a while a Royal Flush and dropped it on him like a safe, which caught him dead-to-rights with only a Pair. Only a pair of excuses, not balls, to immediately deny her accusation by saying either "Perhaps, you misheard me," (...which impugns her conscious mind as the liar...), or "Sleep-talkers don't do it under oath," (...which implies his subconscious mind may blurt untruthful things, but why specifically... that?) Given that shitty hand, Jake said, "I'm outta here!"

Jake plopped down upon the edge of their bed, reached below it for his Vipers (*...Dutch name-brand sneakers...*) and, one by one, slid them on. Laced up now, he launched up angrily and bolted out of their bedroom. Kiernan tucked her diary further down her waistband behind her and ran after Jake down the hall. Shoving him twice, she'd chide, "Where you goin', huh? You're goin' to see him? Run to him, huh, for strength and support?" Her disdain was palpable to Jake as he walked on, but he stopped cold when she said this: "Is that why it's so hard for you to get hard!!!"

Jake whirled around, clutched Kiernan by the throat, raised her up from her bare feet, slammed her into the hallway wall (*...the stucco wall concaved upon impact...*), and pinned her there, glaring at her meekness. She struggled to breathe. She couldn't speak or scream or stop him. She clawed at his two-handed grip around her throat without success or relent. The whites of her eyes now showed petechial hemorrhaging because of the crushing force he applied. It rivaled that of a noose. If looks could kill, Kiernan would have been dead already, and Jake yelled as much, "WOMAN, I WILL KILL YOU! KILL YOU!"

Kiernan, about to faint, believed him.

Suddenly, Jake heard the children in the hallway by their bedroom door, crying. Summer and Chase, in their pajamas, diminished to a high-pitched pleading voice for mercy: "PLEASE, STOP DADDY! STOP!"

Jake let their mother go unceremoniously.

Kiernan dropped to the wood flooring below upon her backside awkwardly. The children fled to her rescue (...sobbing, whining, quaking in fear...) once they saw their father back away from the wreckage he was poised to leave behind. Wife and children saw a monster, not a father, and Jake couldn't dispute that fact in the moment. He fled. He grabbed his keys, wallet, and cell phone in one swoop from the credenza in the foyer. Kiernan and the children jumped at the blast of the front door slammed by Jake. He was gone. Cries bellowed throughout the house, no longer down for the night.

That diary stabbing Kiernan in the back, propped up against that shattered wall, crumbled on the floor, and the children bore down on her with all the love in the world... to feel better. Sandwiched between the two, she wondered tearfully (*...seriously questioned...*): Will I become a divorcee or dead?

[10:47 p.m.]

The night was mild to warm with the slightest breeze from the south. Overcast; crickety.

The neighborhood was pristine and suburban-quiet. Only a few parked cars were curbside on the streets. The rest were tucked inside extravagant two-door or three-door garages. The night air was tinged with the pungent fragrance of wet grass. Meanwhile, the perfectly manicured blocks southward from his townhome—still enraged as he strolled—he needed a friend. He activated his cell phone, and it informed him of all the missed text messages sent by Kevin throughout the day and night. He clearly had troubles tonight too...

Kevin Moran Texted [11:51 a.m.]:
" Jake, we need to talk. Get back to me A.S.A.P.!"

Kevin Moran Texted [12:20 p.m.]:
"What's up? Where are you, dude? Something has come up."

Kevin Moran Texted [1:32 p.m.]:
"It's about that woman I told you about in the restaurant. The "new-hire." Call me instead. Don't text me."

Kevin Moran Texted [3:11 p.m.]:
"I would never ignore your texts. I always take your calls, even at work! Why aren't you getting back to me? It is about Kiernan, isn't it? She's making you not text me after our couples' dinner, right? Call me."

Jake deleted the remainder of Kevin's 14 other texts. Texts that only devolved into accusatory outrage and greater misapplied suspicions, which he had no patience for tonight, especially in light of his ongoing marital trust issues with Kiernan at home. He couldn't absorb more of the same from a friend. Nevertheless, Jake had to chat up Kevin, as the text thread had sown up the fact that they should engage. And it was true, their longtime friendship of twenty-three years never displayed abandonment of the other. Jake's fingers got to work... then he pressed Send.

Jake Montgomery Texted [10:48 p.m.]:
"Tonight. Meet me at the gazebo."

On the other side of things, Kevin, in bed next to Daliah, lay supine staring through the dark at the ceiling above him—incapable of sleeping—alongside his wife in dreamland. He got the notification ding from his cell phone facedown upon the end table bedside. He scooped it up immediately. He read the text from Jake and (...sighing...) typed three words before he pressed Send...

Kevin Moran Texted [10:53 p.m.]:
"On my way."

CHAPTER 13

VISIT #126

(PRESENT-DAY): July 29th
Overmiller-Matta State Prison
Heathcoat, VT
[10:10 a.m.]

Jake Montgomery had earned back his institutional privileges, insofar as that he had been allowed to have contact visits in the Visiting Room with Summer again. No more stinky isolation booths. No more smeared and spotted Plexiglas windows before their faces to speak through, which made inmate visitations feel like a zoo exhibit with an animal in stripes behind the glass, as opposed to their father-daughter time spent. The Visiting Room, however, had its downside too.

Inmates, stepping in white espadrilles and zipped up in white or striped jumpsuits marked with black letters

"D.O.C." on their backs, were oftentimes held off in an anteroom; sometimes close to an hour before they were actually buzzed in and allowed into the physical space of the Visitation Room. The Visiting Room was packed with free folks yet ominously quiet, seated in assigned seats bolted to the tile floors, as they waited for their inmate to push open that pine wood door with the brass knob by the officer's reception desk, capped with CCTV monitors and littered with hand-held radios.

Like a dog let out of the house for the outdoors, the inmate—in this case, Jake—burst through that pine wood door, looked about over seated heads for his daughter Summer, who had risen from her seat near the back of the Visiting Room to draw his attention toward her. His eyes lighted with mirth; he missed her, but... No kissing or hugging was allowed upon greeting the visitor nor during the visit itself. Handshakes upon first contact were highly scrutinized to ward off the passing of contraband between inmate and visitor, but handholding was allowed wherever. It was not the feeling of a homecoming, the contact visit, because the human contact had its soul extracted by prescribed prison protocols and policies.

But this wasn't Summer's first contact visit with her father. They had a decade of this. Both were well-rehearsed to get past the staging phases. Immediately, Summer took her father's hand as they sat down side by side. Their eyes lighted with jitters, not knowing what the other might say or do, and yet though father and daughter knew each other well, in this setting they sensed each other as strangers every time. Crosstalk around them drowned out their initial greetings, but as the other inmates and their visitors settled in around them, Summer and Jake found their normal repartee.

"So, how's Sticks, Daddy?"

"What? Is that a perverse joke?"

"Just trying to kill the lull in the conversation, Dad."

"Sticks died last month."

"What?!"

"Massive stroke. There's no legitimate health care behind these prison walls, Summer. Fate took him. They found him facedown, spread snow-angel style on his cell floor, dead."

"Sorry to hear it, Dad. You really liked him."

"I did."

Summer raised her hand from her lap, laid it flat upon her father's white sleeve starting at the crook of his arm, and slid it down until she reached the back of his hand and braided their fingers together into a single father-daughter fist at the armrest's edge. Jake felt less hardened.

"Dad," asked Summer, "For some reason, your lawyer calls at odd times, and the missed calls catch me when I'm in crisis mode with Sienna. Do you know why he's trying to reach me?"

"My public defender is calling you?" replied Jake, suddenly woozy. His psych meds had kicked in, making it harder to hide from Summer that he had been prescribed anti-psychotics.

Summer's saccadic gaze recognized Jake's face-droop, the darker bags under the eyes of his gaunt, pallid complexion, but his speech was clear. "Yeah," replied Jake, "I was supposed to see him today at 9 a.m. My appeal or something is coming up."

Summer glanced at her swanky Rolex wristwatch. The time showed 10:45 a.m. She demurred, "Dad, I'd say your lawyer is a little late."

"Yeah," answered Jake, almost childlike in demeanor. He felt somewhere between high on weed with the munchies and someone with a thought, if only Summer would give him a true minute to assemble its coherency.

Summer appeared suspicious of this sudden decline in her father's energy, and the longer lulls of silence between questions and answers didn't mitigate those suspicions. She released her father's hand, turned in her seat to face his profile (*head hung lowly*), and insisted, "Dad, we have to start talking about things I want to talk about. It can't be just a one-sided conversation about mundane things with no relevance to my life. I'm a mom and wife now; I leave my family behind to drive an hour and see you, Dad. And it's against the wishes of many people who say that I'm wasting my time coming here. I—"

Jake cut her off. "Fine. What is it that you want to talk about?"

A breakthrough.

Summer, half-shocked, half-eager (*a thousand questions stormed her brain all at once*), leaned into her father and asked, "Who is Shannoah Blakely? And why did she have Mom's gas card that day?"

A man's voice shouted from behind Summer across the room. "DON'T ANSWER THAT!" Summer glanced behind herself and noticed a fat Black man in a cheap grey suit carrying a thin black suitcase in one hand and a thick document of white pages in the other. He advanced quickly toward them in the visiting room. Summer asked, "Who are you?"

"Evans."

"I'm his lawyer." (*Jake nodded while staring at the tile flooring.*) "Attorney Ephraim Evans."

"His lawyer!"

"That's right. You wanna step away from my client, lady? What are you, a cop in plainclothes?"

"Someone from the D.A.'s office trying to compromise and trick my client into a false confession, given the fact that he's on antipsychotic medications?"

Summer, stricken and mortified, screeched, "Psych meds?! Since when?!" She whipped her attention to the right, toward her father. Jake filled in more details. "600 milligrams of Millipres, 100 milligrams of Depakote, and 50 milligrams of Trazodone."

"Yes, sir!" interjected Attorney Evans. He encouraged, "Don't worry, Mr. Montgomery. We'll get you off that too, in addition to the murder charge."

Corrections officers who manned the front desk of

the Visitation Room monitored their CCTV screens below the desktop. They honed in on the commotion emanating from Seating Section [A]; that would be Attorney Evans, Summer, and Jake. Other inmates and visitors in close proximity vanished from security concerns meanwhile. Summer, facing off with the brash attorney, was no longer smiling. She rebuked his prior accusation: "I'm his daughter, by the way, not a D.A. Not affiliated with the D.A.'s office in any form. I am a clerk at the county court level. So, what's this about getting him off his conviction?"

A tinny, mechanized announcement from the overhead PA System alerted all inmates and guests to remain seated in their assigned chairs or they would be properly escorted from the premises.

Immediately, Summer reclaimed her seat beside her father, blankly staring ahead. Attorney Evans ignored the official warning but recalibrated his tone regarding Summer as a friend, not foe, in the decade-long legal morass to get her father exonerated. He bent halfway at the waist, set his suitcase down on the floor by his leg, still held onto the stack of papers in his right hand, and he pleaded with Summer: "I tried calling you numerous times. You didn't return any of my calls."

Summer rolled her eyes. It was still a struggle for her to calm down.

"Here... Just read." He extended the court document to Summer; it was about twenty-three pages thick. It crossed in front of Jake's face. He was out of it. Summer snatched the papers from the attorney and began leafing through them—skimming parts and reading others with angry urgency. Attorney Evans remarked, "Read it and weep." He glanced over at Jake and added, "Your dad's been granted a new trial by the State Supreme Court of Vermont."

Summer half-read, half-skimmed the following:

[P]eyton v. Rowe (*...skimming...*) holding that a state remedy is available (*...skimming...*) **Peyton**, prisoners attacked future sentences which were consecutive to the sentences they were serving. Overruling **McNally v. Hill** (*...skimming...*) the Supreme Court held, thus, this State Court must abide. (*...skimming...*) prisoners could attack the constitutionality of their future sentences without awaiting the expiration of their present sentences (*...skimming...*) Nothing constrained in this Article shall be construed to deprive any prisoner of any right which he may have to contest the legality of his sentence (*...skimming...*) in the case of **Montgomery v. State of Vermont**, therefore, it must stand that the case be REMANDED to the State Supreme Court for curative further review (*...skimming...*) it is so ORDERED...

"Oh, shit!" blurted Summer. The court document nearly slipped from her grasp, but Attorney Evans—*Johnny-on-the-spot*—reached down and took it from Summer. He asserted sprightly, "We have a week to prepare and to appear for arguments. Get ready, Jake!"

The lawyer stood nearby, brimming with satisfaction. He had done his job effectively, if not too well. Summer's glance slowly crawled over her right shoulder toward her father. His blue eyes awaited that direct eye contact like a man waiting for his train already late to the station. Their sights collided and latched on, unblinking. The daughter appeared godsmacked and guilt-ridden. The father decided to be gracious and soft-spoken (the meds helped). Jake reached over, recaptured Summer's trembling, limp hand, and assured her, "I told you I didn't do it."

CHAPTER 14

THEORY OF MIND WHEN IT TROLLS

(FLASHBACK): April 27th
Daliah's End-of-the-month Pedicure Appointment
Tai-Beauty Hair & nails Salon
Uptown Burlington, VT

Daughter Wangni seated Daliah in Salon Chair #4 and assured her, "Mom will be right with you."

"Thank you."

Daliah settled her frumpy brown leather purse down in the empty Salon Chair #5 off to her right. She took a deep breath, reclined backward, unburdened herself of the world like Atlas, and waited to be pampered by Mother Wangni. A lady by happenstance, situated next to Daliah in a pink, velvety, fitted tracksuit in Salon Chair #3, had her feet planted in an Epsom salts footbath, the pre-soak stage of things. She glanced over at Daliah and asked, "Rough day? (*smacking on gum*)"

Daliah perked up from her musical headrests, opened her weary eyes a squinty bit, turned toward the stranger's voice who addressed her kindly (*though annoyingly with gum-smacking*), and answered, "Yes, but it's over with now. I just graded sixty-four book reports all written by fourth graders. Their perspectives on Nancy Drew Mysteries."

"Sounds intense," remarked the lady-stranger, who Daliah thought was gorgeous, though apparently older than she was. Still, gorgeous. What made her less so was her gum-chewing. Every teacher's pet peeve; not tolerated from children, rarely acceptable from adults. Daliah explained, "The mystery novels are supposed to encourage critical-thinking skills as they relate to something called Theory of Mind."

"I don't know what any of those terms mean, but if that is what Barack Hussein Obama is teaching our fourth graders nowadays, our enemies are gonna wipe the floor with us."

Daliah shook her head as she responded, "No, no, no. Our kids are in very good hands, but I've been a terrified teacher for six years."

"It's that Barack Hussein Obama!"

"No, not him. It's the social plague of school shootings in this country. Our gun culture seems more essential than our children's lives. School teachers are sitting ducks without a lake to hide in within today's classrooms. I mean, it was nice of President Obama to shed a tear at the lectern of the White House Press Room back in December, but Sandy Hook rocked me to the core."

The lady-stranger rescinded her Republican talking points gleaned from listening to Rush Limbaugh daily; besides, she failed to bait Daliah into revealing her politics, so she feigned concern for the topic to save face. She said, "All those poor babies lost."

"I know, and I'm trying to have a few of my own before I get too old. My husband—" (*Bingo! The lady-stranger got her woman. She might not have been well-versed in psychological terminology, but she was a professional card dealer employed at a local casino, which made her educated as a people person. The lady-stranger predicted from the moment that Daliah sat beside her that she would tell on herself. Her last name—not common yet well-known around town —confirmed her to be related to no other than Kevin Moran as his sister or spouse. Having heard Daliah declare she had a husband exposed Kevin as a cheating husband and his wife as clueless. Like a feral cat with a field mouse at its paws all of a sudden, Shannoah Blakely decided to play with her food before she ate it... Troll her, she told herself.*)

"Hello!" shouted Daliah at the lady-stranger's blankness.

"Oh, yes! Yes, I'm sorry," stammered Shannoah, blinking incessantly to be present. She pleaded, "Sometimes I get trapped inside my own head. What did you say?"

Daliah asked again, "Do you have children?"

"Actually, I took a pregnancy test this morning, and I found out that I'm with child."

Daliah praised, "What a wonderful development! What precious news! Congratulations! So, are you married?"

"No. Just a guy I met recently. We hit it off well. I can't wait to tell him, though. It's going to stomp the brakes on everything he's got going on. I know that much."

"If you don't mind me asking..." Daliah paused until she recognized in the lady-stranger's countenance that she was amenable. She got The Nod. "How old are you?"

The lady-stranger shaved off thirteen years and lied, saying, "I'm 34."

"That's amazing! Here, I thought you were older than me. You are gorgeous."

"Thank you. I appreciate that. Maybe one day my baby will be a fourth grader in your class. You can teach him or her about Mind Theory or what-not."

The women shared a hearty laugh.

Daliah extended her hand over the armrest between their salon chairs to press flesh with the lady-stranger because, to Daliah's discomfort, too much time had passed for either of them to remain strangers. She introduced herself formally, "I'm Daliah Moran. I didn't catch your name."

"Oh, that's because I didn't throw it." The lady-stranger accepted her hand, pressed flesh limpwristedly, and revealed herself, "My name is Shannoah Blakely."

The women made eye contact with circumspection. Daliah remarked upon Shannoah's name, "It's interesting, your name. What is it? Native American?"

"No, I don't believe so. As the family story goes, my mother's first name is Shannon. My father's was Noah. Their names were merged to make mine. More parents should do that, I think, because we are our parents' creation."

Daliah was taken aback by that secular-sounding belief—"we are our parents' creation"—because the Bible taught her otherwise. Shannoah wasn't Daliah's first encounter with an apostate, so she responded as politely as she could, saying, "Interesting and clever." Daliah's gaze appeared redirected toward Mother Wangni and her daughter below. They had summed up both Daliah and Shannoah's footbaths and started on their nail filings.

"This might sound like a cheap plug, but I am the wife of a car dealership owner (*...Shannoah grinning devilishly...*), and I wouldn't be worth my salt if I failed to ask you... Do you need a deal on a new or used car? I can get you a good deal."

Uproariously laughing to the point of hysterics, Shannoah slapped the armrest repeatedly before she calmed herself to say, "I already bought one two weeks ago. A grey Saab coupe. All the bells and whistles! I got ahold of that deal-offer sheet (*...she made a fist as if holding* *something phallic...*), and it was pretty up there, that thing... the price... I had to pay. (...*chewing gum rapidly*...) The dealer stood firm, but I used my feminine wiles; got on my hands and knees, and I begged the dealer to come... come way down... with that price I had to pay. They shot a new deal-offer in my face. I gobbled that up instantly. Got a new Saab for $4,000 flat!"

"My word! That's cheap! Where'd you get it?"

"Moran's Motors on Maple Street."

"Wow! Who was your dealer? Was it my husband, Kevin?"

"Um, (...*pausing... wondering how far she should take this... so she chickened out and decided to lie*...) I think it was a woman named Miranda?"

"His secretary, Miranda? She's back doing Sales? Hmmph!"

"I suppose," replied Shannoah, who sensed it best to switch topics; however, not in her attempt to become less trolling but worse. She insisted, "We should go on a couple's date. Your hubby and my Boyfriend-Turned-New-Dad, plus you and me. What'd yah think (...*smacking her gum... dripping with sarcasm*...)?"

Missing every insidious microaggression aimed at her ignorance, Daliah, at first surprised by Shannoah's invitation, thought better of it and agreed, "Sure, Kevin and I would love that; in fact, it will be our treat since you're a new Mom. Ever ate at Violets On The Vine?"

Trolling is no fun when the one trolled is completely oblivious... and kind.

Shannoah answered, "That's a bit pricey to eat there. (*...no longer smacking that gum...*) I couldn't."

"No-no! You never mind that. Like I said, it's The Moran's treating you and yours to dinner. What'd you say?"

Known as much for their car dealerships as they were for their wealth and being envious of both, Shannoah Blakely's insatiable contempt for poor saps like Daliah and womanizers like Kevin compelled her to ask, "What if my boyfriend and your husband realized that they can't sit at the same table? They'll hate us for bringing them together, won't they?"

Daliah chortled, "Oh, never!" she insisted, "My Kevin is a doll. He gets along with everybody. Let me tell you about him- (*...Shannoah Blakely, concealing this sly thought: please do, please do...*)"

CHAPTER 15

MISSING: SHANNOAH BLAKELY

(After That Spa Appointment with Daliah...)
Four months later: August 16th
State of Vermont, Missing Person's Division,
[FAX] c.c.: Unit Director, Detective Jamal Rivers
[9:46 a.m.]

"B.O.L.O."
State Police of Vermont
Missing Person's Incident Report No.#
12VT0031

Summary: On 15th August 2013 at 1426 hours, the mother of [Shannoah Blakely], Shannon Reese-Blakely, (68 yrs.), requested the issuance of a "B.O.L.O." (Be On the Look-Out) with regard to a Missing Person's complaint filed naming [Shannoah Blakely] of 234 Not a resident of King Street,

Apartment #12, Leeds, Vermont. Shannon Reese-Blakely of New Hampshire contacted Sgt. C. Bennon and Ofc. L. Akins at the Vermont State Police Barracks, Missing Person's Division, in Barton, Vermont, via Zoom call.

Description: [Shannoah Blakely]

Height: 5' 6 1/2"

Weight: 110-115 lbs.

Hair: Blonde/Dark Brown

Age: 47 years

Eyes: Hazel (green contacts)

Status: Single

Occupation: (Full-time) Card dealer at Standing Stallion Casino & Suites.

[Supplemental]

INVESTIGATIVE SUMMARY: A "B.O.L.O." was issued on 15th August 2013 at 1500 hours in the City of Burlington, Vermont, Washington County, and surrounding areas. An affidavit documenting the necessary probable cause could not be provided because the concerned party aforementioned had suspicions of foul play, sabotage, and/or abduction but nothing discernible at this time. Neighbors of the Missing Person alleged that they last noticed [**Shannoah Blakely**] on the morning of 8th August 2013 driving away alone from her apartment complex parking lot in her grey Saab coupe without issues. [**Shannoah Blakely's**] residence was searched, finding nothing suspicious at this time, and her place of employment, including coworkers, have not heard from [**Shannoah Blakely**] after 8th August 2013...

"Turn off all cell phones!" ordered Detective Jamal Rivers upon entering (...sighing...) with a single sheet of paper in hand. A FAX. He taped it to the conference room white grease board on the wall for the nine other officers in his unit to notice. They sat unstirred in chairs whose right-side armrest flattened out into a desk attachment. A copy of that FAX lay upon each of their desks before them. The brass and blue uniformed men (*...cell phones off...*) read their next assignment. Some reached down by their laces for their matte-black coffee thermoses standing at attention on the tile floor. Just a swig of coffee before receiving instruction from their Unit Chief.

All alert for their morning debriefing. Rivers turned toward his pine wood lectern monikered with the state seal of Vermont and said, "Good morning!" His unit team responded in kind. No eye contact from Detective Rivers. No time for that. He got right to business. "In 2011, this Missing Person's Unit investigated specifically women cases, some 678,000 of them," he confirmed. "Women who simply vanished. In 2012, a better year for Vermont's women. A dip. 661,593 missing women complaints. So far, we are projected to cut into last year's record by 30,000 fewer missing women in Vermont. That's progress for a rural state whose backlog of Missing Person's cases rivals big metropolitan areas like New York City, Philadelphia, and Chicago. We are doing the work in the field, and we are finding women, but the work is not yet done. We got another B.O.L.O. today. You all have a copy before you. A Shannoah Blakely has gone missing. Let's go find her..."

CHAPTER 16

THE BABYSITTER & THE GAZEBO

(FLASHBACK): April 12th
The Links Estates & Townhomes
Fairway Pedestrian Park

[11:56 pm.]

A passerby by happenstance would come upon Jake and Kevin's secret rendezvous. Neesha McGovern, a brilliant high schooler, 17, in her last year at Pine Crest-Inuit Pride High School where all the gated community kids attended, made it her nightly exercise to walk her cat on a leash down by the gazebo. A half-hour brisk, well-lit walk.

Neesha and her four-year-old grey-coated Blue-point Siamese, with a smoky black mask, traipsed off-road, off sidewalks, between nightshade and klieg-light-lit parts of the golf course park, to straddle the straw grass rough.

They navigated the margins of the 8th, 9th, and 10th Greens, which made up the back half of the Fairway Pedestrian Park within the gated community.

The night pushed an intermittent tepid breeze at her face. It was eerily crickety, but overall an uneventful stroll, leading her toward the centerpiece of the park: the cedar wood garden gazebo draped in white string lights. A night attraction. A gauzy beacon. Beloved by adults in the gated community but panned by their children, mostly teens in Neesha's classes.

On weekends, the gated community kids, trapped by their parents' wealth and high expectations (*...verboten to leave the grounds...*) besieged the gazebo as their hangout spot. They blasted music from it, urinated in the flowers around it, made out with each other behind it, and trashed it with spilled cheap beer, empty bottles, and crushed cans. The gated community security force—grey-haired old men, mostly retired golfers, past their bedtimes—traveled on golf carts capped by blue strobe lights. They dispersed the teens loitering each time and cleaned up behind them later.

So, it was rare to see signs of life inside the gazebo past midnight on a school night, especially adult life. The Links Estates & Townhomes gated community, very much upper-crust, was more a retirement resort than a swinger members-only club, thought Neesha. But not tonight. From her vantage point, it appeared to be the goings-on of a secret rendezvous. Close-talkers. Two fit, young-looking, casually dressed White men angrily gesticulating. She couldn't hear much initially because they were speaking in hushed tones.

One of them had mannerisms all too familiar. "That's Mr. Montgomery," Neesha thought. "Who's the other guy?" She had never met Kevin Moran, only heard of him through the kids or prior to being booked to babysit, given the phrase: "We're going out to eat with the Morans." Nothing more discerned or specific or substantial.

Immediately, Neesha scooped up Mojo and stepped back (*...the crickets stopped chirping meanwhile...*) behind black crossbeams of nightshade cast by the tree trunk in front of her and its overhead, low-lying leafy canopy. Even ahead of her view of things, the fairway under klieg lights helped; making anything or anyone standing in the straw grass rough outside its swath of lightness invisible to the naked eye. Neesha's hazelnut coffee-and-two-creamers complexion was also an asset at night and for spying. If Mojo meowed, her cover wouldn't be blown—these natural aesthetics were her ally.

So, she listened from afar—some 70 feet—from the men in the gazebo. Their crosstalk, raised in pitch, leaked from the string-light skeletal framework of the gazebo as soundproof as a tent. Their baritones reverberated down the undulating fairway and up the upsloped greens. Their arguments echoed from the night sky back to earth among the trees in the rough. (*...no geriatric security force in sight to break this up...*) Their secrets aired and ricocheted off the gazebo roof and traveled far to burrow into Neesha's ears unbeknownst to them.

The taller, thinner man in a dark tracksuit said: " (*...incoherent...*) ran here (*...incoherent...*) my wife! (*...incoherent...*) pissed!"

Mr. Montgomery responded: "It's Kiernan! (*...incoherent...*) About us!"

The taller, thinner man in a dark tracksuit said: " (*...incoherent...*) marital problems."

Mr. Montgomery retorted: "Fuck you, dude!"

The other man shot back: "No, fuck you!"

Suddenly, fists flew. Both men tussled to the floor of the gazebo. Fairway klieg lights blacked out on a timer. It's a quarter past midnight. The pressure now falls on the three-quarters moonlight to repel the nightshade, if only the passing traffic of black wafting cirri before its face didn't diminish its ghostly glow. (*...Neesha's cell phone on vibrate indicates a text just arrived...*)

She scrambles for her cell phone tucked inside her windbreaker's inseam pocket. (*...Meow!*) Mojo, not pleased by all the sudden shifts while carried, retracted his nails and clawed into her sweatshirt by the collar, hanging on with his ears perked up and agitated blue eyes chatoyant. Neesha is forced to set him down while on his leash in the straw grass rough as she hurries. She couldn't manage the cell phone and the cat and remain well-hidden. Hunkered down, she reads her lighted screen...

Kiernan Montgomery Texted [12:23 a.m.]:
"I know it's late, but can you babysit? I need to find Jake. He hasn't come home."

Neesha's downcast gaze snapped back from her cell phone up to the milky-white glowing gazebo, upslope in the distance. (*...Oh, my God...*) They're fucking! On the floor of the gazebo, through the cedar wood interstices of the balustrade dripping with webbed white string lights, she saw what she saw. (*...she couldn't hear them, but...*)

Charging the Montgomerys $50.00 an hour to babysit Summer and Chase per norm juxtaposed with witnessing Jake destroy his family, she decided she would watch the kids for free.

Neesha repeatedly asked herself, "What about the kids?" The male selfishness; their Sin of Onan; their depravity out in the open... Neesha contemplated, *"What if it were Mrs. Montgomery who had come to find them, instead of me?"*

The babysitter had had enough. She retreated, tugging Mojo on his leash to come along; shifting straw grass in the rough; their silhouettes and nightshade blending into being undetected. Neesha reached gravelly bike paths and peeled off, jogging downslope with Mojo ahead of her now. She slowed with bated breath halfway down to the 7th Green. Between a water hazard and a sand pit the size of a large pond, and under gauzy-thin pale moonlight, Neesha's chest tightened with terror. She appealed to her cell phone...

Neesha McGovern Texted [12:33 a.m.]:
"I know where Jake is."

Kiernan Montgomery Texted [12:38 a.m.]:
"Where, Neesha?"

Neesha McGovern Texted [12:38 a.m.]:
"The gazebo."

CHAPTER 17
INFIDELITY WAS VICTORY

Sunup... [9:37 a.m.]
The Gazebo

If the cheaters cheat with matching parts, is it still cheating? Kiernan wondered, cheating logic with doubts. A Sisyphean effort, indeed, at seeing Jake in a better light for the sake of her embattled marriage juxtaposed to her near-perfect children.

Though the gazebo didn't have walls per se, Kiernan sensed walls closing in on her, seated there sunning at the scene of infidelity. Though not a witness bearer of it in real-time, its aftermath left ghostly images behind across the cedar wood plank flooring of the gazebo, which she struggled to vanquish. Neesha, the babysitter, had the same problem, and she was on her way to purge herself of those images of Jake by telling Kiernan the truth, which her text confirmed.

Neesha McGovern texted [9:16 a.m.]:
"I'll cut morning class... Be right there."

Unsensed morning light, a refulgent moue upon all things. The sidewinding verdant repurposed fairways actively spritzed by sprinklers misting rainbows midair out in front of her. Monarch butterflies and honeybees gamboled and pollinated crisscrossing rituals. (*...cadent tears marred her mien's steely resolve to appear strong...*) Barn swallows and peewees, sparrows and robins, crickets, achirp, rival rattling cicadae from trees for an ambient mid-symphony to sunrise. (*...her attention snatched by a spry Black-eyed Susan unsprung through the cedar wood floor's crevice...*) A chilly north-by-southwest spring breeze perfumed by the essences of dogwoods and geraniums, yet it belched wet-grass pungency. A clean affluence all over but undercut by a creeping sense of her security and stability choked in vitality. But for the saving grace of Neesha's girl-power honesty and benevolence just now spotted in the distance. Ostensibly, she emerged from ether and sauntered up the green fairways, through the sprinklers, waving. (*...she returns to her seat facing the archway entrance of the gazebo... slyly swipes away tears with her hoody sleeve... while holding that Black-eyed Susan plucked...*) The world, as currently constructed and twirled upon its axis from the gazebo's vantage point, in all, appeared dizzying in sun-soaked misery.

For the first time, Kiernan identified with that wildflower she had plucked: its greenish stem abruptly severed from feeling whole, its orange bloom holding on in vain, not yet shriveled, and it being uprooted unceremoniously, unnecessarily, and unfortunately. A part of life, this. You come up from the ground planted firmly in who you are, and within the direction you must go. The roots have been set and feeding under that sun, then suddenly you are plucked by Fate...*just for sport.*

That's life!

Neesha, a little wet from the sprinklers she had traveled through, ascended toward the cedar wood gazebo stairs and placed down her backpack. Now under the roof-shade in an outfit akin to a Catholic schoolgirl's uniform but being unholy in its snug-fitting ensemble. Her shiny brown legs for days well-exposed. A form-fitted white collared blouse, sleeves rolled up to the crooks of her arms and untucked. The blouse strategically unbuttoned to show supple cleavage and the frilly red-lace trim to her bra. White ankle-height socks peeked a wee above the tops of her matte-black penny loafers; to die for, thought Kiernan. She felt underdressed next to Neesha, who greeted her with a hug, and dropped the Black-eyed Susan, meanwhile. Immediately, Neesha sensed something sharp and blocky stab her in her midsection during their embrace, which she had learned later Kiernan carried her diary tucked in her hoody's muff-pocket. The gazebo's octagonal bench seating pivoted Neesha closer to Kiernan and face-to-face with her. Kiernan's unblinking eye contact with Neesha, at first blush, waxed intimidation a bit, but she told Kiernan everything from Jake's gazebo sex to Jake hitting Chase.

"What do you mean he hit Chase?! When?!" screeched Kiernan.

"Three days ago. When you took Summer to her Birthday Spa Day. I arrived at your house a little late. Didn't want to admit that at the time, but Chase was on his backside already when I got inside. He was crying in the hallway in front of your bedroom door. Mr. Montgomery yelled at us both; in fact, I had to take Chase out on the stoop. Calm him down a while. I kinda said some stuff to Chase about his father that I should not have."

"What did you tell him?"

"I compared Mr. Montgomery to a snake. I'm sorry."

Kiernan liked the comparison. "Well," she said, "he is a snake."

Her tone suddenly miffed added, "And after what you've witnessed of my family life falling off the edge, we are on a first-name basis now. Call me Kiernan."

Neesha, out of a colloquial habit or an unwavering respect for her elders, ignored Kiernan's advice. The babysitter decided to switch topics from Chase to Jake and insisted, "I had never seen Mr. Montgomery look like that before, Mrs. Montgomery. He looked like a totally different person to me."

"He was unrecognizable to us too," carped Kiernan. "He bashed my head into the wall, strangled me, and threatened to kill me."

"Oh, my God! Did the kids see all of this?"

"Oh, my, yes! Neesha. If they hadn't cried out for him to stop, I might be dead."

"Damn men, I think I'm gonna be bi," chirped Neesha. She launched up abruptly and started a pacer's rumination in front of Kiernan who watched her like a pendulum and getting sleepy. Neesha, mid-paces at each of the turns, gazed outward. Beyond the gazebo's post-beams. (...Kiernan waited for Neesha to say something...) Beyond the lengths of the sun-soaked green fairways. Beyond the regrets and resentments as the Montgomerys' babysitter, and that reality snapped back her farsightedness to a nearsightedness which by happenstance landed upon a curious find. A sharply detailed carving which romantically marred the archway post-beam of the gazebo.

"Look, Mrs. Montgomery!" Neesha pointed, which guided Kiernan from her seat. Immediately, she sighted the carving in the cedar wood directly out in front of herself at eye level in the archway's post-beam. Kiernan smirked mirthlessly, devastated. She raised her hand toward its declaration. The carving's puerile rebellion beneath her fingertips, she sensed it like reading Braille... or betrayal.

Neesha sidled up closely behind Kiernan. Kiernan turned to Neesha's profile just over her shoulder and muttered, "He's wretched."

Neesha still hadn't come to the same conclusion. "Why wretched instead of romantic? It's to you, Mrs. Montgomery. He made it for you."

Kiernan stepped away from it, returned to her seat, dug in her hoody's muff pocket to extract her diary—time to chronicle this sick shit. Kiernan sighed and said, "'K.M.' can stand for Kiernan Montgomery, which it doesn't, because we never screwed in a gazebo. Or it can be the initials of Kevin Moran, which I'm certain Kevin made that statement himself, because that's not Jake's handwriting. Jake always crosses the 'J' in his name... always."

"Who is Kevin Moran? Does he live here in The Links like us?"

"Yes," answered Kiernan as Neesha turned and watched her pen a diary entry. She interrupted, "Is he married too?"

"Yes," said Kiernan, then she closed her diary to admit to Neesha what she planned to pen. "Have you heard the saying, or hear your parents warn, 'To tell the truth and shame the devil.' (...Neesha nodding...) Here, Jake has lied... proudly brought the devil delight... put up his middle finger to God. He's no longer a true man, nor a good father, nor a devout husband, but a dog that has marked his territory. Apparently, infidelity was victory. To both married men, infidelity was victory. What is victory if you've lost your family or without a trophy in the end or the slightest applause?"

Kiernan reopened her diary, took up the pen nestled between the pages, and with her head craned down started to write. A sliver of sunlight lighted her penmanship. Neesha watched Kiernan, this time not comfortable with interrupting the process. The moment... a diary entry in real-time commanded the same respect as being in a library or listening to a eulogizer or a mother nursing her baby—silence.

Songbirds of all kinds and colors, swooping from trees to land, settling down on the gazebo railing from time to time or aimed skyward, and louder throughout the morning. It reminded Neesha time had gotten away from her. She only promised to cut morning class, not the day entire. When Kiernan appeared to take a break for further thought upon what to write next, Neesha saw that as an opportunity to speak respectfully. "I should be getting back."

"Thank you for coming. And though I slipped into grown-folks talk with my babysitter, I'd never ask you to lie to your mother. If she asks you what we talked about... tell her. Tell her that a woman needs to know when her husband is fooling around. (...she scoffs self-deprecatingly... thinking out loud...) But a wife never thinks, if it happens, that the other woman will be a man."

"I'm sorry, Mrs. Montgomery."

"Again, thank you."

"For what? I ruined your marriage."

"No, Jake did that. You just watched him do it from behind trees. Truth, unlike lies, does not ruin things. Don't irk me with pity, or tax yourself with guilt, or shame all men because of Jake. He won't get away with what he's done to this family."

Neesha turned to walk away, out of the gazebo's roof-shade into the burning sunlight, but she stopped short of taking the second step downwards. An unspoken question nagged her. She turned to Kiernan, clutching her backpack straps, and glanced down at Kiernan's diary resting open upon her lap. She asked, "What if he finds that?"

Kiernan's response, with the palpable sense she had longed for Neesha to ask that very question, she insisted, "Jake mustn't ever find this diary... nor the rest of them." Kiernan paused. (*...thinking...*) She leaned forward where she sat under the roof-shade and pleaded, "You can't tell your mother."

"I won't. What do you need?"

"In case something happens to me, here's the plan..."

CHAPTER 18

MISSING: KIERNAN ALLISON KLÜGER MONTGOMERY

(... After That Morning Meeting in The Gazebo with Neesha...)
Four months later: August 14
State of Vermont, Missing Person's Unit
[FAX] c.c. Unit Director, Detective Jamal Rivers
[9:15 a.m.]

"B.O.L.O."
State Police of Vermont
Missing Person's Incident Report NO. #
12VT0030

Summary: On 10th August 2013 at 1804 hours, the eldest sister of [**Kiernan Allison Klüger Montgomery**], Gracey Mae Kluger (47 yrs.), requested the issuance of a **"B.O.L.O."** (... Be On The

Lookout...) with regard for a Missing Person's complaint filed naming [**Kiernan Allison Klüger Montgomery**] of 2301 VeeJay Singh Drive, The Links Townhomes & Estates, Burlington, Vermont. Not a resident of Vermont, Gracey Mae Kluger of Fairbanks, Alaska, contacted Sgt. V. Vess and Cpl. P. Gutiérrez at the Vermont State Police Barracks, Missing Person's Unit in Barton, Vermont by phone.

Description:

Height: 5' 10" - 5' 11"

Weight: 115 lbs. - 125 lbs.

Hair: Chestnut-brown (long shoulder-length)

Age: 42

Eyes: Green

Status: Married with two children

Occupation: Retired

[Supplemental]

Investigative Summary: A "**Be On The Lookout**" ("**B.O.L.O.**") was issued on 10th August 2013 at 1804 hours in the City of Burlington, Washington County and its surrounding areas. An affidavit documenting the necessary probable cause was provided to the F.B.I. and A.T.F. A .22 caliber Remington Thunderbolt registered to [Kiernan Allison Klüger Montgomery] is missing, considered stolen from the residence. The gun-safety lockbox was found unfastened and abandoned at the residence. The Missing Person in question, [**Kiernan Allison Klüger Montgomery**], was last seen in the residence by her children named Summer and Chase, including her husband Jake Montgomery, prior to her disappearance, and their leaving for a movie night on August 9th, 2013 at 2030 hours or thereabouts. [**Kiernan Allison Klüger Montgomery**]'s family residence was searched to find nothing of note at this time. The family has been informed by law enforcement to make contact immediately should any new information materialize.

It was a long flight from Fairbanks, Alaska—*leaving her wonderful log cabin and peaceful, untouched evergreen wilderness behind*—to come back East. To pick up the pieces of a shattered family. Her family. To take care of her niece, Summer, and her nephew, Chase, since Kiernan, their mother, her sister, disappeared for weeks so far. Their father's arrest and subsequent incarceration shortly thereafter with more charges pending, gave her no choice but to come back East. The children had no one else.

Aunt Gracey never wanted children, and it's why she didn't have any of her own nor marry, but after little Chase opened the front door to her arrival, Summer fled the living room sectional for her bedroom in tears, leaving Chase behind to ask the question, "Are you gonna be our new Mommy now?"

Aunt Gracey knew Alaska would have to wait. Vermont was home now. And to answer Chase's heartfelt question, she replied, "I'm just here to help your Mommy until she comes back."

It's lies like that one, whereby adults tell themselves

they seek to spare the children further pain, though really it's to avoid the role of being a bearer of even greater bad news, and anymore, lying by omission isn't seen as lying at all but as *intolerability as virtue.*

CHAPTER 19

JAKE SERGYI MONTGOMERY V. THE STATE OF VERMONT

(PRESENT-DAY).: August 14th
ZOOM-CALL GALLERY

Deputy Attorney General of Vermont, Grant LaPlant
Montpelier, VT
Attorney Ephraim Evans, 1st Assistant Public Defender
Heathcoat, VT
The Honorable President Judge, Connor O'Cromby
Montpelier, VT
[9:06 a.m.]

The aesthetics of justice: the courtroom theatre; the judge's bench; the gavel; the stenographer's station; the horizontal alignments of the past jurists captured in memoriam within painted portraits gilded-framed; the HD-TV monitors which symbolize a modernized court for the public to view at all angles indoors; the jury and witness stands but a foot apart for intimate engagements; the side-by-side conference tables and chairs for each opposing party, and even the harsh lighting ceilingward from dusty light fixtures—all of it vanishes behind the emphatics of adversarial argument, legal precedent, procedural decorum, eventual judgment and adjournment, because nothing else matters in the Court of Law after one is referred to criminally as... DEFENDANT.

A short redhead with a bob-cut styled hairdo bounced by in a snug navy-blue pants suit and bolo tie cinching her Ruth Bader Ginsberg-inspired frilly collared blouse closed. She walked upon dark flats up the side stairs to the judge's bench and connected the Zoom call. She confirmed that all parties were present and accounted for to the parties themselves inside their Zoom call gallery boxes before she saw about the judge who was running a little late. (*...literally, just came out of chambers as she glanced back behind herself...*)

President Judge O'Cromby, a tall, frail, and pale-looking man; grey-haired behind the ears and bald up top. His squinty brown eyes studied lawyers, defendants, testifiers under oath, victims—people in general outside the courtroom theatre—like they were specimens. He didn't need glasses to correct his perception of them either. All things were clear to him after hearing arguments or testimony given the evidence. Evidence in a case only bolstered what he believed about a case all along. He was Old School. Direct. No bullshit in his courtroom, and his rulings, past or present, didn't favor one side or the other more or less—straight down the middle—he was fair. In his courtroom, it was about what he thought the case, testimony, evidence, and the rule of law dictated, not his ego or career aspirations.

That simple: the law.

The President Judge made his way up the side steps to his bench. The I.T. Communications Director with the bob-cut hairdo pointed out that the parties were on standby and visible upon his computer screen when he was ready. After the President Judge raised a curious brow at the I.T. Communications Director's hairstyle, he got right at things, struck his gavel once, and the I.T. Communications Director cleared the bench for her station below with the clerks. Deputy Attorney General of Vermont, Grant LaPlant, got his cue, stood from behind his table on screen so the judge could see his respect even outside of his courtroom, and he greeted the court, "Good Morning, Your Honor." A block up State Street was the Attorney General's Office Conference Room A2.

"Morning, sir," said Attorney Evans for the defense. Jake seated beside him at a round table with two styrofoam cups of water nearby for each of them. Attorney Evans didn't do obsequious or ceremonial or suck-up acts in court, and he instructed Jake to be the same way. Jake merely nodded at the judge on screen from the Overmiller-Matta State Prison, some twenty-seven miles northeast of Montpelier where the State

Supreme Court was located, and where President Judge Connor O'Cromby shuffled his papers and said, "Good morning, all. I do see that all parties are present and accounted for in this criminal matter, including the defendant, so let's get to opening arguments. No time to waste.... *Defense?*"

"Yes, Your Honor!" shouted Attorney Evans, as he glanced down at his laptop from where he sat well-dressed in a dark suit beside Jake in a white buttoned-up jumpsuit. Attorney Evans straightened his red-colored Windsor knot and argued, "I'm here to speak on behalf of the defendant Jake Montgomery who is present beside me here at the state prison where he is currently confined. Your Honor, our application for Post-Conviction Relief also moved a writ of error coram nobis in the County Court. The same claim which is before us now..."

"...Your Honor, we weren't allowed to strike or cross-examine witnesses, yet those said witnesses were permitted to testify before a Grand Jury. Those witnesses, employees of the Pine Crest Hotel or Motel, found the only decedent in this criminal matter, Kevin Moran, in Room 204. Our two Motions for Liminine filed in order to set aside their testimony were denied. Critical evidence has been concealed from the jury regarding two Missing Persons, namely Shannoah Blakely and the defendant's own wife, Kiernan Montgomery. (*...Jake's thinking: this judge is not even looking up from his papers...*) We've contended from the beginning, since evidence and witnesses disappear, memories fade, and events lose their perspectives, that the defendant's rights throughout have been adversely circumvented by the Washington County prosecutors when at trial, they were allowed to try three cases as one..."

"...They accused and convicted Jake Montgomery of murdering Shannoah Blakely, Kiernan Montgomery, and Kevin Moran. In so doing, the jury never heard nor deliberated upon evidence which showed Missing Persons Incident Reports Numbered 12VT0030 and 12VT0031 with regard to Kiernan Montgomery and Shannoah Blakely. They are not presumed dead, by the way, and must be considered still alive. There's DNA evidence in one of the cases linking Kevin Moran to the defendant, yes, Your Honor, but it's due to a prior interaction, not samples lifted from the crime scene known as Room 204 itself..."

"...On the internet, because this is a cause célèbre, Your Honor, no gag orders issued, Facebook followers, some 206,000 of them approximately and growing, have Direct Message accounts, quasi-affidavits as it were, witnessing and sending pics of Kiernan Montgomery in Singapore working out in a gym, and we don't have reason to believe that these are Deep Fakes, Your Honor. There are pics of Mrs. Montgomery hiding her face, coming out of an office building in Singapore, and we believe that she has returned to her place of work as C.O.O. of AgriCare. Additionally, there have been multiple witness sightings of Shannoah Blakely. Pics that she's either sending—not sent—sending to Facebook Friends or Direct Messaging to other platforms like Twitter and Instagram. These are active accounts, Your Honor. How can this be when both women are dead since 2013 as alleged by the prosecutors? The fact that county prosecutors have failed to track down and interrogate these witness sightings' locations around the world, or these 'WIT-NESS-SEZ' in particular, is their failure to inculpate the defendant. It's not the defense's cross to bear, but it is our Ace-In-The-Hole..."

"... The defendant did not receive a fair trial in 2013, Your Honor; actually, it is this 3-in-1 criminal case that has impaired his ability as the accused to properly defend himself on the merits..." (...pausing...) Attorney Evans reached for his cup of water, took a swig of it, and Jake meanwhile spied Evans' worried countenance concerned for his chances. Evans recognized on his laptop screen that the judge wasn't impressed with his argument; more fluff than law, as judges say about public defenders over their desks in chambers. He knew he had to bring it, and what "it" was, was U.S. Supreme Court precedent.

He sat down his styrofoam cup and proceeded with his voice raised a pitch: "The defendant was denied the right to confront these witnesses who worked at the motel, yet they appeared before a Grand Jury and indicted him!" Evans insisted, "That can't be The American Way nor an act of jurisprudence! The defendant did not present any waiver of his confrontation rights as alleged by the county prosecutors. A writ of error has been deployed to contest the validity of future, as well as present, restraints, Your Honor. See the U.S. Supreme Court ruling *Peyton v. Rowe*, 1968, Your Honor. Prompt adjudication of the defendant's constitutional claims today is as compelling as was Rowe's then, as it pertains to Meaningful Factual Inquiries before memories grow cold..."

"...It is not a fact that Kiernan Montgomery is dead. It is not a fact that Shannoah Blakely is dead, but it is a fact that Kevin Moran is dead. The defendant, nonetheless, has been convicted and sentenced to 25 to 45 years for the murders of three people, not just one; thus, the '3-in-1 murder case,' Your Honor. Clearly, the jury trial and its deliberations altered the truth, and thereby the truth could not be truthfully discerned. The county prosecutors misled the court and the jury at trial for personal gain because the truth was hidden." Evans cleared his throat and continued, "For all intents and purposes, Shannoah Blakely and Kiernan Montgomery are still alive somewhere. (*...Jake, weeping and nodding, glanced up at his attorney speaking for him...*) The defense, humbly, requests of this court to cast aside the 2013 guilty verdict and free this defendant outright so that the defendant can be with his family; or should the court decide to re-try him, allow the defendant to properly retain legal representation to build an adequate defense at re-trial while out on bail. Thank you, Your Honor."

Evans took a seat beside Jake, rested his elbows on

the table, and folded his hands into a fist, pressing it against his mouth pensively. President Judge O'Cromby shifted his gaze downward toward the dimly lit gallery box where Deputy Attorney Grant LaPlant was seated. The judge's glare said: It's your turn.

The deputy attorney general remained seated and flatly argued, "Yes, Your Honor. This case has been troubling for my office for some time. It was handed up to me from the Washington County Prosecutor's office in Burlington, and I've done my best with this case given its gravity and depravity in scope; crimes which this defendant perpetrated..." (*...A clever twist, thought Evans; concede that the criminal case is faulty, then sucker-punch with that it is still worthy of prosecution...*) "...The State believes that it can make its case against this defendant for the murders —all three of them—regarding Kevin Moran, Kiernan Montgomery, and Shannoah Blakely. Daliah Moran, widow of Kevin Moran, testified at trial that Kevin had come home with numerous cuts and bruises to his hands, face, and body. A split lip, she added. She testified that it looked like he had been in a fight on the night of April 12, 2013. An autopsy of Kevin Moran's mutilated corpse showed that he was in more than a fight, but had suffered some 22 to 23 stabbing puncture wounds; additionally, the defendant's semen was also found inside the victim. Sexual assault was not charged in this case, but the Attorney General's Office in Montpelier did not charge this case initially; the Washington County prosecutors in Burlington did. Moreover, at the time of the defendant's arrest, booking photographs showed these cuts and bruises; numerous scratches and abrasions which Ms. Moran spoke of. Kevin Moran's blood was found under the defendant's fingernails, and there wasn't a single defensive wound on the victim, which proves he was ambushed...."

"...Kiernan Montgomery's body and Shannoah Blakely's body, we concede, have never been found, but the State has an argument for this, which we cannot disclose at this time since the case is ongoing. We were able to effectively indict this defendant, linking him to the murders of his wife and Shannoah Blakely, because the motel employees turned over the defendant's disposed-of clothing encased—actually preserved—in plastic, after they spotted him putting it inside their dumpster. The State tested the DNA on those items of clothing, and it came back positive for trace evidence of DNA commixtures belonging to both Mrs. Montgomery and Shannoah Blakely. The chances of that outfit linking the defendant himself to the murder of two missing persons is 1-in-100 million. The defendant, we believe, knows where the bodies are buried, as it were, and the State believes it can prove that this defendant murdered Kiernan Montgomery, Shannoah Blakely, and Kevin Moran— all three. We ask that the Court, respectfully, deny this defendant's request for the verdict to be remanded or for a retrial, effectively dismissing his PCRA application. Thank you, Your Honor."

The Honorable President Judge O'Cromby took a

beat, glanced down at his papers, then back at the gallery of the parties. He didn't need a minute. He was certain he had heard enough. He firmly responded, "All of these missing and/or dead people had a voice snuffed out, and for some reason, justice for these victims has been delayed. The prosecution's attempt, once again, to re-litigate Shannoah Blakely and Kiernan Montgomery's Missing Persons cases as murder cases, furthermore alleging that the defendant had something to do with it when murder has not been determined regarding them, given the scant physical evidence, is disheartening. The State, in its ten years working on this open case, should have more than a bag of dirty laundry to convict this defendant..."

"...With that said: Must the conviction of this defendant be tossed out? Or would it be more prudent to downgrade the charging docket to better suit the offenses perpetrated in part rather than in full for the sake of jurisprudence? I see no precedent for that, however. If the petitioner contends that he had been prejudiced by the ten-year delay, and/or a Grand Jury indictment that he never presented a waiver for to confront said witnesses who found these clothes was misinformation. This is critical. How can this claim be adjudicated? If I have too many questions and no answers to substantiate a ruling that denies a defendant's contention that he had been deprived of his constitutional rights, then I cannot soundly rule against that contention..."

"...I refuse to join the opinion of the higher court,

understanding that to remand this case for further curative proceedings is prudent but inconsistent with its opinion. To present leave upon the ultimate question, whether Vermont must dismiss the verdict against the petitioner, I am compelled to set aside such verdict only for the purposes of giving the petitioner a just trial, which had been denied him in 2013. This much is required by the Due Process Clause of the Fourteenth Amendment and not incorporation of the Sixth Amendment's speedy trial provision into the Fourteenth...Wherefore, I'll set bail at $200,000, and the retrial date will be discerned within seven business days, submitted to the clerk... (*...Evans and Jake can be seen hugging exuberantly pleased by the ruling before it is stated in full...*) and to the parties forthwith, this hearing's adjourned."

Gavel stricken sharply...

The I.T. Communications Director disengaged the Zoom-Call from the judge's side of things, and the remaining parties saw on their laptop and computer screens the court's wallpaper—the state seal of Vermont.

Jake, seated with his head in his hands and weeping without tears, was comforted by Attorney Evans, who cheered, "We did it! We did it!" Evans stood up, gathered his papers, stuffed them haphazardly into his suitcase, and glanced down at Jake. He urged, "Now, if you put up the townhouse as collateral, you can post bail."

Jake appeared exasperated. He rolled his eyes at Evans, who whined, "What's wrong?"

"I don't own the townhome in Burlington anymore," Jake replied, contempt evident in his tone.

"Well, who does?" Evans asked, presuming, "The eldest, Summer, right?"

"No!" Jake retorted bluntly, "Fucking Chase."

CHAPTER 20

FINALLY, CHASE MONTGOMERY IN THE FLESH!

Three days later...
Gunther's & Gilly's Cross-fit Gym & Shooting Ranges
Burlington, VT
[7:06 p.m.]

Formerly an airplane hangar for commercial Seven-Forty-Sevens, Gunther's Gym boasted a sprawling space featuring a world-renowned rock wall stretching as high as twelve stories. The wall measured ten RV lengths wide and was equipped with its own rain, wind, and snow blowers indoors. The gym also showcased five weightlifting pits, five treadmill avenues (with twenty machines each), eight aerobic studios, and a mile-long runner's track that circled the rock wall midmost high, like a hula hoop. Gunther's offered stationary bikes, rowing machines, and two sand derby race tracks out back, but none of these attractions drew Chase to the gym that day.

He sought out the shooting ranges.

Gunther's entrance was an automated sliding glass door, with motion sensors detecting Chase as soon as his step hit the curbside black rubber mats. Immediately met with the odors of human sweat, ATV exhaust, and burning leather, Chase carried a grey-colored gun case in one hand, nursing a creatine-laced fruit smoothie in the other, and left-shouldered a bloated red gym bag (*he considered weightlifting afterwards*).

Taller than his father at 6'5", Chase was a strapping 20-year-old with fair hair styled in a crew cut, clean-shaven, and possessing rugged good looks. His devastatingly honest tanzanite-blue eyes were hidden behind Aviator-style Ray Bans. He approached the front desk, scanned his membership card under the red-laser reader, and Leah, the gym's receptionist, glanced up from her cell phone with terror in her eyes at the sight of Chase. Unbeknownst to him, Leah, tapping as if a spy on a mission, composed herself and managed a shaky smile. Chase, moving on, raised a curious brow.

Immediately, Leah texted her contact...

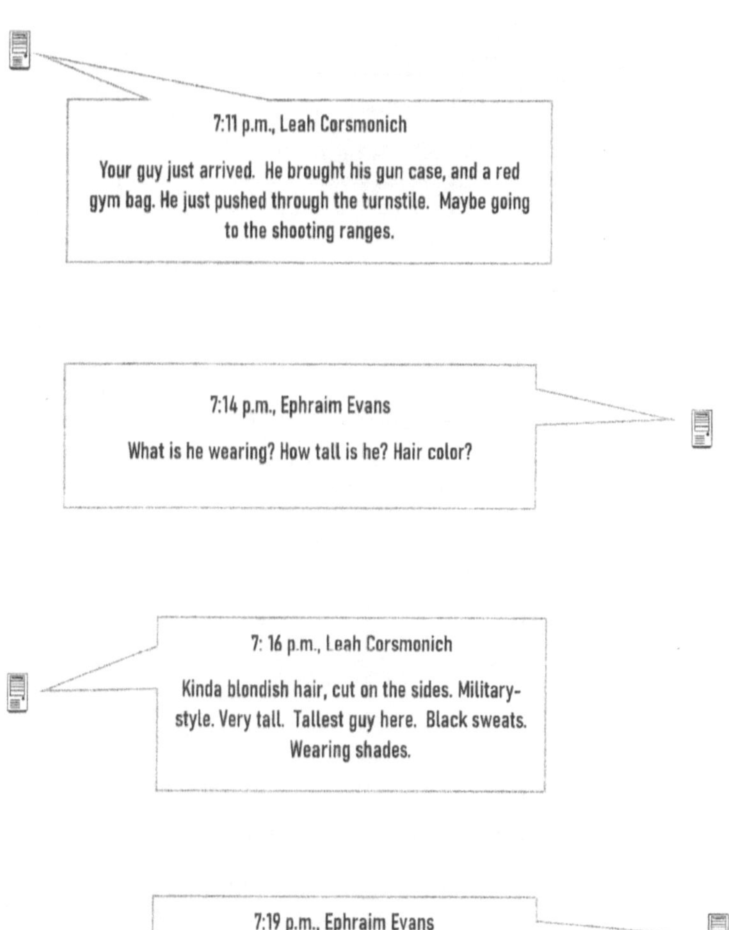
7:11 p.m., Leah Corsmonich
Your guy just arrived. He brought his gun case, and a red gym bag. He just pushed through the turnstile. Maybe going to the shooting ranges.
7:14 p.m., Ephraim Evans
What is he wearing? How tall is he? Hair color?
7: 16 p.m., Leah Corsmonich
Kinda blondish hair, cut on the sides. Military-style. Very tall. Tallest guy here. Black sweats. Wearing shades.
7:19 p.m., Ephraim Evans
What is he doing? Weightlifting? Rockclimbing?

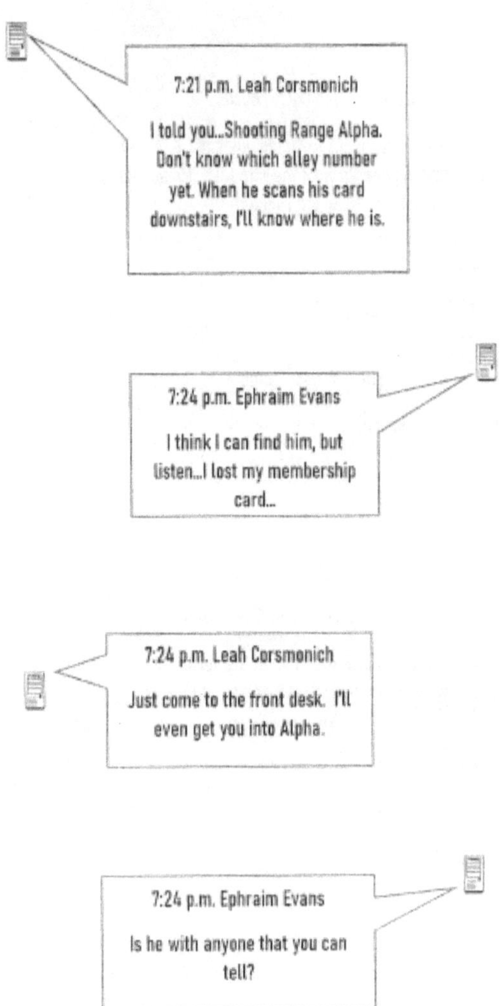
7:21 p.m. Leah Corsmonich
I told you...Shooting Range Alpha. Don't know which alley number yet. When he scans his card downstairs, I'll know where he is.
7:24 p.m. Ephraim Evans
I think I can find him, but listen...I lost my membership card...
7:24 p.m. Leah Corsmonich
Just come to the front desk. I'll even get you into Alpha.
7:24 p.m. Ephraim Evans
Is he with anyone that you can tell?

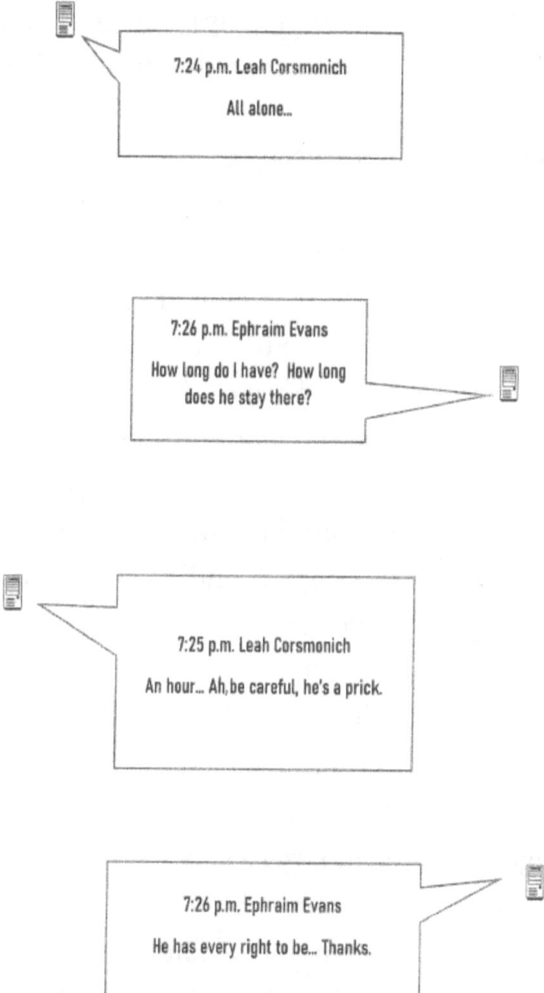

Halfway through the well-lit gym, Leah, tracking Chase's cocksure glide in his all-black form-fitted Nike sweat suit, watched from behind members exercising on universal weightlifting machines and other equipment. The suit accentuated Chase's bulging deltoids, traps, biceps, and the curvature of his track-star buttocks—a physical specimen indeed, a gym-rat who used his target practice days as rest periods from weightlifting throughout the week.

Chase zig-zagged through the crowded gym of weightlifters, treadmillers, and stationary bikers, sauntering past the massive rock wall. The techno music blasting from the front of Gunther's to its rear space channeled foot traffic toward the closed black-painted door labeled *Alpha-Beta Shooting Ranges.* Chase pushed through that door, and the loud, throbbing techno music quickly faded behind him as he approached the handrails of the top landing staircase. He scampered down a couple of flights and was thrust into a windowless, white-walled sally port. He encountered two black-painted doors: the left one marked Alpha Shooting Range, and the right marked Beta Shooting Range. Chase reached for the silver handle of the left door and entered an unadorned windowless anteroom with a locker cage and a secondary steel door.

Inside the locker cage, visible through a glassless window, sat a young girl on a barstool. Her nametag read Amy. She glanced up from her school book, set it aside, and activated her work mode, nodding as a greeting at Chase.

No returned response.

Chase removed his Ray-Bans, pocketed them, and pointed around Amy's head to the shelves stocked with protective eye and ear headgear. He selected both items and placed his gun case on the lithe countertop of the locker cage for scanning. There was no exchange of words during the transaction. Amy reached down for her red-laser gun reader and scanned the barcode on the side of Chase's gun case, registering it to Alpha Shooting Range #8 for his Sig Sauer 9mm semi-automatic handgun. This was standard procedure. Meanwhile, Chase set down his smoothie, scanned his gym membership card under the shooting range's red-laser card reader on the countertop, then pocketed it. Grabbing his gun case, eye and ear headgear, and smoothie, he turned toward the secondary steel door that Amy buzzed open for him. Live gunfire spilled into the quiet anteroom from behind the door as Chase pushed through it. Amy said, "Thank you for your serv—"

The steel door shut on her customer service salutations.

Chase overheard Amy, the Locker Cage attendant, but he had tired of coming to the gym and staff misperceiving him as active military, a veteran, or a cop. It was common patronage for law enforcement and military members to target practice at Gunther's Shooting Ranges daily, and it was easy to lump Chase in with them. He had their same erect posture, muscular physique, and no-nonsense countenance. Merely 20 years old, Chase seldom smiled, whether his Ray-Bans concealed the truth of his moods or not. When he entered a room, he emanated a young man who had gone through some things. Not akin to law enforcement chasing down drug dealers on the beat... some things; not comparable to servicemen and women on their second, third, or fourth tour of duty in an armed conflict... some things; however, he harbored feelings as a man who lived without a mother declared missing and without a father due to incarceration since he was ten years old... some things. What's worse: some things weren't fully divulged to him because adult decision-makers—Aunt Gracey and Summer, 18 years old at the time—decided it was best to salvage whatever innocence remained of his childhood. Chase, 15, in 2018, learned the truth that his mother was presumed dead and murdered by his incarcerated father, but it was a day or so before the reading of his mother's will. Pshaw!

Nevertheless, lying by omission, it affected him like a service member on active duty who had come upon a sleeper improvised explosive device, only set to go off when the truth had naturally come to light. No, it didn't blow up body parts akin to a service member in that predicament, but it destroyed Chase's ability to trust anyone ever. Losing trust in everything and everyone cultivated his depression, triggered his acute anxiety, and created his PTSD. He was diagnosed at 13 but refused to take his medications since 15; since the reading of the will; since his mom was presumed dead, no longer a missing person; or since he needed answers for closure, which would have made life worth living. Some things... not even a multi-million-dollar inheritance could cure, assuage, or help.

So, he'd come to Gunther's to blow off steam, forgive his Aunt Gracey nonetheless, reconcile with his sister who thought it was best to lie to him too (*his only friend*), and prepare for the day his father ever got released from prison by making reservations for Alpha Shooting Range #8. His church and confessional. His true faith and only savior. (*Not the one that allows moms to go missing for a decade and then murdered...*) This God. His Holiness... target practice.

GAT!... GAT!... GAT!... GAT!... GAT!... GAT!... (live gunfire rounds)

...And any prayers that hadn't been granted, sins not absolved, or feelings left unexpressed, Chase recognized at the click-click end of a magazine, he must reload, aim, and fire...

GAT!... GAT!... GAT!... GAT!... GAT!... GAT!... (live gunfire rounds)

...And after thoughts of suicide had overridden the one thousand ways he imagined his mother's demise—*a fact that no one knew with certainty*—Chase reached inside of his gun case, slammed a full magazine into the handgrip of his 9mm pistol, aimed it downrange, and unloaded...

GAT!... GAT!... GAT!... GAT!... GAT!... GAT!... (live gunfire rounds)

...Shooting in tears sometimes at the paper target downrange whose physiognomy reminded him of his father, who allegedly killed his mother; of law enforcement, who searched Washington County entirely for her body; or at God itself, who sacrificed his only begotten son to spare the rest of mankind, allegedly. If Chase's paper target, brought up to his windowless window from downrange for review, revealed more bullet holes in the shaded areas of the body than the shaded area of the head, he'd self-correct, reload, aim, and shoot...

GAT!... GAT!... GAT!... GAT!... GAT!... GAT!... (live gunfire rounds)

An unlooked-for presence seized upon Chase from behind him and angled a pointed finger down upon his shoulder. It jabbed him twice. Immediately, Chase stopped shooting downrange, whipped his attention behind himself, and noticed a smiley, fat Black man in a cheap grey suit with a black suitcase in his grasp. Over the thunderous gunfire rounds of other shooters at his back, Attorney Evans shouted, "WELL... WELL... WELL... CHASE MONTGOMERY IN THE FLESH!"

Chase started to pack up but shouted, "WHO THE FUCK ARE YOU?!"

"I AM YOUR FATHER'S LAWYER! WOW! YOU FAVOR HIM... A BLONDER VERSION, BUT..." he muttered, "...On steroids, perhaps?" Chase didn't hear Evans' last remark.

A cessation in gunfire quieted the space. Chase asked, "How did you find me? Who told you I would be here at this time, at this range? Why are you watching me?"

Abruptly, live gunfire rounds resumed all around at a deafening duration. Attorney Evans yelled to be heard, "SUSPICIOUS MUCH?!" He smiled, which wasn't well-received by Chase, who had since put his gun in his gun case, snapped it shut, and slid it inside of his red gym bag. His smoothie, which sat sweating on the pine wood ledge countertop, had been thrown in the small trash bin below the ledge. Evans detected Chase was about to flee, so he scurried to pop open his suitcase and pulled out a 23-page court document revealing the Opinion of the State Supreme Court of Vermont—Jake's new trial papers, essentially. He plopped it down upon the pine wood ledge, waist-high by Chase, who glared at it briefly. Attorney Evans said, "READ IT! IT'S YOUR SERVICE COPY! YOU WILL BE INTERESTED TO KNOW THAT YOUR FATHER WAS GRANTED A NEW TRIAL. HE CAN BE BAILED OUT NOW! HE NEEDS YOU!"

"I DON'T CARE ABOUT HIS NEEDS," said Chase, who shouldered his red gym bag bloated with his things, ready to leave. But he added, "FUCK HIM! EXCUSE ME... LET ME GET PAST."

Attorney Evans refused to oblige him. He shouted, "LISTEN, KID! YOUR DAD DIDN'T DO IT! HE DIDN'T KILL YOUR MOTHER! NO MATTER HOW MANY TIMES YOU COME DOWN HERE AND SHOOT AT THAT TARGET DOWN THERE! IT'S JUST PUTTING POCK MARKS IN PAPER, NOT THE PERPETRATOR YOU IMAGINE IT TO BE! IT'S NOT YOUR DAD! IT'S NOT YOUR FAULT! IT'S NOT GOING TO FIX THE PAST!"

"AGAIN! FUCK YOU, SIR!" exclaimed Chase, who sought his exit. He brushed past Attorney Evans, who smirked at Chase's brashness. By happenstance, Attorney Evans glanced down and spotted that Shooting Range #8's pine wood ledge countertop appeared clean of all things. Attorney Evans' knowing smile broadened before he muttered, "*Son of a gun...*"

He recognized that Chase had swiped a little more than his gun case and red gym bag but also Jake's court Opinion.

CHAPTER 21

A SNAKE

(FLASHBACK); April 10th
The Montgomery's Townhome
[1:05 p.m.]

Thoughts and feelings, as much as they are our own, can be taken over by another. Corralled like reins; snapped to turn one's thoughts and feelings toward directions another desires, and until those reins, another drives, also manipulates a human being like gelding. Never thinking or feeling another's breaking-in gelding but child-raising, yet that's not whatsoever another's doing. Thoughts and feelings remember everything... wrote Kiernan in her diary after she had learned from Neesha that Jake had hit Chase.

The *Why* never told... until now.

No alarm clock needed, the sun... blinding. No headache anymore, his nap... fading. Chase, squinty-eyed, shot up in bed, rubbing them. The ruckus outside their sundrenched bedroom window was what stirred him. Blue jays quarreling in the large sycamore in the backyard outside but three feet away. He and Summer's curtain-drawn bedroom window, she had left ajar a smidge to let in fresh air. Its venetian blinds yanked halfway up to let in sunlight. Blue jays aside, it was a beautiful day out there, and Chase decided he should get up and take a bike ride down to the pedestrian park bike paths.

Attention turned from the bedroom window and toward the bedroom door behind himself, he noticed a strategically-placed note tee-peed beside his Snoopy digital alarm clock on his bedside end table. The time showed one-ten. He spun himself on his denim-covered rear over to the other side of things, scooped up the note, and read it quickly...

Mom and I went out for my Birthday Spa Day at the Tai-Beauty Salon... Ah-ha! Told you I'd still be able to go! How's your head? (LOL). Mom called Neesha to babysit you... Again, Ah-ha! Be back soon. 13 kicks-ass! Sucks to be 10!
The Birthday Girl,
Summer

Chase tossed Summer's note onto his unmade bed behind himself, and he met the wood flooring to cross the hall for the bathroom. He made a beeline for it. He took a piss. A quick flush followed. Poorly washed his hands thereafter. As he headed out of the bathroom, he heard smatterings of chatter—*mechanized, not natural*—spill out from down the dusky end of the hall. His parent's bedroom. Their door partially closed. He knew Summer and Mom weren't home... no Neesha that he could hear about nor see...

Maybe Dad was in his room still?

Chase sauntered down the hall on sock feet toward his parent's bedroom. He overheard weird groans, also mechanized, but followed by heavy breathing. He advanced forward quietly. His quickening heart's pace in his throat; oddly, smiling, though. He heard his father's voice in a hushed tone say, "Send me the pic... *let me see that.*"

Chase reached his parent's bedroom door, pushed it forward quietly, and he peeked past the threshold. In a blur. In a flash. Before the father noticed the son, and why the son hadn't called him father or dad since. He spied Jake with his bare back turned, facing the sunny bedroom window, his one hand gripping his animated cell phone upturned like a hand-held mirror angled toward his face, his other hand gripping himself but reflecting shock that he had been caught with his pants down.

"Oh sh*t!" blurted Jake before he stopped, hiked up his grey sweatpants, and charged after little Chase. Cell phone in hand.

Chase thought and felt within that nanosecond of his father's advance that he had done nothing to fear; he had done nothing to flee; he had done nothing to forgive. Innocence, which Jake snatched up by the arm singlehandedly, was likened to a limp trash bag. The horrified confusion in Chase not yet taught what else penises can do besides urinate; off his sockfeet and punched by Jake's cell phone-hand four blunt times to the side of his head.

Chase cried a caterwaul.

The cell phone Jake's shock made him forget to put down, put in pocket, or put to better use. He had put it to his boy to make the point: "YOU DON'T WALK IN ON YOUR FATHER!"

Neesha, unlooked-for, arrived on the scene, ran halfway up the hall, and stopped, which grabbed Jake's attention from outside of his blind rage. Little else she could do but watch Jake throw Chase to the wood flooring below. Chase's neck snapped back, crashing the back of his head upon the wood flooring. Dazed, he had the presence of mind to scoot backward on his back and elbows. Fleeing in fear, as Jake lorded shirtless at the bedroom door, Neesha coaxed Chase to come faster toward her down the hall. Afraid of what Jake might do next to abuse little Chase. "That's it..." she encouraged, crouched down part way. She got ahold of him and said, "Get up! Come on! Let's leave!"

Jake yelled, "Watch him! Get him out of here! Leave!"

A moot point, because Neesha led Chase forward from behind hurriedly, stroking his shoulders meanwhile as he sobbed toward the front door. Neesha heard behind herself Jake slam his bedroom door and lock it. Good riddance, she thought. She told little Chase, "Come on, let's go outside for some fresh air. It's a beautiful day out there."

"Okay?" answered little Chase, who whined pitifully beaten, not bruised, but a bearer of bane.

The Montgomery Townhome's red-painted wood door had been drawn to a close by Neesha after Chase sat down upon the shaded grey concrete step of the front stoop, sobbing. She sat down, sidled up next to him, and little Chase turned to her crying even harder. She hugged him tighter as he quaked in her arms. His scrawny physique, which she hoped one day would get big and strong, she assured, "Everything will be alright. You'll see."

The sunny bucolic spring day, so warm and evergreen-fragrant out in front of them. The cul-de-sac appeared cheery with ebullient, highly vocal pre-teens riding dirty bikes or kicking a soccer ball or racing remote-controlled stock cars around the Singh Drive water fountain rotary. Outdoors glorious versus indoors being grim. Neesha saw this and told little Chase, "It'll be okay. I'm still a kid too and had it rough. You'll bounce back. Look at those kids out there. They had days like this one too."

Chase merely sobbed in her bosom, turned away

from the sun, from the neighborhood, from the pain. Neesha rubbed his back in circles to soothe him to a quiet. From sobs to sniffles, the babysitter's tactic seemed to work. Chase raised his head slightly, showing a tear-soaked face and snotty nose. He whined, "I didn't do anything wrong. I didn't know what it was (*...stammering...*) I just... he was... I didn't know what it was!"

"What was what, Chase?" Neesha pressed, but little Chase shut down, burying his face again in her sweatshirt. Neesha stroked Chase's long, dark blonde wavy hair, saying, "Shhh! I understand." (*...Chase sniffles...*)

Neesha lifted her sights outward, sunward, yet inward. Chase craved consolation, reparation, and inspiration, she thought. Seeing the neighborhood kids in the light of joy while one kid clung to her in dark despair. Her sense of helplessness more intolerable than any possibility of saying the wrong thing to him about his father. A father she too caught doing something in a gazebo she didn't want to rehash or relive or respect. Hoping little Chase was listening (...and he was...), Neesha analogized people as animals, saying, "You know how people are dog lovers, or like me, cat lovers (...Chase nodded his head squirreled away in her bosom...)? So, you've got those weird folks out there who like reptiles as pets too. They believe having a turtle or an iguana or a frog is cool; or, sometimes, more cool to them... a snake."

Chase reared up his gaze, looking up at Neesha from beneath her jawline, yet still found her brown eyes gazing sunward at the neighborhood kids playing. She continued, "There's nothing loving or pet-like about a snake in the home. Yet and still, some people keep and feed garter snakes, rattlesnakes, albino boa constrictors, pythons—you name it... Now, anything, I believe, which doesn't give you eye contact you can't trust as a pet... or a person. But let's stick to snakes. Snakes don't have legs, which means they must slither, and if anything slithers, it exists in life as the lowest-of-the-low... Snakes are nothing more than a mouth, so, of course, they're gonna bite, right?"

Chase nodded.

"...I'll never understand these snake-lovers of the world, Chase. It's like they're begging to get bitten, then get pissed after they get bitten. Now, Chase, you know I love me some Mrs. Montgomery, right?" Neesha glanced down at him. Chase's sights upturned nodded, as he quietly replied, "Yes."

"That said," Neesha concluded, "sadly, your mom's a snake-lover, and Mr. Montgomery (*...she paused...*) he's your father, but (*...a longer pause...*) he's a snake!"

Since the age of 10, Chase had never forgotten that characterization of his father.

CHAPTER 22

SUMMER'S CALL FROM CHASE TURNED

(PRESENT-DAY): August 9th
Darren & Summer Korda's Ranch-style Home
Suburbs of Burlington, VT
[11:40 p.m.]

"Summer, you can't—" (*...then she pulled that rabbit out of a hat...*) Chase remembered seeing Summer pull Jake's cell phone from behind her back, grinning like the devil on her birthday, and Jake distracted from disciplining Summer after she attacked him. Chase remembered that morning in his parents' bedroom like it was yesterday, even though it happened ten years ago. It hurt, still. Not his head, his heart. He oftentimes imagined what degree of discipline Summer would've had to endure if, indeed, Jake had a spine. Would it have been the loss of TV privileges for a few days, or no allowance for that week, or no more spa days with Mom for a month? Chase could only imagine, because the past can't truly be relived, and even if it could be, Jake rarely or half-heartedly disciplined Summer growing up anyway, so what would be the point of even imagining justice a decade hence? This frustration triggered what forged Summer into a Daddy's Girl and left Chase to become a Momma's Boy.

Kiernan, like Chase, noticed Jake's every bias, blind spot, and favoritism reserved for Summer. What mother worth her salt wouldn't seek to balance the scales a bit, spare the son from feelings of slightedness, diminishment, or abandonment by the father? It's that toxic childhood dynamic between the siblings, then or since, that informed their adulthood decisions family-wise.

Summer attended every courtroom proceeding which led to Jake being found guilty of murder, Chase nary one of them. Summer had visited Jake in state prison every month for a decade; Chase wouldn't dare. Summer believed Jake had been falsely accused; Chase contended he was guilty as fuck. But where these siblings disagreed—Big Sis and Lil' Bro—they loved one another despite their differences. No argument there.

Summer and her husband Darren slept sandwiching their three-year-old daughter Sienna in her twin-sized Rainbow Goblins-accented bed until she had fallen asleep. Now Mom and Dad found themselves stuck in rigid resting poses for an hour, Charlie horses abound between them, without regrets. Little Sienna had hooked herself to her parents' arms and legs, keeping them in place and, likened to a live wire, one move from under her would stir her awake. It would reactivate the cry for that ice cream cone she was deprived of at dinner because she failed to eat her carrots, and for trying to barter her way out of eating her carrots if she'd pick up her toys in the hallway instead. A smart, manipulative girl, which reminded Summer of herself.

And still, Summer and Darren wanted to have two more just like her.

Each parent heard their cell phone, but only one of them was right that it was theirs. Darren raised his head, mussed hair and bleary-eyed, and over the tiny shoulder of Sienna facing him in bed. She was still asleep... thank God! Summer, on the other side of Sienna, reached behind herself, and it was her cell phone on vibrate in her jeans back pocket. She sighed before she rolled out from underneath Sienna's clever leg-and-arm pseudo-live-wire traps. Doing so undetected by her... and grinning. Darren whispered, "Go ahead, I got her. Tell Chase I said hi."

"Thanks, sweetie," whispered Summer.

Summer fled Sienna's dark bedroom for the dim-lit hallway, answered the late phone call—knowing who it was—whispering brusquely, "Give me a sec. Let me get to the kitchen."

"Okay," whispered Uncle Chase, knowing why Summer was whispering but not himself on the childless end of things.

Three minutes lapsed.

"Okay?" chirped Summer clearly. A vibrant voice. "What's up, Lil' brother?"

Chase asked, "Did you read it?"

"Help me out here with a clue. Read what? Sienna's been on a tear today. Darren's upset Trump might face a criminal trial during the RNC Convention, and between work and Mom-brain, I don't know (...sighs...) what year this is? 2023, right?" she chortled.

Chase sounded doleful when he replied, "Jake's court opinion. This ruling."

"Oh, I read it five times. In fact, it's right here on the countertop. Darren read it too. Stunning, isn't it? Wait! How'd you get a copy? I was gonna make you a copy from mine at work when I got the chance, but when I got the chance... Mom-brain... I forgot to do it."

"I was at the shooting range at the gym today, and I got a surprise visit from Jake's public defender. A guy named Evans. He put a guilt trip on me something thick. He wants me to bail out Jake from jail. It seems he's eligible. You know anything about this?"

"I do."

"Speak."

They were entering into treacherous territory. Summer wanted her father out of jail, and though she could bail him out herself, she refused to do it out of respect for Chase's sensitivity on the issue. However, she had hoped Chase would react with grace, not from a grudge, and disappointment set in. Chase asked, "Why are you quiet?"

"I'm just listening."

"I asked you a question, though."

"What, Chase? Are you gonna do it? Bail him out? I wish I could see your eyes right now, because you say more with them than when you speak sometimes."

"So, you do know how awkward it would be living with Jake again in this house where we lost Mom."

"I can imagine. Chase, listen... I will support you if you don't want to bail out Dad." (*...a long pause ensued...*)

Summer sounded worried. She pressed, "Are you still there?"

"How can you still call him that?"

"Call him what? Dad?" Summer sighed at peak frustration, then she replied, "We didn't have a choice in the matter of whom our parents should be. God's domain. I didn't have the greatest connection to Mom growing up because Mom wasn't all show-tunes and fairy dust, as you would like to believe. I felt tremendously loved by Dad in our house, so Dad wasn't all fire and brimstone, as you would like to believe. You call Mom Mom, but she was no Mary Poppins. And I call Dad Dad because he's not Satan. I honor and respect both of my parents; warts and all."

"C'mon, Summer! No legalese with me. You're not at work, it's just us. You read that court opinion. We grew up in the same household together. You and I both know

Mom through and through, but can you honestly say—with all that favoritism you got—that 'you knew' Jake?"

"Favoritism?"

"And you always make excuses for him!"

"No-no, Chase! No excuses made but forgiveness. Hope someone does that for you in life, and if not family to rely on to afford you such, then God help you in that very cold, unforgiving world out there. Be careful with this point of view, Lil' Brother. You have a lot to learn at 20."

"I HAVE a lot to learn?" chirped Chase contemptuously.

"Yes, Chase, you do. I love my father. Was he a piece of shit when he hit Mom or you? Definitely. Do I trust him? Sometimes on some things, but you and Mom didn't trust him, so I consider that factor too because that distrust just might be valid. Might be. I appreciate people with different viewpoints; being complicated and not trainable like pets. All I know is when he looks at me, I know I'm his daughter. What he is, I am."

"A murderer?"

"Oh geez, Chase! He's a complicated, not-so-easy-to-sum-up, flawed human being like you and me."

"Let's DE-complicate things, then. You got the court opinion by you, right?"

"Yes, why? It's right here on the countertop."

"Open it to the Arguments page. Page 6. Read the second paragraph, seventh line down."

Plaintively, Summer said, "I don't know where you are going with this."

"Just read it." Chase said, and Summer proceeded to read aloud: "...The chances of that outfit linking the defendant hisself, (*pausing*) to the murder of two missing persons is...' C'mon, I'm not about to do this!"

Chase emphasized the point: "It says, '1-in-100 million...' Summer! It goes on, though, here: ...The defendant, we believe, knows where the bodies are buried...' When are you going to wake up, Summer? He did it! He had Mom—our Mom—killed."

Summer seethed in her rebuttal, "Fine, you want to play this game, Chase? Turn to page 5 of the opinion... Um, (*...she fingered the sentences as she perused...*) right here! No, where is it. Yes, here, it says, ...There are pics of Mrs. Montgomery hiding her face, coming out of an office building in Singapore...' Chase, that's where Mom planned to transfer her job from Boston to there. Remember Dad convinced her to retire early, the move to Burlington, all that, saying, *'A bird in the hand is worth more than two in the bush.'* There were hundreds of thousands of Facebook friends, Instagram users, and Twitter followers who said they saw Mom still alive, not just me. I saw the video. Like it says in the opinion, they are not deep fakes! It's really Mom alive and well in 2023!"

To Summer's ear, the silence was piercing from the other end of things until Chase asked, "You really believe Mom is still alive?"

"Chase, Dad was with us that night Mom disappeared from our lives. We went to the movies, remember? To see, um... The Hunger Games sequel or something. We got back home, WITH DAD I MIGHT ADD, who never left our side. Mom, gone! Just gone. How do you answer for that one? Mom always aspired to get back into the game after raising us, and we were pretty self-sufficient. I was 13, you were 10. We had Neesha waiting in the wings for whatever. Mom always wanted to be the one who called the shots. She got her drive by outsmarting and outlasting her male counterparts, and being a housewife was no substitute."

Chase escaped his sister's informed conjecture and espoused criminal probable cause; he argued, "What about Mom's missing .22 caliber Remington Thunderbolt pistol? The gun case emptied out, even of ammo, abandoned underneath their bed? Nowhere to be found on any of her properties in other states. Her cell phone never found or answered if called? Her prolific writing—diaries and such—not one note to her children? No time for that or... what, Summer? None of her clothes or shoes or important papers or her passports packed up? All still in closets; still in boxes, or still in drawers after her disappearance? None of her money withdrawn from the banks. No money transfer made, not even to Singapore where you think she lives. Not one debit from her bank cards. No credit card transactions. Wake the fuck up, Summer!"

"Why was Mom's gas card found in Shannoah

Blakely's car?" carped Summer, but Chase had grown exhausted by the wall he sensed beating his head against. Yet in a last-ditch effort for clarity, he asked, "So, you believe Jake's defense theory at jury trial that he had an affair with Blakely? That Mom found out, confronted Blakely in her car, which led to a physical altercation, which led to Mom losing her gas card, which led to murder, because of the missing pistol Mom had to have shot her, right? After all that bullshit, you believe Mom fled the country, resumed her life as a businesswoman in Singapore as C.O.O. of AgriCare? This all sounds reasonable beyond a shadow of a doubt—to you?"

"Chase, can we stop?"

"Summer, do you believe Shannoah Blakely is still alive?"

"No. Evidence in court showed that there was too much blood loss inside her car for her to survive that much spillage."

"Fine, now Kevin... Is he still alive to you?"

"No, I could've gone to his funeral. Daliah invited me. I learned that it was an open casket, and his body was in it, so..."

"Speaking of Daliah... she was like an aunt to us. I forgot to tell you this, but I saw her in the supermarket in Burlington a week ago. She was pushing her cart down the frozen section aisle, coming toward me, and I spoke. This woman passed by me like I wasn't there. Like she never heard me, but we made eye contact. She simply ignored me. I was like... pissed. Both of our families have been torn apart by Jake. Do you believe Mom hurt her best friend by killing Kevin, too?"

"Chase, I don't know any—"

"No-no, Summer! You talk of Facebook followers as evidence. What about your father's DNA inside Kevin's ass, Summer (*...she gasped...*)! Mom did that too, somehow, huh?"

"What is it you want me to say, Chase? The courts, the lawyers, the law enforcement agencies investigated this case for over a decade and think Dad deserves a new trial because he didn't get a fair one the first time. They don't think he did it, so..."

"That's a very liberal reading of this opinion, Summer. If he didn't kill him, who did? If you need me to, I'll make one plus one equal three for you. As in three dead people in this fucked-up equation. Who else would do this? Who else has lied like him? Who else threatened to do just this, as we heard him in the hall when we were kids, Summer!"

(*...a long pause... she could be heard sighing...*)

"Mom, she... she... (*stammering...*) had assets out the wazoo, Chase. Millions, Chase! Some millions Dad didn't even know about. Someone might have wanted that, I mean—"

"So now she's dead again to you? I thought she was living it up in Singapore?"

"Stop!"

"C'mon Sis, you can't have it both ways. This is what

I mean by you making excuses for him. This has nothing to do with forgiveness."

"All I know is Dad's getting a retrial. The Supreme Court of Vermont believes he's not a killer on some level. I wish I knew who killed Kevin Moran. I wish I knew why Mom's gas card was inside Blakely's car, all bloodied. Listen... Has Dad lied to me? Sure. But is he a murderer? I'm the one who visited him for years in state prison, Chase. Not you. I just don't see it. You can't be this way against your blood, Chase. You are better than this. Stronger than this. You are."

Chase considered his sister's plea and responded sniveling, "He's the lowest of the low."

"Please bail him out, Chase." Cried Summer, "I don't want to do it because I know you will never forgive me. Never speak to me again. I'll lose you forever if I bail him out. He's Dad, Chase. You should do it for the family."

Chase mumbled, "So you will break my heart, betray Mom's undying love to spare Jake from his own fate?"

"I love him. I love you. I love this family. You two, one day, will come together as one. I swear it. The universe works that way. (...*pausing*...) Chase, please. I love you."

"I know that you love me, but (...*whimpering*...) you love him more."

"Chase, I—"

She heard that he ended the call abruptly.

CHAPTER 23

INTOLERABILITY AS VIRTUE

(FLASHBACK) August 9th
The Montgomery Townhome
[5:13 p.m.]

We confront problems in life in three ways: getting it over with because we anticipate losing, proving to ourselves that we're not afraid of losing, or going toe-to-toe with it because losing is not an option... wrote Kiernan in her diary earlier in the day.

(... ♫ "Somebody That I Used To Know" by Gotye blares in the background♪... and snapping her fingers, humming along to the popular Number #1 Hit song...) Kiernan decided to confront the problem of infidelity with the hopes of some A-1 female solidarity in tow. She dressed in her bedroom's cozy bathroom to get ready for Happy Hour. However, the date itself had yet to be confirmed as a go. (*...facing*

the bathroom's lighted vanity mirror... red lipstick on her lips pristine... eyeliner-penciled eyebrows popping sharply... dark-brown hair up in a slicked braided French Twist flawless... red and white cow-patch patterned print dress hemmed just over the knee and hugging her hips and bosom lovely... open-toed red patent leather stilettos stepping to To-The-Nines...)

The plan: Contact Neesha, the babysitter, and pay her for two hours to watch the kids (*...check...*). Don't tell Jake a damn thing wherever he is, and give Neesha the heads-up to remain silent (*...check...*). Text Daliah Moran and insist that she meet for Happy Hour at Street-Side Harry's in Evanston (*...pausing...*). Kiernan turned down the volume of her J-Heart Radio station and typed...

Kiernan Montgomery Texted [5:21 p.m.]:
"Are you busy? Can we meet at Street-Side Harry's for Happy Hour? Drinks on me."

Daliah Moran Texted [5:31 p.m.]:
"A bit short notice, but Kevin's at the dealership until late. Dinner doesn't have to be ready for a couple of hours yet. So, yes, let's do it!"

Kiernan Montgomery Texted [5:34 p.m.]:
"See you there in 20 to 30 minutes."

Daliah Moran Texted [5:35 p.m.]:
"Is something wrong?"

Kiernan read Daliah's reply text, but she turned off her cell phone. She planned to go toe-to-toe with her about this problem of infidelity between their husbands, and losing her amid the turmoil wasn't an option.

Later... Approaching Street-Side Harry's Diner
(... *On the corner of Sycamore & West Main Streets...*)
Downtown Evanston, VT

[6:13 p.m.]

It was hot; gauzy-thin cirri blushed the azure-brilliant skies overhead. Buttery complexioned hues tinted the humid sunlight, as the sun itself in transit dipped behind the low-lying brick and mortar landscape of the mid-sized city, horizonward. If there was a breeze, it had blown rather scarcely and unsensed.

Kiernan paralleled parked on Sycamore Street; a dusky, quiet, upper-crust residential avenue narrowed by privately owned brownstone townhomes capped by mansard roofs, sidewalks lined by thinning deciduous trees chirping, as she strode (...click-clack...click-clack...) in those expensive red leather stilettos upon silted uneven sidewalk. Her purse shouldered and clutched. She turned rightwards on the corner onto West Main Street; smacked in the face by the main artery of Downtown Evanston bursting alive. Bumper-to-bumper traffic to her left thrummed. To her right, a family-owned pizzeria, hairdresser's salon, a Starbucks, scores of boutiques ranging from women's clothing to homemade wicker furniture, and a vintage movie theatre; even a piano store. Someone's graceful fingering played a Steinway indoors; a master on the keys. Classical music—a pirouette of sound in B-Flat—spilled out onto West Main en pointe in her wake. The traffic to her left was a din.

Nearing Street-Side Harry's cordoned-off section for curbside dining, she sensed her heartbeat flitting like a moth in flight, because the inexplicable energy she approached was her kind of flame. And she pondered—even as passersby (...males entirely...), half appeared arrogant, half appeared prurient, but they all introvertedly said Hmmph! with raised brows at her ass in that red-and-white cow patch pattern print dress glued to her womanly curves. Nevertheless, such crude Downtown Life, reminiscent of Boston, was something she had missed: the ordinary people drably dressed but with colorful temerity shooting out of their glares, and the savory smells of street cuisine, and the rich diversity of music unlooked-for; meeting wine glasses upturned and clashing sounding like chimes in cheers, the business-attired and the casually dressed sunning and seated crunched-in enjoying Street-Side Harry's curbside dining, also bearing side-eye sizing-up any newcomers, specifically keen on Kiernan who'd pulled out a chair from the vacant petite dinette table amongst their chatter. No, pardon me with the utmost style.

Now seated cross-legged and alert waiting on Daliah, Kiernan's despair and lover-scorned shock, well warded-off over these past few months, snuck in through a crack in her mental shields, because she recollected Daliah's damn-near lyrical life perspective over the years: ...If you need me, I'll appear; if you concede to me, I'm fair; and as long as I live and breathe, it's because of my husband; my air...

Kiernan heard a car door slam nearby on West Main. Over her exposed left shoulder, she turned and immediately noticed Daliah's smiley advance proceed around the hood of her beige Camry sedan; parallel-parked curbside. She stepped in brown leather-strapped sandals, khaki shorts, and a flowing eggshell-white collared blouse whose two opened buttons at the top revealed a thick neck dripping with several gold necklaces. She shouldered her frumpy, brown leather purse. Not to lose sight of her huge engagement ring on her ring finger blinking in the sunset light. A smiley, lighthearted teacher of modest means, yes, but it was noticeable, besides her size eighteen waddle, that Daliah had money in excess.

Just not as much as Kiernan.

Kiernan stood up to greet Daliah with a kiss on the cheek. Daliah and Kiernan took their seats oppositely at the table. All smiles. Pleasantries. Subtle laughter. A little nervousness between the two of them. They never went out without their husbands, and while Daliah couldn't help but feel suspicious of the Happy Hour date, Kiernan was grateful that two intelligent women could simply talk without men around.

A sharp blade of limp dusky sunlight cut across Daliah's sights as she glanced up to meet the call of the waiter who sought to take their drink orders. She looked at Kiernan for approval, as she would if Kevin had sat across from her, and she sensed herself a little out of her element having to order for herself. Kiernan already knew what she wanted, and she slightly enjoyed the internal struggle Daliah suffered alongside the waiter about what to order in the moment.

"Ummm..." Daliah mused, "You told me so many drink options." She frowned up at the waiter standing to the right of her. He tried valiantly to help her, "Ma'am, you can go with a wine cooler for starters. Is there any flavor that you like best?"

"...Sound?"

(...*Kiernan, ever so slightly, shaking her head and stifling a grin...*)

Daliah said, "Oh yes, I love strawberries, I think."

The waiter smiled kindly and asked, "How does a strawberry daiquiri wine cooler sound?"

"Lovely, and I thank you for being so patient with me."

"Sure, Ma'am." Assured the waiter, then he turned to Kiernan whose certitude came flat and quick, "Rum & Coke."

"Be right back!" chirped the waiter.

The two women snuck glances back behind themselves to mind their purses hanging from the backs of their metal chairs, and Kiernan said, "I'm glad you came."

"Me too. It's a lovely night. Warm. Evanston's a quaint little town. I have been through here many times to get to Burnham, but I hadn't stopped once until now. I appreciate this, Kiernan." Daliah sounded chipper, then she noticed the whites of Kiernan's eyes. They were bloodshot, whether by fatigue or tears. Daliah refused to believe that anyone in her life could be unhappy, so she asked, "Little sleep?"

"It's been a taxing couple of months since we last talked. I've had some stuff on my mind which I felt challenged to tell you about."

"Oh really, why?"

The waiter arrived with the drinks on a platter. He set down Daliah's wine cooler and a wine glass first, followed by Kiernan's Rum & Coke on the rocks. Kiernan nodded at his polite service, grabbed her cool glass filled to the rim, craned her lips toward it carefully, took a swig (...wincing...), and gasped, "Good stuff…" Daliah poured her wine cooler into the wine glass and waited for Kiernan to answer her question before she imbibed. Kiernan responded, "Do you remember when we ate at that restaurant, Violets On The Vine?"

Daliah nodded pensively.

"Did you happen to overhear the guys talking about a woman named Shannoah Blakely? Do you know her?"

"As a matter of fact, I do know her. I met her at the salon. A wonderful woman."

"Really?"

"Yes," answered Daliah. Kiernan looked stricken and flabbergasted, as Daliah appeared too pleased by the mention of the other woman in her life. Kiernan had surmised this woman to be Kevin's secret mistress, which wouldn't make sense since Jake and Kevin were having sexual relations.

"Is something the matter, Kiernan?" Daliah took a drink.

"What about this woman, Shannoah?"

"Well, she hasn't contacted me yet, but she knows the offer for dinner still stands. Kevin and me, she and the boyfriend, together. She works at a casino as a card dealer, she told me."

"A card dealer? Why did Jake tell me she was a new hire at Kevin's dealership?"

"Oh, no… She recently bought a grey Saab from our dealership, but she's a card dealer. I can see how Jake might have conflated the two jobs; card dealer… car dealership."

"Hmmm… I don't know…"

"Oh!" blurted Daliah. She swatted the back of Kiernan's hand that rested flat on the table. She added, "She's pregnant too."

"This Shannoah Blakely is pregnant?"

"Yep. She seemed pretty happy about it. It's why I invited her to dinner, the boyfriend too. She should be far along by now. It's been some four months since April when we met in the salon."

"Young girl?"

"Well, actually, I'm a year older than she is. I felt stupid when she told me her age, because she looks older."

"You said she works at the casino?"

"Yes, I'm sure that's what she told me."

"I'm going to find her. There's only one casino in Burlington. So, do you have a cell phone number for her?"

"No, she has mine. I left it up to her whether to make contact or not for that couple's dinner date because she was intimidated by going to Violets On The Vine. But, um, what are you planning?"

Kiernan dismissed the question by drinking the last of her Rum & Coke. She turned in her seat, raised her empty cold glass, which her waiter spotted from the bar through the street-side window of the diner. He hurried to make a fresh drink. Kiernan asked, "You need a refill?"

"I haven't finished this one," fretted Daliah. "What's wrong, Kiernan?"

"If you had to pick Kevin's best quality, which one would it be?"

Daliah perked up at the question and answered, "His ambition, definitely."

The waiter arrived with Kiernan's refill of Rum & Coke. She responded warmly upon taking it from his platter. She turned to Daliah, who appeared mid-sip of her wine glass, half-filled with strawberry wine cooler. Kiernan made Daliah pause with this question, "Now be honest. (...Daliah nodding eagerly...) What's Kevin's worst quality?"

Kiernan expected to hear something like Kevin lying sometimes, cheating at board games, or keeping secrets for no just cause—something equivalent to infidelity that would make it easier to transition into the controversial topic she hoped to broach with Daliah. Instead, Daliah responded, "Again, his ambition."

"How so?" asked Kiernan, then took a quick sip of her drink.

"Well, he has this saying. It's his life motto: *'If you ain't got what you should get, you're getting got...'* Personally, I don't like the refrain because it's gotten him into some hot water before."

"I'm listening."

"Like that time he and Jake stole Kevin's mother's car—drunk off their asses. (...she chortled...) They wrecked it off campus. It was a dare that made him do it. Another time, he promised a competitor he wouldn't buy the last supply of German-made Jeep Wranglers because the market would reject them. This encouraged his competitor to overstock on sedans instead. But Kevin knew the market was thirsty for jeeps, not sedans. It duped his competitor to go all-in on sedans. Kevin made hundreds of thousands from those jeeps sold, and his competitor couldn't move the sedans off his lot, which bankrupted him in Royceville."

"Jesus!"

"Yes, it was kinda slimy, but it's his ambition that drove him and made him not care afterward."

"We need to talk about Kevin now, Daliah."

"Okay?" replied Daliah worriedly. Kiernan added, "...And Jake."

"Oh, Kay!" chirped Daliah before she told Kiernan what she had long known. "Those two for damn near 23 years have been pranking, goofing around, getting into stuff since they were next-door dorm-mates at Penn State. I—"

"This is serious, Daliah."

Daliah quieted immediately. She stared intently at Kiernan's eyes, searching for the truth before she was to hear it. She answered, "I'm listening."

Kiernan leaned in, placed her elbows on the table, braided her hands together into a tight fist, and confessed, "Jake and Kevin are lovers."

Mooneyed, Daliah screeched shock in a single word: "What?!"

"It's been going on for some time right under our noses. I found out in April from my babysitter."

Daliah's face trembled. She closed her eyes to hold back tears. She found it impossible to attend reason. She backed away from the table, her eyes flashing with rage as she found Kiernan with more to say, "Daliah, they were caught having sex in the gazebo in the park."

"Stop!" screamed Daliah, "Just stop!"

Indeed, Harry's Diner curbside customer service stopped. Its patrons seated around Kiernan and Daliah outdoors stopped eating, drinking, or thinking briefly because the outburst was their dessert. Though traffic on West Main Street still flowed, and the Earth continued to spin on its axis, Kiernan sensed otherwise due to sheer public embarrassment, which made her existence feel entirely stopped.

Kiernan debated whether she had teetered on the edge of losing a good friend or if she had lost grip with reality in such a confession, which might either bind them closer together or make their injuries mutually exclusive. It was up to Daliah at this point. Kiernan's head had stopped spinning, but not the world. She realized that the town's traffic was never stuck; she was. As patrons feigned to mind their own business at their tables, Daliah would leave no doubt as to where their friendship stood anymore. She shouted, "You lying bitch!"

Instead of common sense, there was static. Instead of being convinced, there was panic. Instead of evidence of sisterhood, there was fallacy; the idea that a woman cannot survive without a man. At her breaking point, Kiernan stiffened her resolve against die-hard romantics, semantic arguments, and theatrical crying, and she cut Daliah off by screaming, "SHUT THE FUCK UP!"

That drew public attention and turned the opinion against Kiernan...

"No!" shot back Daliah. "It's not enough to lie about there being another woman. No! You have to lie and make my husband out to be the kind of man who would sleep with yours!" Daliah jumped from her seat, pointed at Kiernan's face, and insisted, "You are sick! It's not true!"

"It is true."

"It's not!"

"But it is."

"You lie!"

Kiernan stood up to Daliah and pleaded calmly, "Don't let the men win. You are my friend."

"You are not my friend."

Everyone inside Harry's and curbside had a front-row seat to this loud spectacle between longtime friends at Curbside Table #3. Daliah, beet-red in the face, cried plaintively, "Why are you doing this to me?! You know I had a rough year! I gave up teaching! I can't get pregnant!" she whined. Suddenly, she picked up her emptied wine cooler bottle from the table and smashed it against the sidewalk. Patrons in close proximity recoiled in fear from the explosion of glass shards. She screamed again at Kiernan, "MY HUSBAND, I LIVE AND BREATHE! I HOPE YOU DIE! YOU ARE SO EVIL! I HOPE YOU DIE!"

"Sweet Jesus, Daliah! I'd never lie to—"

Daliah screeched, "LIAR! LIAR! LIAR!"

She grabbed the leather strap of her brown purse from the chair-back and bolted for her parked car, clumsily and in a fit of anger. Kiernan and the other patrons watched as Daliah ducked into her sedan and slammed the driver-side door closed. All heard her start the engine—almost flooding it—and punch the gas pedal simultaneously. Patrons cringed as Daliah rammed into the bumper of the car parked in front of hers, then repeated the offense in reverse when she shifted gears and backed into the vehicle parked behind hers. She continued this backward and forwards, causing significant damage, as she wedged out of the curbside space into oncoming traffic. Horns blared all around her, and a multitude of one-finger salutes were raised from car windows as she peeled off down West Main Street under a dusky veil until she vanished.

Kiernan sat back down in her seat, aghast at the spectacle.

Two aggrieved Black teenagers emerged from the front door of Harry's. Their uniforms and aprons revealed that they worked at the diner. Harry, the owner, followed them out, making it clear they were not pleased as the car-crash victims of Kiernan's Happy Hour têt-à-têt. The teenagers looked close to tears with their hands braided behind their heads, mouths agape, and Harry exclaiming, "This is fucked up!" The damage was significant. Kiernan saw this and immediately made eye contact with her waiter through the diner's street-side window. She waved him over. He nodded, wiped his hands with a white towel, and bolted from behind the bar to meet Kiernan at Curbside Table #3. Kiernan rummaged through her purse and pulled out her diary, wallet, and checkbook. She opened the checkbook, shuffled through the pages, and found some unmarked checks. She quickly wrote out two checks for $10,000 each, leaving the "Pay to the Order of" line blank for the teenagers to fill in their own names. On the Memo Line, she wrote... ***For Car Damage***

Her waiter arrived. Kiernan turned and handed him the two checks, saying, "Give these to those boys over there and tell Harry that I'm sorry for my friend." Patrons seated nearby overheard the waiter gush, "Oh, Ma'am, they will appreciate this money. Sharif and Raymond are new here. Just bus boys, really... and I'm sure they couldn't afford those repairs." He fawned over the amounts written on the checks, pinched between his fingers, and was shocked when Kiernan snatched them back.

"What the—!" he exclaimed.

"Calm down," Kiernan said, and muttered, "Wait a sec."

She ripped the checks into halves twice and stuffed the shreds into the back of her checkbook. Then, she turned to fresh checks, re-gripped her pen tightly, and angled it toward the check's prompting lines. The waiter's attention was fixed over her shoulder as she wrote:

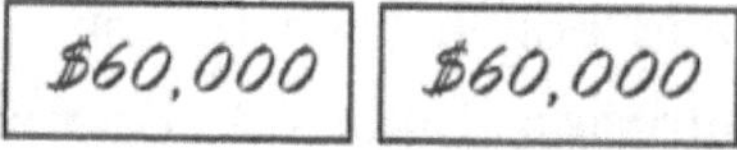

The waiter blurted, "WHOA!"

"Shh!" spurned Kiernan, as she wrote on the Memo Line... ***For New Car***

Kiernan separated the two checks from the checkbook's seam, glanced up at the waiter, and instructed, "Now when you give these checks to them, tell them that I only require two things: One, that they DO NOT... buy the car from any Moran Motor's Used & New Cars Dealership, and, Two, DO NOT... come over here! I don't need thanks. If they want to wave, that's fine, but I don't want to get involved. All they have to do is write their names on the Pay To line, and I'll make sure my bank honors those checks."

"Sure thing, Ma'am, I'll tell 'em," responded the waiter excitedly.

As she put her pen down, the waiter bolted to perform the task. Immediately, Kiernan blushed as she heard a sudden eruption of boyhood joy and some curse words in disbelief from behind her, as the waiter tried to quiet his fellow employees and relay Kiernan's instructions to honor the checks.

Owner Harry Glotz and the Black teenage boys, with knowing smiles, waved in Kiernan's direction at Curbside Table #3. However, she appeared otherwise distracted, craning downwards into her purse as if looking for something.

Not at all. She didn't want attention, adoration, or affirmation. She heard Glotz telling the boys, "Okay, you lucky bastards! Back to work!" He corralled them back inside the diner through the front door, leaving their damaged vehicles curbside as though they were street trash.

Kiernan went to the second thing that lay upon the metal table in front of her: her beige alligator-skinned wallet. She extracted a crisp $100 bill from it. She raised her empty, sweating glass a touch and pinned her $100 below its weight so that any upturned wind might not run away with it before her waiter had a chance to retrieve it. She put the checkbook and wallet back in her purse, then turned to the first item she had picked up—the only thing that could make this Happy Hour date a gesture of sound reason: her diary. She cracked it open to the last entry she had written that morning. She slid the diary's pen out of its leathery sheath. She returned to that page and then the paragraph where she had left off. A paragraph that, ostensibly, called for the results of the Happy Hour with Daliah. She re-read the unfinished entry. Her finger raced below the lines of her cursive, its prevailing thought being a sentence that considered...

...losing is not an option...

Then she angled her pen after its punctuation to craft a follow-up thought to that sentence, which concluded...

...I lost anyway... I lost a friend...

Perchance due to the check-writing spree, too preoccupied to notice it before, but in her curbside dining section alongside the diner's street-side window, a few public whispers raised in their pitches above the sounds of adjacent street traffic, smattering into chatter whose hubris gained momentum and reached decibels too pronounced to ignore. Given their pitter-patter of pointed derision:

...There was a better way of telling her friend about her husband's cheating.. So tactless... (some opined)... She should've just let sleeping dogs lie... So thoughtless... (some espoused)... Whatcha' don't know can't hurt ya; now she's hurt when she wasn't before... So unnecessary... (some believed)... Oh, what a bitch to that poor woman, I would've wished her dead too... So cold-blooded... (some empathized)... Their husbands just

gave them free Go-Have-An-Affair-Yourself cards, and she did that instead?... (some rationalized)... With friends like her, enemies are a pleasure!... So crazy... (some joked)... Principles are like knives; remember they are sharp; don't cut yourself... (one couple made clarion, not so under their breath).

The waiter noticed through the street-side diner's window that his charitable, well-dressed patron was having a hard time stuffing her things angrily into her purse. What's the matter now, he thought. The waiter abandoned the bar again. From indoors to outdoors, a starry night now above his head, fresh pine-scented air, and a cool intermittent breeze. Street traffic was but a hush. As Kiernan turned on her heels, they collided.

"Excuse me!" effused the waiter, half-smiling, half-embarrassed. Kiernan scoffed, clutched her purse, and sought to get past him. He blocked her kindly and persisted, "Ma'am? I'm sorry that your Happy Hour at Harry's hasn't been too happy at all. Please, it's after seven. Will you let us offer you a complimentary dinner?"

"No!" yelled Kiernan with a finger wag in tow. "Don't you dare pity me!"

"Ma'am, I'm sorr—"

Kiernan brushed past him, snaked around the curbside seating of tables patronized by her nameless, faceless detractors, and onto the sidewalk, where passerby helped her vanish from the waiter's view. Now running in stilettos on uneven grey pavement, she couldn't get away fast enough to reach her parked car curbside around the corner on Sycamore Street. Desperate to get home to her kids, having decided that divorcing Jake was on the horizon, and haunted by Daliah's curse of death upon her, she had become afraid for everyone involved, least of all herself, and yet...

What we wish for, Fate will fish for.

CHAPTER 24

KISMET OR KARMA OR KILLJOY

(PRESENT-DAY): August 27h
Washington County Correctional Facility
("W.C.C.F.")
Cellblock 3A, Cell-6 (ground floor)
[7:47 a.m.]

Jake, a 10-year state inmate downgraded to a county inmate eligible for release, had developed over the years an institutional-inherited pathological preference for claiming the top bunk in a cell. However, Cell-6 had not been assigned to Jake first for him to earn "first dibs" (*...unwritten rules in inmate etiquette...*) whereby he could say where one inmate sleeps over another. That honor would fall to his cellmate in the top bunk, J.J. Brown, a convicted pedophile who recidivated while on parole due to no fault of his own.

Inmate Brown was caught within 100 feet of a school

while a city contractor directed with his crew to fix a water main break. One of the multiple problems with Megan's Law is a legal tool which hammers a nail with a very broad Mac Truck. Jake didn't care to listen to Brown's expletive-laden characterizations of Washington County's Adult Probation Office any more than he wanted to remain situated below Brown in the bottom bunk of Cell-6, to which inmate J.J. Brown told Jake, "Deal with it. You'll be a free man soon enough."

Noisome disadvantages came with sleeping in a cell on the bottom bunk: (one) it got the foot traffic (*...the inmate with "first dibs" on the top bunk had to hoist himself up somehow to get into bed...*), and (two) the bottom bunk was situated on the same plane and within close proximity to the toilet by a foot or less. (*...bottom bunk inmates, literally, slept where both inmates shit, pissed, spat, and farted...*) A prison bunk bed, though never constructed to be comfortable, was functional; though never where a man wanted to sleep, it was what it was; though never hoping to wake up after dosing off incarcerated, the inmate found himself more times than not meeting sunup.

Over the cell block's PA system, its mechanized announcement broadcasted: "DAYROOM, COMMENCE!...DAYROOM, COMMENCE!" (...a schoolhouse bell sounded...) A corrections officer stationed inside a mirrored-glass central-command module set on a higher plane over the block officer's desk inside the cell block pushed a button. The action opened every cell door on cell block 3A, which included Jake's cell door. Stirred awake by this and the plashing vacuum-sucking sounds of a flushed toilet behind his head, Brown, Jake's cellmate, standing over the toilet, fixed his hunter-green jumpsuit closed and exited the cell. No washing of hands or face. No brushing of teeth or hair. No apologies for the noise or farting.

That's good morning in jail; a toilet flush.

Nevertheless, good riddance, thought Jake.

Lying there tethered to fatigue while being pulled toward the life of the cell block now aroused, he couldn't silence the sounds of clanging institutional steel being slammed against itself, or the distortions and squeals from hand-held radios clamped to the utility belts of corrections officers on the move accompanied by the jangling of their keys, and then there was the noise inmates had a stake in which heightened the cacophony of institutionalization: the dayroom TV.

And this morning's variation came in the annoying form of Disney's Beauty & The Beast.

Jake couldn't sleep. He got out of bed. He brushed his teeth, washed his face, and made himself a plastic cup of coffee at the sink in Cell-6. With that steaming cup in hand, he sauntered out onto the cell block. From beneath a tier, at ground level, Jake entered the dayroom as if he had come in from a side entrance in a theater or auditorium. An open floor plan in front of him with rows of silvery metal benches bolted to the grey tile floor. Each bench ably sat five inmates from end to end, and presently only one metal bench was clean of any inmates. He turned his attention leftward and glanced up at the dayroom TV—the bane of his existence—angled downward toward the bench seating in the dayroom. Posted to the cinder-block wall on high and as high up from the floor as a basketball in from a court, Jake recognized with quick astonishment—yes!—about 15 inmates in hunter-green jumpsuits were drawn to watching Beauty & The Beast.

Some even hummed its songs...

They appeared moved by, if not enthralled by it, if not actually watching this shit in jail. Killers and rapists and drug dealers and pedophiles and burglars and... Jake be damned if the newly exonerated followed suit. Over the heads of about 15 inmates, toward the corrections officer's black-painted desk stationed opposite himself in the dayroom, Jake yelled, "Channel-check!"

Smatterings of discontent ascended from the benched inmates, Jake's cellmate among them, which only triggered Jake's ire more so. He pressed, "Are you kidding me with this bullshit?!...Fricken cartoons?"

Corrections Officer Georgetta Jarvis, middle-aged, over 12 years employed as a corrections officer, over men which was why she married a woman, over 300 pounds, over six-foot tall, and over Jake said, "You know the rules, and we've been over this. Get the votes! Majority rules to change the channel."

Officer Jarvis grabbed the remote control from her desk drawer, struggled to rise on achy knees, advanced toward the benched inmates opposite Jake, and asked him, "Didn't see you getting votes."

"Votes!" chirped Jake, "This is bullshit!"

"Mr. Montgomery, I know in the state prison system inmates have their own TVs in their cells. Here, in the county jail, we share one TV, and it's this one above my head, and what these men are currently watching is Beauty & The Beast."

"Fuck that!" yelled Jake, gripping his coffee, still not spilling a drop as he argued, "I can't catch the news in the morning like- I don't know...--every fucking American at 8 a.m.? Only children start their day with cartoons in the morning..."

An outburst from one of the benched inmates interjected, "FUCK YOU!"

Jake glanced down at them, not knowing who said it, and shouted, "No! Fuck you, asshole!"

Officer Jarvis interrupted, "Aren't you supposed to get bailed out soon, Mr. Montgomery? Why do you even care about what's on this TV when you'll be going home to watch your own?"

Jake responded (*a little choked-up...*), "Because I don't know if I'm going home, lady! I don't know if or when I'll get bailed out. It's my family. It's complicated."

A benched inmate, closest to Jake, snagged his attention after he blurted, "I bet it is when you murder them."

In a flash of rage, Jake doused him with his hot coffee, spiked the plastic cup off the inmate's forehead, and reared up his fists. He shouted, "Get up, asshole! Come on! Come on!" The nameless inmate sat shocked and drenched and blinded. Unable to take Jake up on his challenge to fight. A white towel sailed through the air, all of a sudden, and it was caught by Jake's cellmate Mr. Brown, who threw it atop the head of the inmate dripping coffee and rubbing his eyes. He dabbed the towel to his face, as Jake lorded over him with his fists ready to fight. The nameless inmate wouldn't take Jake up on his challenge, which led to Officer Jarvis' next order, "Lock it in, Montgomery! Lock it in!"

Jake glared down at the pitiful inmate, now dried off, that towel roped around his neck but afraid to stand. Again, the same rage in Jake's brilliant cobalt-blue eyes that Kiernan witnessed squeezed and pulled off her feet against the wall in The Montgomery Townhome ten years ago. Officer Jarvis again ordered, "Take it in, Montgomery, or I'll call the team and put you in the hole for a month."

Jake obeyed her order.

CLANG!!!

By automation, Cell-6 cell door locked shut behind Jake after it was clear to control-command that he was safely inside his cell. He plopped down on his bottom bunk, head in his hands, and seething about what to do next. He couldn't take much more waiting for Chase to do right by him. It had been a week; not a letter, not a phone call, not a visit from Summer. No news. That's all he wanted was news. Good news, perhaps.

Unlooked-for, a knock and visitor at his cell door snagged Jake's attention to the right of himself. Framed by the lithe cell door window appeared a tall, big Black man known on the cell block for saying very little though a young guy, and for killing a White man at a Trump rally, though he wasn't sentenced to life for it. Inmates called him Mittens, but his government name was Raymond Samuel Thell. The story goes, at an Ignite the Right Rally in Barton in November 2020, after Election Day results were being contested by Trump, a White man yelled the N-word as Trump ranted from the podium about Condoleezza Rice and The Bush Administration during The Afghan War days. If anything will make a Black man remember his roots amid an almost-all White Trump Rally is to shout out the N-word while referring to an intelligent Black woman; Democrat or Republican. Thell confronted the White man who stood behind him one bleacher seat up in the crowd and demanded that the bigot stop saying the N-word. The conversation didn't go well. After the bigot wouldn't stop spitting the racial slur of the utmost historical venom from his rants, even while arguing with Thell, Thell proceeded to charge and choke the bigot *(...wearing Trump-swag red mittens...)* crushing his windpipe. Killing the bigot instantly in cold blood.

Jake approached his cell door window cautiously, knowing these facts and rumors about this inmate, and asked, "What's up, *Mittens*?"

Thell responded through the glass, "Don't call me that."

"Okay, I apologize."

"You wanna watch the news, I gather?"

"Yeah, but I'm locked in now; probably for the rest of the day."

"Your cell has a good view of the dayroom TV from here, though."

"I know that. Seeing the TV is not the problem. It's what they have on it right now. *Oh well*, it doesn't matter. I can't get the votes."

Thell squinted seriously at Jake before putting the question to him directly, "Do you wanna watch CNN or WCAX this morning?"

Jake raised a curious brow and answered, "Local news...WCAX, so I can know what's going on in Burlington."

"Is that where you are from, Burlington?"

"Yes, and you?"

"Evanston, a small town."

"I know where that is. I took my wife there many times. One of our favorite spots to eat is there...a Harry's Stree—"

"Street-Side Diner," Thell finished Jake's sentence and said, "Harry Glotz used to own the place. Now his son does. I used to work there as a bus boy. I think it was...2013. I was 19. Some woman, though, a fat lady pissed off, crashed my little Camry Tercel where I had it parked in front of the diner. I guess she was trying to get out of the diner something fierce and backed into my bumper. Dislodged it pretty bad and what-not! Then some rich lady stepped in, seeing this from outside the diner, sent her waiter over to give me and another bus boy checks for $60,000 each because she hit my boy's car too. He was parked in front of the fat lady's car. I bought a new car that year, too."

"Wow! That's a lot of dough!"

"You White people got it like that, though."

Both inmates stood eye-to-eye. A single-pane glass window between them; each having had concealed being offended by the other, however their reasons were as much unlooked-for as they were unrelated. Jake was secretly offended by the racial microaggressions in Thell's last comment, and Thell was secretly offended Jake made no connection that that woman's charitable act ten years ago, which changed his life significantly, and his missing wife were one and the same person. A missing wife Jake had been linked to murdering most notoriously. Thell spied Jake's altercation with that other inmate from his cell window earlier. Thell overheard the inmate bring up Jake's criminal case before being splashed with coffee. Thell remembered that that woman's check, the highlight of his teenage life as the recipient of it, had the name Kiernan Montgomery emblazoned upon it, and its address had come out of Burlington. Jake had just confirmed that he, too, hailed from Burlington. Harry's Street-Side Diner being he and his wife's favorite spot. Montgomery, not a common surname in Vermont, but locally only one Montgomery millionairess could throw $120,000 in checks at a couple of Black bus boys as if they were soiled napkins. Thell considered, maybe, Jake hadn't been told about the incident or bread upon waters from Kiernan Montgomery, but it was odd to meet the missing woman's husband in jail, concluded Thell. Coincidence? Or was it, deduced Thell, *kismet or karma or killjoy*?

Thell assured, "I'll be right back."

Jake watched Thell move through his cell door window. The man who frowned upon being called Mittens walked over to the officer's desk and talked with Officer Jarvis. Her chin planted atop her fist, elbowing the desk at first, she listened to Thell. Whatever he was saying, Jake couldn't overhear, but Officer Jarvis appeared receptive to it. Thell, a large black man, appeared to eclipse Officer Jarvis, but she formed a smile eventually... that stayed in place. *What was he saying to her?* wondered Jake.

Suddenly, Officer Jarvis raised her chin from her fist and used that hand to reach into her upper desk drawer to extract from it the remote control to the cellblock TV. She pointed it lazily to the side of herself, as Thell's lips moved—Jake read them... he told her the channel—and from the TV screen, Beauty & The Beast switched in an instant to WCAX Eyewitness News. Jake smiled immediately at the sight of this. He won! And without a single vote cast. No election needed. Jake couldn't resist the thought; *Trump would've liked that.*

Thell left the officer's desk and headed toward his cell. For a split second's glance leftwards, over the seated heads of inmates in the dayroom, he found Jake's face pressed against the glass of his cell door's window. He spotted Jake's thumbs up in gratitude. However, on the other side of things, Jake recognized in Thell's mien—however slight and quickly erased—a sense of sadness or disappointment or lingering hurt in him; or perhaps it was all three emotions. Odd, thought Jake as Thell vanished into the shadowy confines of his cell across from his own.

The news station's jingle cautioned BREAKING NEWS throughout the cellblock. Jake's attention snagged, he noticed on the TV screen a familiar sight. A sweeping roving camera shot whose overview from a helicopter had trained down upon a bucolic Crystal Lake State Park; specifically, the area of Lookout Point. The chyron below the live shot read: *HUMAN REMAINS FOUND AT LOOKOUT POINT...*

[8:28 a.m.]
(...LIVE ON THE SCENE...)
Crystal Lake State Park, Lookout Point
Barton, VT

"...Today at Crystal Lake, all Vermonters mourn the

loss of two females found dead here at Lookout Point. A location fraught with accidental falls or intentional suicides over the years, it has claimed two more lives according to eyewitness accounts. Two rock climbers who would like to remain anonymous, but willing to speak to us on WCAX Eyewitness News this morning..."

Dana McCutchins, the crime-beat reporter for WCAX Eyewitness News, tilted her grip upon her black foamed microphone and aimed it toward the black-bearded mouth of a man standing beside his fiancée—*she stood just outside of the live camera shot*—willing to talk to viewers. Dana asked, "Will you please tell our viewers what you saw down there?"

Rock Climber #1: "Yeah, man, my fiancée and I often come here to rock climb. I own Gunther's & Gilly's Cross-Fit Gym and Shooting Ranges in Burlington, so —" needless plug in the face of a tragedy compelled his fiancée to nudge herself into the live shot... he got the hint... "Yeah, go ahead sweetie, tell 'em what you saw!"

Rock Climber #2: "I descended first... (Jake recognized her instantly... Kevin's secretary...) tracking my guy, here, on his way down. I was his spotter, you know? And as my guy here was halfway down his rope, I stepped back and nearly sprained my ankle on what I believed to be a large rock, like softball-sized, but I looked down and noticed that it was a hairy skull. Hell, I thought, God damn it! I got the heebie-jeebies. You don't expect to find something like that out here. It's beautiful out here."

Rock Climber #1: (Teeters into the live shot) "We even saw a wedding band still on one of the bones out there. I guess it was a hand or a finger or something. Obviously, the bodies have been out there in the wild for some time, and animals must've got ahold of them, because bones are scattered all over down there. Those ladies didn't just fall; they were pushed or something. I ain't no detective, but it's definitely suspicious. Even the cops down there are saying so, right, Miranda?"

Rock Climber #2: "That's right! It was terrifying. I'm just a secretary that sells cars for a living. Maybe for too long after this. I'm ready to retire, get married, and leave this place. But I love Vermont and the wilderness out here." (Weeping-ripe... her fiancé reeled her in with a half hug) "It's scary that someone would do this to women."

"Indeed, it is scary. Well, thank you for your harrowing accounts of what you've found down there." The reporter pulled back her microphone and announced into it, "Live from Lookout Point at Crystal Lake State Park. Back to you, Gary... in studio."

[8:45 a.m.] Washington County Correctional Facility

(Jake swallowed hard)

In studio, the news anchor got his turn to ask questions of the next guest. Enter Detective Jamal Rivers, Missing Person's Unit Chief, State Police of Vermont. That's what Jake read from the chyron below the officer's camera shot. A black man with a sharply manicured black beard, shiny dark-brown skin, and a no-nonsense glare and tone to his vernacular. A serious big-shot with serious big-shot duties, and the WCAX Eyewitness News anchor Gary Glenn peppered him with these questions: *"How was it possible to discern gender within 24 hours of finding the human remains?" "How long were those human remains out there in the woods?" "Is it suspected who these human remains belong to as to why his Missing Person's unit is on the case?" "Now, one of the rock climbers on the scene mentioned a wedding ring being upon one of the skeletal remains, and since wedding rings have oftentimes personalized engravings, is it possible that the police already know the names of these victims?"*

Detective Rivers answered in detail every one of Gary Glenn's pointed questions save for the last one, to which he replied, "No comment."

(*Commercial break*)

Otherworldly transfixed upon the Breaking News coverage, Jake never noticed the cell door open automatically upon its metal track from right-to-left in front of his near-catatonic face, nor had he sensed his cellmate J.J. Brown enter Cell-6 having brushed right past him; even as the cell door slid to a gradual closing and locked itself securely rather loudly, Jake stood in place unflinchingly. Brown had since stepped upon Jake's bottom bunk to hoist himself up to his top bunk; propped up his pillow to cushion his head; retrieved his James Rollins novel and cracked it open rather closely to his face for a good read. From time to time, Brown peeked over the horizon of his paperback novel, past his sock feet, and through the metal interstices of the top bunk footboard to see the back of Jake's head. His standing there. His face pressed up against the glass window of the cell door. Wordless.

What was he thinking about?

Unexpectedly, a tinny, breathy, distorted announcement barked out of the Cell-6 intercom speaker just above the light switch, which was within a couple of inches of where Jake stood at the cell door. Officer Jarvis yelled, "Montgomery!" No response, so she yelled twice, "Montgomery! Montgomery!"

Brown shot upright in the top bunk, and he yelled, "Jake! Answer that!"

Jake startled, jolted out of his own head, back to Earth and in jail again, snagged by the brusque New England accent of Brown's, not Officer Jarvis'. He scrambled to hit the red-response button to transmit his voice back to the officer's module. He leaned forward into the intercom speaker and answered, "Yes. Montgomery, here!"

"Pack your shit!" ordered Officer Jarvis, "A Chase Montgomery just bailed you out! Go watch your own T.V., asshole!"

"Wow!" delighted Brown, "Dude! You're going home. Just so you know, your plastic coffee cup is still laying out there on the dayroom floor. Nobody picked it up. You better pack your property, dude, before they change their minds. (...he chortled...) You'll still be in the bottom bunk, though."

Brown stopped talking. He recognized Jake's body

language. It was quaking slightly around the shoulders of his jumpsuit. Brown assumed, "You see dude, this is why you shouldn't watch the news. It'll depress you."

Jake wouldn't turn his head nor start to pack nor acknowledge his cellmate. He needed a minute—as tears tracked his cheeks and clung to his jawline in the form of droplets until they splashed against his upturned collar. No one ever saw Jake cry, and he aimed to keep it that way.

A decade long overdue those tears.

. . . Annus Horribilis, 20†8

(Aunt Gracey's Memory)

- *Just two months in, an 18-year-old student of Stoneman-Douglas High School concealed an AR-15-style semi-automatic rifle. He ambushed, shot, and killed 14 fellow classmates in their classrooms and hallways in Parkland, Florida.*

- *The Tree of Life Synagogue mass shooter, a white supremacist, concealed an AR-15-style semi-automatic rifle. He ambushed, shot, and killed 11 Jewish faithful in Pittsburgh, Pennsylvania.*

- *Aunt Gracey's pyrrhic victory over The Links Townhomes & Estates Homeowner's Association came after a long four-year legal dispute. The organization unsealed the court transcripts, divulging the 2013 murder case and the Missing Person's Incident Report "B.O.L.O.'s," along with public rumors about the Montgomerys' swinger's lifestyle, which included gazebo-sex on the back Nine in the gated community. Despite the doxing attempts to influence the court, it ruled that Aunt Gracey didn't have to relocate from or sell the Montgomery Tutor Townhome, but 86% of the home's equity was lost.*

- *Aunt Gracey was forced to sell her log cabin in Fairbanks, Alaska, to live full-time with Chase, 15, and raise him as the legal guardian in The Montgomery Tutor Townhome in Burlington,*

Vermont. Being back East and the designated stepmother-type was her lifelong nightmare come true.

- *Summer, now 18 in 2018, leaves home for college and rarely looks back.*

- *Daliah Moran suffered a massive stroke. She survived but decided to sell Moran Motors New & Used Cars —27 car dealerships throughout New England—to a local competitor for only $1.00.*

- *Kiernan Allison Kluger Montgomery was declared dead (without evidence of a body) by the State of Vermont Coroner's Office on August 9th, 2018.*

CHAPTER 25

THE UNBEARABLE RIGHTNESS OF POSTHUMOUS THOUGHTS

(FLASHBACK): August 10th
The Law Offices of Angus & Merriman-Hockley
Uptown Burlington, VT
[11:21 a.m.]

Death desires the decedent's last rites called, the mourner's caterwaul, a eulogizer's choked-up stall, and the reign as the Be-All End-All... wrote Kiernan in her diary back in 2013 after she learned from Neesha that Jake cheated on her. Though not divorced, she decided to extract Jake from the family will thereafter and scribed: ***I must have the final word.***

A row home converted into a law firm, sandwiched between a Greasy Spoon and a car garage in the grittiest parts of Burlington, was where Aunt Gracey led the Montgomery children for the reading of the will: Kiernan Montgomery's Last Will & Testament.

Collin Angus, a Senator Sanders look-and-sound-alike probate attorney, retained by Kiernan in the event of her death and after Jake had threatened to kill her on the night of April 12th five years ago, explained to Aunt Gracey and the Montgomery children, "Kiernan also dissolved the marital will that included your father's last wishes; moreover, in your mother's version, which excluded mention of your father, it will serve to supplant the marital will going forward, and it stands alone uncontested due to Jake Montgomery's conviction and current imprisonment. He has lost the right."

"Are you sure about that?" chirped Summer.

Attorney Angus couldn't discern whether her question, accompanied by a leer, stirred proceedings in defense of her father's honor or on behalf of her remaining family's interests. Nonetheless, she was a principal beneficiary in the will and not a minor at 18 years of age; therefore, he couldn't dismiss her concerns out of hand. He responded, "I'll make absolutely certain of it for you, because we've anticipated this question."

Attorney Angus reached for his cell phone tucked within his dark-blue blazer's inseam pocket, pulled it out, and started a text thread with his partner across the hall, who had a direct line to the Deputy Attorney General of Vermont.

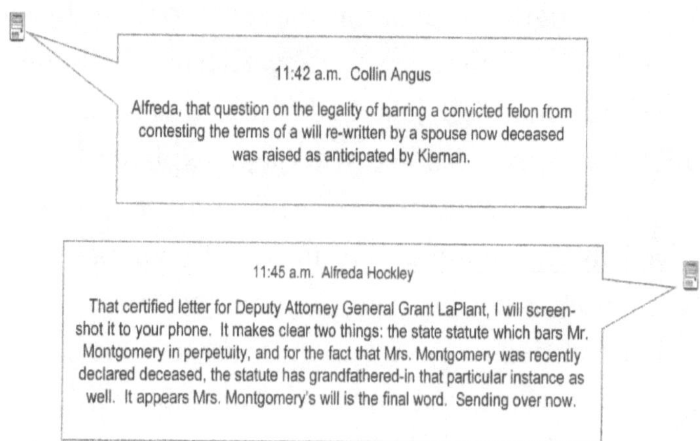

Attorney Angus returned his cell phone to his blazer's inseam pocket, turned to the family more broadly in his sights, (*...seeing Summer in his periphery...*), and reported matter-of-factly, "Deputy Attorney General Grant LaPlant has confirmed that Mr. Montgomery has lost the right to contest the terms in this current will. A copy of his certified letter will be entered into the record and submitted as an attachment to the beneficiary's receipt of this will and mailed to your address forthwith to end any confusion."

Chase delighted short of cheering, high-fiving, or live-streaming his Machiavellian grin.

Seated side-by-side in hardback cherry wood chairs with armrests, Aunt Gracey and Summer appeared situated at the right and left of Chase—all dressed in black formals (*tilted-brimmed petite hats with black veils attached for the ladies, and a black silky tie and white pocket square for the gentleman*)—in front of Mr. Angus's cherry wood vintage 19th-century desk, clean of all things save for a sealed, unmarked manila envelope, which he cut into with a rigid, arthritic pointer finger.

He pulled from the torn envelope a stack of crisp white papers. Meanwhile, Chase reached over and grabbed Summer's white-gloved hand where it lay limply over the edge of the armrest. He squeezed it, not letting go, supportively, anticipatorily, and fearfully. He was poised to hear his mother's voice through that of her probate attorney's brusqueness.

Terrifying...

Aunt Gracey sensed this fear palpably emanating from Chase, as she glanced over to the left of herself. In a half-whisper, as the attorney rustled the stack of papers into a certain order, she assured Chase, "Everything will be just fine." Summer refused to return Chase's affections through hand-holding, but she at least allowed her white-gloved hand to be crushed by her little brother with expressionless consent. Then Mr. Angus read the following:

"I, Kiernan Allison Klüger (*Chase nodded as he noticed that his mom notably divorced herself from the Montgomery name ceremoniously though not legally*), in the event of my death, it is my wish to speak lovingly of my youngest half-sister Jenna Kluger-Patrelli. My two children have lived deprived of your energetic beauty and fierce intelligence because of one family dispute we had after Dad died.

You would've made a wonderful aunt to my two children and a friend to me had we reconciled properly before my death. I never stopped thinking of you, which my diaries will attest, and for that reason, I bequeath The Montgomery Florida Vacation ranch-style home in St. Petersburg, Florida, on 1059 North Grant Street. Additionally, I bequeath $10,000 of my shareholdings in Red Maple Technologies, formerly known as AgriCare, in your name, and $25,000 in cash, whereby the Law Offices of Angus, Merriman & Hockley will transfer the money into whatever bank account of your choosing (*Summer and Aunt Gracey concealed the identical thought and feeling at the exact coeval: She's never let bygones be bygones; why give her anything?*)...

"...To my eldest sister Gracey Mae Kluger of Fairbanks, Alaska, though we have fought constantly as children, as my own children have followed suit, we've loved each other enduringly as adults, as my children will learn from you how to follow suit. (*Sniffles from Aunt Gracey snagged Chase's attention, and he reached over to grasp her adorned hand supportively...*)

"...I appoint you power of attorney over The Montgomery Estate until Summer or Chase have aged 18 years and/or graduated from high school, whichever comes first. I will deem you executor of the children's Trust Funds until they have aged 18 years and/or graduated from high school, whichever event occurs first. Both appointments run concurrently from this day forward and until Summer and Chase reach their 18th birthdays and/or graduate from high school, whichever event occurs first. Thereafter, Gracey, your appointments will expire, and the Law Offices of Angus, Merriman & Hockley will transfer all monies, assets, properties, and shareholdings to Summer Kristina Teresa Montgomery and Chase Colton Montgomery..."

"...As an aside, it must be said that I know my demise and subsequent decisions all but made you a mother to my children, and you never aspired to such a role; in fact, your entire life since college has been spent in fear of having children. My demise by proxy has disrupted your life's trajectory, possibly even your beloved commune with nature and the wilderness out West, and this most certainly has incited your fears and anxiety going forward. I know, Big Sis... I know, and I'm sorry..."

Aunt Gracey sobbed uncontrollably.

Mr. Angus stopped the reading of the will. Perfunctorily, he reached beside himself for his bottom desk drawer, pulled it open, and extracted from its hollow depths a fresh box of Kleenex. He handed it over his desk toward Chase's reach. Chase grabbed it, tilted it toward Aunt Gracey, who plucked out a couple of sheets and dabbed her eyes and cheeks, careful of her makeup. She apologized pitifully and composed herself only briefly, or until Summer teetered forward in her chair, glanced over Chase to insist, "Aunt Gracey, we love you, and thank you for all that you do for us."

Aunt Gracey broke down again... plaintively.

Summer sat back as Chase launched up and cradled

Aunt Gracey around her neck and shoulders, dislodging her tiny black hat and veil combo. She bewailed, rocking inside his warm embrace. Chase reminded her, "We've been through worse. We are family now. We'll get through this."

Attorney Angus, throughout his unsung legal career, had encountered thousands of these heart-wrenching episodes whereby the inexplicable power of the Last Will & Testament was undeniable in its pull to induce tears. As every probate lawyer had done before him, he argued within himself whether it was the power of the cold legal document per se, *or the unbearable rightness of posthumous thoughts.*

Aunt Gracey steeled herself eventually. Chase sat down, and as a family, which had been through hell and back, managed to return their attention toward Attorney Angus seated across from them and listened intently. Mr. Angus resumed, "Therefore, Gracey, I bequeath $1.8 million in cash to you, and the Boston condo that the Montgomery family left behind after my retirement. I bought the building as well in 2011; this too is yours as landlord to collect rent from its tenants or your right to sell it as property owner. Your choice. I bequeath $15,000 of my shareholdings in Red Maple Technologies, formerly known as AgriCare, now in your name. The Montgomery Family Vacation Motor Boat you've always loved and is docked along a pier in Provincetown, I bequeath to you. You've always wanted a boat to fish in Alaska. You now have the means to move that boat there and fish there, should you so desire... enjoy! I would have bequeathed more to you in honor of your sacrifices, but I have two children to take care of for the rest of their lives and for generations to come. I must safeguard their future..."

Aunt Gracey interrupted, "I'm satisfied, Sis." She glanced ceilingward, repeating, "I'm satisfied."

Mr. Angus continued, "To my son, Chase Colton Montgomery (*Chase released Summer's white-gloved hand*)... much beloved, and at all costs remember to take care of your sister. Become a man that other men respect and that other women deem decent. With that said, I bequeath the Montgomery Family Tutor Townhome situated at The Links Townhomes & Estates in Burlington, Vermont. When you have aged 18 years and/or have graduated high school, whichever event occurs first, it is yours. The attorneys at the Law Offices of Angus, Merriman & Hockley will assure safe transfer of the deed to your name. I bequeath $40,000 of my shareholdings in Red Maple Technologies, formerly known as AgriCare, now in your name but in a trust. You might benefit from its value when you've aged 18 years and/or graduated from high school, whichever event occurs first. The Oceanside property in Rehoboth, Delaware, which houses 30 tenants, I bequeath to your trust. You will become landlord of this property after you've aged 18 years and/or graduated high school, whichever event occurs first. You may collect their rents as your income, or you may sell it as the property owner and invest. Your choice..."

"...As an aside, I must confess, after I retired, convinced by Jake to accept the buy-out in that severance package worth $1.3 million dollars, I, unbeknownst to him, re-invested half of it back into Red Maple Technologies, formerly known as AgriCare, for the sake of financial safety. I did not believe we could survive on Jake's salary as an insurance salesman, despite his drive and belief. I never looked back at that investment until Jake threatened to kill me. I pulled out all of my investments, liquidating it all, and converting it into cash. Cash, which I knew would be impossible to hide from Jake for too long, so I banked it in a hedge-fund offshore account in Singapore for safekeeping and/or in the event of my death. If the latter occurred, it would have triggered financial authorities to reconnect with three New England-based banks here to make pay-outs relative to the beneficiaries named in this will. All of it governed by the newly named power of attorney, Gracey Mae Kluger, and the Law Offices of Angus, Merriman & Hockley..."

"... Thus, to my son, Chase, I bequeath the sum of $8.5 million dollars (*his mouth rendered agape—Summer's too...*) in cash assets..."

"*Oh, shit!*" blurted Aunt Gracey.

Attorney Angus continued undisturbed, "...Now in your name, Chase, to be received in full after you've aged 18 years and/or graduated from high school, whichever event occurs first..." Chase could not draw his mouth shut. He could not move a muscle. He could not stop his cadent tears. Summer, this time, reached over white-gloved and grasped his hand supportively over the armrest. Oppositely, Aunt Gracey grabbed his other hand, balled it inside her fist, and kissed the back of his hand. She then hung onto him, reached over, and rubbed his suit sleeve that lay upon his armrest, assuring him, "Your mother loved you very much," she said. "That much is clear."

Crosstalk notwithstanding, Attorney Angus read on, "...Additionally for Chase, (*Summer's eyes glazed over... she mutters, 'What's left?'—no one heard her coherently...*) What next involves another beneficiary..." Attorney Angus winced, perplexed and annoyed at this development as though the script had caught him off guard. He read onward: "...returning to your attention shortly, but it is important and necessary to bear regard for my daughter..."

(*Attorney Angus cleared his throat...*) "To my first-born, the ferociously intelligent, foremost beautiful, Summer Kristina Teresa Montgomery. I know when you heard your name expressed in full growing up, it oftentimes signaled trouble, but that was then; this is now. Not today. A daddy's girl, indeed, but I've believed to my last breath that a parent's love has no rival. The mother-daughter relationship has been fraught with growing pains and confrontation since the beginning of time. We were normal throughout the annals of history. You illuminate all the things which make you daring, pugnacious, strategic, confident, rational, fearless, smart, and forgiving. Before I had you, I wanted a daughter to be better than I ever was as a woman. When I learned that I was having a daughter, I promised myself to teach you both ways of being a woman endowed to run a company while being down-to-earth legitimately to keep a household; have hundreds of employees who would admire you as a boss, as well as have children who would adore you as Mom; develop a keenness to select only the kind of man who comforted your womanhood, and never competed with it; and he'd acknowledge such womanhood as strength in partnership, not a strength to put down. You will be that kind of woman, Summer. I'm sure of it." (*...Summer whimpered, swiped at her tears, knowing better of her name, better of her purpose, and better of her mother...*) "To my daughter, Summer," announced emphatically by Attorney Angus, "I bequeath my first home. A starter home, which I never sold nor rented out to anyone. It may need repairs, but it's a ranch-style home in the suburbs of Burlington, the Pinehurst neighborhood on 420 Nottingham Lane. I saved it for you. It will be in your trust until you have aged 18 years and/or graduated from high school, whichever event occurs first. I bequeath the remainder of my shareholdings (*an amount that wasn't disclosed, but Chase's shares were higher*) of Red Maple Technologies, formerly known as AgriCare, now in your name. They will be put in your trust until you have aged 18 years and/or graduated from high school, whichever event occurs first. I bequeath to you all of my jewelry, clothing, and other accoutrements, which has been appraised at $960,000. These valuables will be placed in a safe deposit box, and your Aunt Gracey, being the key holder, will relinquish it to you after you have aged 18 years and/or graduated from high school, whichever event occurs first..."

"... And, lastly, to my daughter, I bequeath to you the sum of $8.5 million dollars in cash assets. Monies that will be placed in your trust until you have aged 18 years and/or graduated from high school, whichever event occurs first. To my... Wait!" exclaimed Attorney Angus.

The probate lawyer, stricken and perplexed, flipped ahead a few pages and shook his head incredulously amid re-study of the document. On the other side of the desk, the Montgomery family appeared curious, anxious, and worried. With his head down, still flipping pages, Mr. Angus muttered, "There's been a mistake."

Aunt Gracey carped, "What?!"

The probate lawyer explained, "So, here at the law firm, there are three partners: Hockley, Merriman, and myself. Whenever we take on a client with a large estate having several beneficiaries, we split our duties and work our expertise together to get it right with respect for the wishes of the decedent. It's to avoid errors. Well, we have an error going on here anyway. It's a small one but fixable."

"Tell us the mistake, sir," pleaded Aunt Gracey.

"Well, there seems to be a fifth beneficiary whom we

haven't summoned to appear here with you all today, and that beneficiary should be here."

"A fifth?" chirped Summer, displeased.

"Wow! Where?" asked Chase. "Who?"

"Yeah, who?" complained Aunt Gracey. "There better not be a surprise, illegitimate kid of Jake's running around Vermont that we didn't know about until now."

"No, no, please," stressed Attorney Angus, but he asked, "Who is Neesha McGovern?"

"What about her?" asked Aunt Gracey, sounding frustrated. She wondered aloud, "How is she the fifth?"

Summer rolled her eyes and answered, "Because Mom treated her like my older sister or somebody. She loved that girl growing up."

"So, yes," added Attorney Angus, "I'm sorry for the mishap, but it appears that my partner was cautioned not to summon Ms. Jenna Klüger-Petrelli because the decedent anticipated her being a no-show when this day came. Where the error arose, my partner made out summonses for only the immediate family without distinction for the unrelated beneficiaries and overlooked Ms. McGovern. That's the way I believe it happened. Nonetheless, I must read her quite intricate portion of the will."

"What's coming to her?" asked Summer. She counted the cash assets in her head. "I got $8.5 million. Chase got $8.5 million. Aunt Gracey got $1.8 million, and Aunt Jenna got $25,000, so that's roughly $19 million. How much were Mom's total cash assets again?"

"$27 million dollars," replied Attorney Angus.

"What?" carped sharply Aunt Gracey. "The babysitter is getting the remainder of that... which is what?... um?"

"$8 million!" blurted Summer in contempt.

"This is all improper," interjected Attorney Angus. "I cannot disclose what the fifth beneficiary will inherit without first reading it to her. I'm not done with the reading of this will. Please don't skip ahead of the process with conjecture."

Chase considered aloud, "Well, if that's what she got, $8 million, that's even with us, not more than us. That's fair."

"Yes, it's fair, Chase, if you are a Montgomery," chirped Summer. "Not a McGovern. She was employed by us, not related to us."

Aunt Gracey listened to her niece and nephew, who rarely agreed on anything, but she sided with Chase, saying, "Your mother was always generous with money. She shared with strangers since we were kids. I remember she would get pissed too if they tried to thank her afterward. She would get embarrassed by her own generous heart. We shouldn't find fault with her if she gave your babysitter $8 million. It's her own money to do what she wants with it. She earned it, not us, and we want for nothing more than what we have, right? We are fine."

"But what about Dad?" pressed Summer. "What does he have?"

Chase turned to Summer and yelled, "He's a jailbird! He's in a jail cell. That's what he has!" Summer rolled her eyes at Chase while looking at the lawyer across the desk.

"Come on, children, stop. Not here," chided Aunt Gracey.

"Is there any way that we can make contact with Neesha McGovern by phone?" asked Attorney Angus as an open question to the family seated before him.

"I don't know her phone number," replied Aunt Gracey. She asked Summer, "Do you?"

"No."

Chase blurted it out: "802-555-6213."

Summer pursed her lips, half-disappointed and with half-disbelief. Attorney Angus plucked his cell phone out of his inseam pocket once again. He dialed Neesha's phone number as recollected from rote by Chase. He heard it ringing and was quick to push a button to switch the outgoing call to speaker mode. Everyone in the office now overheard the ringing of the phone and awaited Neesha to pick up. Instead, it was her mother who answered, "Hello?"

Chase shook his head immediately at Attorney Angus.

"Is this Neesha McGovern?" asked the probate lawyer, slow to recognize the relevance of Chase shaking his head. It dawned on him only now. He rephrased his question. "May I speak with Neesha McGovern?"

"Who is this?"

"Collin Angus with the law firm Angus, Merriman & Hockley."

"What is this about?"

"A will. Neesha's been named a beneficiary, and I need to speak with her."

"She gettin' any money?"

"Ma'am, I really can't... um... Is Neesha present in the home?"

"Is this about them Montgomery White folks that got their hooks in her?"

The family collectively raised a brow, chortled, or appeared flabbergasted.

Attorney Angus answered, "Ma'am, I don't know what you mean by that. However, I can't disclose the things you wish to know. Maybe if Neesha can call me back, I—"

"Hold on... Hold on... I'll get her."

The family seated side-by-side-by-side didn't know what to expect or what to do next. It didn't sit well anymore. Summer blurted, "Well, where is she?"

"Give her a minute," rebutted Chase, but he muttered, "This is kinda weird."

Aunt Gracey said to Attorney Angus, "Just hang up. She's taking too long. We've got business of our own still going here."

Attorney Angus ignored the family entirely. He trained his ear closer to his cell phone, which lay flat upon his cherry wood desk. He detected a slight swooshing sound advancing toward the phone on the other end. Slipper-feet, he deduced... swoosh-swoosh... swoosh-swoosh. Neesha's mother could be heard saying, "It's some lawyer..." Afterward, Neesha's voice came in loud and clear.

"Hello?"

"Yes!" shouted Attorney Angus. "Hello, Neesha McGovern?"

"Yes."

"...Of 1212 Bubba Watson Court, The Links Townhomes and Estates?"

"That's my Mom's address, yes."

"But not yours?"

"I'm not a kid anymore. Why? Who is this? What do you want?"

"Okay, first, I must tell you that I have you on speakerphone. In the room with me are some friends of yours—Chase Montgomery, Summer Montgomery, and Gracey Mae Kluger. We are all present for the reading of the will left behind by the late Ms. Kluger, who employed you as her babysitter and who you know as Mrs. Kiernan Montgomery. She named you a beneficiary in her will. Shall I continue?"

A long pause... 14 seconds long.

After considering all sides, recognizing the consequences if she didn't continue the call, and the morning-after promise she made to Mrs. Montgomery, Neesha humbly answered, "Yes."

"Fine, I should inform you that it is the fault of my law firm that you are not here with us in the office. You should've received a summons to appear and be here in person, so may I proceed with the reading portion over the phone herefrom as it relates to you in the will?"

"Yes."

"Good-good... okay!" exclaimed an exhausted Attorney Angus. Neesha could hear papers being shuffled on the other end. Unexpectedly, Chase shouted, "Hello, Neesha!"

She responded sprightly, "Hey, Chase!"

"So, we are to presume you are not a minor, Ms. McGovern?" asked Attorney Angus.

"No, I'm 22 years old."

"So, I'm just going to read your portion, and you listen along, okay?"

"Okay."

"So..." (*reading ahead... no more thinking, no more mistakes...*) "To my babysitter, Neesha McGovern, you have been more of a girlfriend to me than a babysitter for my children. You've seen me at my best and worst and sometimes in the same day. You've watched over my children and protected my best honor in my absence. You've told me the truth when even my husband would not, and I cannot pay you back for all that you've done, but I will try herefrom. To Neesha Sadee McGovern, I bequeath $900,000 dollars, which the Law Firm of Angus, Merriman & Hockley will transmit to her bank accounts and/or in any form or denomination she prefers forthwith. I bequeath to the college of her choice the sum of $500,000, as a college trust fund only accessible by a university financial office, and should Neesha choose to pursue her college degree, that pursuit will be paid-in-full. And, lastly, as this rejoins that which I bequeath my son Chase, but that which Neesha McGovern is In-The-Know. These series of questions must be asked of her to confirm that she will abide by that which she promised me in the gazebo. Neesha McGovern, do you recall the conversation you had with Kiernan Kluger Montgomery on April 12th, 2013?"

Neesha responded, "I do."

"Neesha McGovern, do you swear to uphold the terms of 'the plan' devised by Kiernan Kluger Montgomery on April 12th, 2013?"

Neesha responded, "I will."

"Lastly, Neesha McGovern, you are not to disclose what you know here and now, but do you recall the location of the items that are to be bequeathed to Chase Colton Montgomery when he has aged 18 years?"

Neesha responded, "I recall."

"Well, Ms. McGovern, I have your address and phone number. I'll have my partner Alfreda Hockley call you later today or tomorrow to get your particulars, such as bank routing numbers, to effectuate money transfers regarding your inheritance. As it pertains to your college education, we have brochures here that we can send you to get you started. There are universities with whom the law firm works well with their registrars if you get overwhelmed with the process; we'll help with that too. We're here to help you, okay?"

"Okay, and thanks," said Neesha.

"Contact us anytime, but again, we'll contact you later today. I have something else to do here with the family."

"Goodbye," said Attorney Angus. Chase, distantly from the background, shouted, "Love you, Neesha!"

"Love you, too!" she giggled.

Proceedings righted from sideways, Attorney Angus turned to Summer and corrected her past calculations of the testator's remaining cash reserves from $8 million dollars to a smidge less at $7.6 million dollars (he insisted, to be precise...), which transitioned the reading of the will toward its last testament: The F.M.E. It had become an invariable prerequisite to inform Kiernan's nouveau riche of her overarching plan for the $7.6 million dollars. Something she had scripted last in the will, organized first with the banks, which involved the law firm of Angus, Merriman & Hockley to facilitate for the next decade. It was dubbed the Family Maintenancc Endowment. Disposable cash only for family access to cover any future costs ranging from home restorations to property taxes; from lawyers' fees accrued to payouts necessary for settling lawsuits against them. It was there for them. How to Be A Millionaire successfully, as it were, tasked Attorney Angus to be detailed and specific with them for about an hour.

However, Neesha Sadee McGovern, also technically a millionaire thanks to Kiernan, on the other end of things, had not been made obliged to such White People-oriented tutorials carried out in the posh law offices of Angus, Merriman & Hockley. Left to fend for herself—the Black People way—Neesha still had been positioned as the unlooked-for important fifth beneficiary. The only person keen on the whereabouts of Kiernan's diaries, which she wasn't allowed to divulge on that conference call, but understood why... sorta. What would have been the difference, she considered with black-and-white thinking, Chase finding out at 15 years old that his father was a lying, cheating snake as opposed to three years later at 18? But, she thought, I'll keep the whereabouts of her diaries a secret away from Chase a little longer... The truth is true, and sometimes it doesn't age well, Neesha believed. A fact Kiernan Montgomery knew all too well, if not to a devastating effect. She may have lost her life because of it; delayed truth.

Neesha recognized that, despite being In-The-Know about many things, she didn't really know The Montgomerys at all. She wouldn't learn until five years later that Chase and Summer had become millionaires overnight after the reading of the will, although she was on the tail-end of the call during it. Similarly, Neesha had no idea Kiernan planned to include her in the will, but she later discovered she had been present in the gazebo while Kiernan made those arrangements. Kiernan's morning-after plan to keep her diaries safe was a mere errand. Speaking of plans, Neesha thought she had seen it all the night she caught Jake and Kevin together in the gazebo, but she hadn't.

Had Neesha stayed hidden with her cat Mojo behind that tree and continued spying for just twenty more minutes, she would have been In-The-Know and could have reported back to Kiernan about Jake and Kevin's plans for Taking Out the Trash. What seemed like an innocuous phrase actually had a murderous connotation when revisited.

CHAPTER 26

THE BABYSITTER & THE GAZEBO (REVISITED)

(FLASHBACK): April 12th
The Links Estates & Townhomes
Fairway Pedestrian Park (The Gazebo)
[10:48 p.m.]

Jake Montgomery texted [10:48 p.m.]:
"Tonight. Meet me at the gazebo."

Kevin's cell phone notifies him of Jake's text, a text he would have missed if he wasn't already awake, staring ceilingward, lost inside his own thoughts, and beside his wife Daliah, who was asleep and snoring slightly.

Kevin Moran texted [10:53 p.m.]:
"On my way."

Kevin & Daliah Moran's Estate

Meanwhile... [11:21 p.m.]:

Kevin flees his home out the back door in a dark-colored Penn State tracksuit. Jogging, not breaking a sweat, toward the pedestrian park. Cell phone and keys jangling inside his pockets, and strapped to his ankle, he concealed a black lambskin sheath which encased a twelve-inch dagger engraved "Memento Mori." A gift, originally bought for Jake, which he kept for himself.

He made his way past Jake's unlighted townhome, which meant he only had four more residential blocks to go. He kept a ragged jogging pace. Residential streets melted away to gravelly bike paths and sinuous grey concrete walking paths, which converted into carpet-flat green fescue. Fairways as soft as running upon stripped mattresses under moonlight converted into upsloped greens. Greens after greens, watching out for water hazards and sand pits under klieg lights until in sight appeared the 9th Green—and nestled downslope, the gazebo illuminated gauzy-white by stringed lights—yonder lay the 10th Green. At this point, Kevin stopped his jogger's pace to a brisk walk. He couldn't see Jake yet, but he sensed he was somewhere sitting inside the gazebo; pissed probably, he imagined. And he was right.

†

[11:15 p.m.] Five minutes earlier...

Neesha slipped out of the back door of her home, mindful not to let the screen door slam shut via its tightly wound springs and wake her mom. She led Mojo out in front of her first, then guided both the back door and screen door silently to a closing. She lived 8 blocks away from the Moran's Estate on Tiger Woods Lane (*...unbeknownst to Neesha...*), but only 3 blocks away from The Montgomery's Tutor Townhome on (*...Vijay.....*) Singh Drive. Neesha donned a dark blue windbreaker with her cell phone on vibrate tucked in its black mesh inseam pocket. Mojo, on his dark-colored leash, walked ahead of her pace...

In the gazebo, Jake glanced down at his wristwatch as he paced inside. The time showed eleven-twenty-five. He shifted his attention eastward toward the lighted fairways, past the gazebo's cedar-arched entryway to the fairways, and he noticed a lanky, tall, shadowy figure of a man (*...It's Kevin, finally; he told himself...*) walking over the hump of the 9th Green.

[11:28 p.m.]

Kevin sauntered out of the klieg-lighted nightshade into the whitish hues of the gazebo up its front staircase inside, and Jake lambasted Kevin with his first words, "What took you so long?"

"Dude, I frickin' ran here!" he said with his arms outstretched from his sides pleadingly. He reached the top step under the cedar roof of the gazebo and explained, "I'm not as close to the park as you, remember? Besides, I was in bed with my wife! What happened? Why do you look so pissed?"

"It's Kiernan!" Jake whined, then he stammered, "She... She... I—"

Kevin interjected, "What, dude?"

"She knows, man. She knows!"

Jake's worries appeared palpable, piqued, and painstaking.

"Calm down. What does she know exactly?"

"About us."

"There is no... us. Where was us when I texted you all day? I have my own marital problems at the moment."

"Fuck you, dude!" blasted Jake. He stepped to Kevin. Face-to-face with him now, he warned, "You don't get to bail on me again, buddy." Jake wagged his finger at him and said, "You did this same shit back in college when we got caught then."

They stared at each other without flinching, blinking,

or forgiving. Nearly speaking into each other's mouths, Kevin, apparently seething, said, "There you go again bringing up the fucking past, bro! Throwing it in my—(...smack!)..."

Kevin's head whipped from center to left, then back to center again, fuming. Jake glared back at him with insolence and intolerance. He told him, "Shut the fuck up!"

†

[11:56 p.m.] Some 70 to 80 feet outside the gazebo...

Neesha squinted from behind the girth of a tree in the rough. She recognized one of the male voices as familiar—*damn-near family*. Quizzically, she muttered, "Mr. Montgomery?"

The other man's voice, however, was a stranger to her, but she overheard him confess, "I got the girl pregnant. (*...incoherent utterances now from her vantage point, then the stranger's voice carried well again...*) Man, if you ain't getting what you should get, you're getting got!"

Such a stupid refrain.

Jake tolerated it for decades, but this was the last time. Unbeknownst to Kevin, Jake had formed a fist at his side and blindsided him with a vicious uppercut. A sucker punch that sent Kevin flying backward, stopped by the cedar wood railing, where he braced himself, dumbstricken. He hollered, "Fuck you, dickhead!"

[12:01 a.m.] Meanwhile...

Back behind the nightshade, the klieg lights of the park had extinguished upon a timer. Unceremoniously, the Links Pedestrian Park appeared down for the night. The same complexion as the night overhead; a starlessness which wafted black veils of cirri across the glowing half-face of the moon. The gazebo's drapery of string lights was the only beacon. Neesha hunkered down. (*...Oh! she thought—fisticuffs!*) She wondered who was the other man in the gazebo losing the fight to Mr. Montgomery?

Kevin, dazed and gloomy, swung back. He threw himself farther than his punch. A glancing blow which Jake ducked. He punched Kevin in the gut. Air left him like vomit as he doubled over, clutching himself. Advantage as apparent as aggrieved, Jake punched downward where Kevin's head loomed lowly. A blow that whipped his head in the opposite direction. Kevin's anchorman-styled perfect fair-haired hairdo stood on end; mussed. They each tasted blood at this point in the fight. Metaphorically, Jake tasted blood with a vengeance, while Kevin actually tasted it on his tongue. Jake threw another devastating punch that landed just behind Kevin's left ear, and it was comparable to being slapped across the face by a brick. Dazed, Kevin's knees buckled against his own will to stand upright. The blow made him drop his fists. His body betrayed him worse than his friend with that first uppercut. Kevin went down. On his hands and knees, Kevin faced the cedar wood flooring, half-aware that sometimes in life a man gets beaten in a fair one, and then he noticed—half-aware—that Jake stood flat-footed a little too close to him.

Swiftly, Kevin see-sawed his upper body weight forwardly upon his hands flattened against the cedar wood flooring, paired his legs together as thick as a log in sweatpants, and, as hard as he could, whipped them against the backs of Jake's ankles. Jake crumbled backward and hit his head on the gazebo railing behind him on the way down. Concussed at this point, hearing wind chimes though the gazebo hadn't dangled any, Jake, upon his back, realized Kevin, in one fell swoop, straddled him. Shit! he thought. Advantage as assaultive as aspired. Kevin's flurry of punches ensued. Each blow torqued Jake's head backward. Floppy jet-black hair bounced off the cedar wood flooring repeatedly, in the same manner that a speed bag bounces off its wooden backstop after a prizefighter catches rhythm. Jake's defensive posture, pleading hands upturned and flailing in front of his face, proved the worst failing guards. Kevin punched by them, hitting Jake square in the face more times than not. A rain of blows with thunderous impact was not deflected, not deked, or not done. Kevin roared with exuberant rage until Jake's drooping head appeared too unswerving as opposed to unconscious.

Kevin stopped mid-punch. He noticed the physical damage he had rendered upon his lifelong friend: the purplish bulbous swollen pair of black eyes, the split lip, the smashed-in nose (...not broken...), the red-blotchy bruised forehead, and the blood...so much blood. None of it spotted the gazebo's cedar wood flooring, however. Odd. Jake's lengthy wisps of jet-black hair appeared matted to his face, due to the gooey commixture of blood and sweat. Kevin's anger against his friend quickly turned into care for him.

"Jake! Jake!" he yelled down at Jake's face. "Wake up, bro! *No-no-no-no!* Bro, *wake up!"*

From left to right and then back in reverse, Kevin had shifted, shaken, or shuffled Jake's face. Jake wouldn't come to. Kevin's indelicate aid failed to make Jake's cobalt-blue eyes uncross. Swollen black eyes no wider than slits. Grossly bloodshot. Eyes that failed to right themselves and drop from those pallid skies of unconsciousness up in his head. Kevin couldn't make Jake more aware, alert, or agleam. A resistance not to come back to Earth, as it were, yet still apparently breathing in that space. Kevin's last resort, smacking Jake's cheeks lightly and calling his name...

A thing that never worked was a never thing that worked.

Jake's eyes descended from those skies up in his head, swerved back to Earth, and his natural blue lights relumed with survivor's fire. Jake appeared jarred. Latently, vertical lightning strikes of pain crossed Jake's field of vision upon his seeking forward focus. The moment he tried to raise his eyelids beyond what swollenness allowed or tested his sight clearer against what petechial hemorrhaging smeared, or tried to visualize depth and perception without distortion or pain, his eyes stayed open-slits; his sight remained blurry; his depth perception contorted whitish ceiling light as splintered triangulated iridescent halos after every sore blink. Jake recognized that he had risen his head from the floor of a knockout, and that he had lost the fight.

He always lost to Kevin.

Jake found it difficult to breathe with Kevin sitting on him, but his head position blocked the overhead ceiling light, likened to an eclipse of the sun, so there was that. Not only was one made to lose some... and lose some, Jake thought. I'm forced to accept being crushed but for relief of mere sight without pain. Seeing that Jake was conscious, Kevin's profusion of apologies sounded sincerely plaintive, "Bro, I'm so sorry! Please, I'm sorry! Jake?"

"Get off me."

"Jake?"

"Let me up."

"Jake, just listen to me. I should've taken it on the chin. We shouldn't have fought. I was being glib, and I was in the wrong. I—"

Jake sighed before he said, "This wasn't the first time

that you kicked my ass, Kevin. Stop, just stop. I've lost everything. Do you... (*...sobbing pitifully...*) understand me? My kids! (*...lip quavering sobs...*) My family life! (*...whining...*) I just know Kiernan is going to divorce me after this! I won't be able to see my children... (*...Kevin slid down the length of Jake's torso, lowered his face closer to Jake's...*) She'll make sure of that. Lawyers will get involved. They'll be fatherless, except I won't be dead. I'm fuc—"

Kevin's mouth devoured Jake's entire.

They both tasted pennies upon their writhing tongues inside each other's mouths, but they knew instantly that it was blood, which cost them nothing; in fact, it made their long hungry kiss—to Jake—that much more priceless. Or was it a hidden tax upon everything that they loved, which was the way Kevin sensed it? But a morally bankrupt man would sell his soul for self-loathing if that transaction might present a greater opportunity...

Kevin Concealed from Jake's Reality: Opportunities are neutral vehicles, but it is man who is fallible, cynical, or immoral with drive.

The Result: Infidelity was victory.

Jake Concealed from Kevin's Reality: Actual injury **[is]** the human being; its degree of severity blinds what it sees; binds you and me to pain.

The Result: Intolerability as virtue.

In the gazebo, both fully clothed in dark-blue or grey-colored sweatpants with matching sweatshirts, Kevin motioned from the straddled position into the plank position over Jake. In other words, Kevin relinquished his dominance over Jake. They lay together as equals. Meanwhile, Kevin caressed Jake's bruised and bloodied face the entire time he worked his mouth over Jake's. The kiss, which felt like drowning to the other because neither had come up for air, underscored an inseparable duration not well-practiced but passionately expressed. They hadn't screwed since college, more than 16 years ago, and they groaned into each other's mouths achingly while kissing at this reunion. Their saliva-slickened tongues twisted at angles, maneuvering like slugs inside dark warm caves, mating. Licentious licks, which paled in primal aggression to their working hands and writhing hips below. Unraveling drawstrings to their sweatpants. Sweatpants that covered upturned, erect penises bulging past their navels. Clashing swords, as it were, through their sweatpants. Their lower halves frictional and mimicking movements yet to come. Sweatshirts rolled up inadvertently, exposing navels, pubic hair, heads of penises as they writhed stomach-to-stomach, pelvis-to-pelvis. Through the thin cotton fibers of their clothing, they sensed a gooey wetness. Pre-ejaculate in thin webs over their waistbands. Continuous writhing below, but above the two working mouths at the risk of ejaculation too soon. Drowning and groaning up top; sticky and slick writhing down below. What felt like spiders pervading upon them on the gazebo's cedar wood flooring were prickly chills down their spines.

[12:21 a.m.] In the rough...

Neesha spied them, appalled. Amid a struggle to manage her cat Mojo, who was getting squirrely after her cell phone on vibrate alerted her of an incoming text, she was forced to set him down in the rough, holding onto his leash. She scrambled to extract her cell phone from her windbreaker's inseam pocket. She turned her attention from what appeared to be Mr. Montgomery's make-out session on the floor of the gazebo to her cell phone's lighted screen. From behind the tree, tucked away in the nightshade, Neesha read...

Kiernan Montgomery Texted [12:23 a.m.]:
"I know it's late, but can you babysit? I need to find Jake.
He hasn't come home."

Neesha glanced up from her glowing cell phone screen back through the darkness and the action. Oh, my God! She appeared taken aback, having recognized, They're fucking!

Upon the cedar wood flooring of the gazebo, Jake had rolled Kevin onto the front of his dark-blue sweats, then roped his right arm under him, lifting him up only as far as to reposition him upon his hands flattened against the cedar wood flooring and his bent knees spread apart.

Doggie-style.

On his knees, Jake scooted up, just behind Kevin's rear, which was upturned and pitching a tent in his grey sweatpants, which he yanked down—his own before Kevin's. Only Kevin's bare ass was exposed. Kevin glanced over his back at Jake poised to lean in, and through a half-whisper, he said, "Fuck me, Jake."

Without spit or grease or remorse, Jake's hands-free plunge inside of Kevin made both of them hiss. They arched their backs and craned their foreheads ceilingward; one due to pleasure and the other due to pain, which was a pleasure—in and out... in and out... in and out... What delicious pain. Jake kept Kevin's nates splayed with both hands as he worked his pelvic thrusts —in and out... *in and out... in and out...* Kevin groaned, tensed up, and cussed, "*Fuck, yeah!*"

Whatsoever few soul-deep connections remain, even that which man believes man has incurred from God, nothing touches the human soul more pointedly than anal sex.

Tighter and firmer than any masturbator's grip—*in and out... in and out... in and out...* Slicker and warmer than any oral copulation's slobber—*in and out... in and out... in and out...* Deeper and grittier than any woman's vagina —*in and out... in and out... in and out...* Kevin's anus likened to a fortress with a busted-in gate, despite continued warm contractile resistance to every invasion.

Jake's penis, that battering ram, sensed as flambeau gone too steep. Jake scratched the surface of a back wall, accompanied by feathery cool slaps of his swinging scrotum belatedly against Kevin's burning perineum—akin to the penis inside the vagina while the man fondles the woman's clitoris; anal sex and the collisions had with swinging testicles from behind... erotically ticklish; every violent pelvic thrust by Jake stretched the head of his penis to hit the prostate—in and out... in and out... in and out... Massaging out squirts of Kevin's orgasmic semen, meanwhile, floorward.

[12:32 a.m.] Retreating from nightshade and the rough...

The babysitter had had enough. She appealed to her cell phone...

Neesha McGovern Texted [12:33 a.m.]:
"I know where Jake is."

Kiernan Montgomery Texted [12:38 a.m.]:
"Where, Neesha?"

Neesha McGovern Texted [12:38 a.m.]:
"The gazebo."

Neesha fled after that final text. Had she remained hidden out of sight and outlasted the male public displays of perfidy in the distance, it would have interested Kiernan far more to learn from her babysitter that the phrase "Taking Out the Trash" doesn't always mean that.

Jake neared climax, quaking uncontrollably while inside Kevin, and he got vocal, "Promise me (...*groaning*...) you'll never (...*hissing*...) fuck another woman (...*labored panting*...) not even Daliah...Promise me!"

This was the opportunity Kevin sought—his Getting Jake Before Jake Knew He Was Got—with the side of his face pressed down against the cedar wood flooring (...rolling his eyes...waiting for Jake to finish...), he squeezed out a response, "I won't...I promise."

Jake met an inviolate exultation of the unintelligible kind vis-à-vis an orgasm rather ne plus ultra, which triggered a gusher of warm semen inside Kevin. With jerky hips, Jake roared, "Ugh! UGH! (...*squirt*...) Oh, my

God... (*...squirt...*) Oh, my God... Oh, my God. (*...squirt...*) Fuck, yeah!"

He collapsed outstretched over Kevin's back, as flat as a table with give. Kevin decided to torture Jake poised to pull out. He flexed his PC muscles, and Jake shivered to the awesome power behind the grip. A cork-popping sound emitted after Jake reached down and pulled out his dying erection by hand. Jake couldn't see Kevin's mischievous grin toward the night and the gazebo railing.

Infidelity was victory to Kevin, but not the finale.

The husbands, to their wives at home, dressed quickly on their backs, floorward. They then rose to their feet, one after the other, and turned their gazes suspiciously toward the nightshade. Only now had it occurred to them that it might be too risky. Relieved that no one had spotted them (*...or so they presumed...*).

Jake and Kevin sat apart from each other upon the cedar wood benches in the gazebo. Pivoted face-to-face, they surveyed each other's facial wounds with a quiet recognition that the fighting from earlier had been puerile. It didn't need to be said; thus, the quiet at first blush. A few minutes passed before Jake spoke first.

"So, what do we do now?"

"I don't know. I still got a woman pregnant. I'm a dad, Jake. A lying dad at that."

"Is she going to get an abortion?"

"I don't know, Jake. I just got the news at work. She

called me today at lunch and just blurted it out, like... like... a threat, almost."

"A threat? She wants money out of you? Give it to her."

"I don't know what she wants yet, but how does it look that I got the other woman knocked up, but not my own wife of 12 years?"

"Our wives, *man*... If they only knew."

"You got that right."

The two husbands with wives shared a chuckle (*...shaking their heads simultaneously...*). Jake launched up from the bench and walked over to the balustrade. He gripped the railing by the gazebo's archway entrance and cast a distant gaze out into the crickety, breezeless, mild evening. Peaceful. He danced with his thoughts, reminiscing about the great sex he just had with Kevin. Kevin walked over, stood behind Jake, saw no one was around, hooked his fingers onto Jake's sweatpants waistband in front of him, and pushed his genitals—in his sweatpants, still erect, halfwise—(*Jake sensed him against his buttocks...thoughts of Round Tow Ensured...*)

Jake, knowing Kevin all too well, asked, "What do you want?"

"What do you mean?" asked Kevin with a smile in his voice, which Jake didn't need to glance behind himself to notice but knew it existed behind his ear.

"Ask. What do you want me to do?"

"Well, now that you forced me into it..."

Jake cut him off, "I'm not forcing you into shit! I just

don't want the games. I'm not in the mood. I have to get back to whatever home I've got left. What do you want from me?"

Kevin reached down toward his left ankle, hiked up his sweatpants there, unfastened the cross-strap over the black leathery hilt, pulled the 12-inch dagger out of its sheath slowly, reared it over his head, and stabbed it into the archway post-beam. The dagger was at eye-level with Jake, an inch from the side of his face, but he didn't flinch. He had been waiting for an excuse to do that. Kevin asked, "Do you love me?"

Kevin started on his carving as Jake side-eyed Kevin's action and responded, "You already know the answer to that question."

"Confirm it, tonight."

Jake admitted, "I love you."

"And that's what this will read," said Kevin while he put the finishing touches on the shape of a heart and the initials J.M. loves K.M. inside its narrow field of space. Jake saw what the carving read in his periphery and said, "That's dangerous."

"I thought you said Kiernan already knew about us?"

"She does, *I think.*"

"And what are we going to do about that?" asked Kevin as he returned the 12-inch dagger to its sheath strapped to his lower calf and covered it with the length of his sweatpants. He added, "That can't stand... *her knowing*, you know."

Jake frowned and asked, "What do you mean, 'can't stand'?"

Kevin spoke in hushed tones by Jake's ear, and Jake spoke into the night. To each other, this was man-talk. Kevin reiterated, "You have a problem at home, and so do I."

"And?"

"And... Kiernan's going to divorce you. Intolerable. She's going to win in court because the scorned wife claiming irreconcilable differences, given the backdrop of infidelity... but The Other Woman in your case is me? Libel in the Court of Law... Intolerable. Plus, the woman's worth millions. Good luck finding a lawyer on your salary with the battery of divorce lawyers she's going to throw at you. Intolerable. She comes from a family worth millions. She makes my couple of millions in the bank and string of car dealerships look like pocket change and just a corner bodega. Intolerable. She's going to wipe the floor with you in the custody-of-the-children battle. Can you say, one weekend a month and two holidays a year, if that? Which won’t include Thanksgiving or Christmas, because whatever relatives you do have are back in Serbia. So, you'll negotiate for whatever remains, and that's the worst holidays, like Labor Day Weekend when you're off from work or Easter, and you believe in nothing. At the end of negotiations, you won't come out with two holidays a year, given your one cheap lawyer versus her high-powered 5 or 7 from a Fifth Avenue law firm. They'll make certain on appeal, that's if you win, that you get at least one of them! Intolerable. Yeah, you'll come out with alimony, but you'll have legal fees in the hundreds of thousands to pay off, and you'll end up going back to Pennsylvania, maybe State College, with our Penn State connections and our fraternity looking out for you. Yes, one of our guys who did well out of Engineering School or Finance, they'll give you a handout with a real job that pays well, so you can get back on your feet. You'll end up living modestly, doing whatever, and you'll call me looking for help or whatever else, but Daliah will be in my ear on the other side warning me to cut you loose. Intolerable. And it will all be Kiernan's fault."

Jake white-knuckled the gazebo railing, aglow as if it were Kiernan's throat, and Kevin's arms around Jake from behind snuggled in more. He then upturned his lips to nibble on Jake's earlobe. One man's coquettishness sensed as another man's contretemps. Jake tilted his head away from Kevin, a clear rebuke of Kevin's pestering affections, before he whined, "Stop."

Kevin repeated that word again, *"Intolerable."*

"What, then?" whined Jake. "You're the business mind, not me. Tell me what to do."

"Well, I said this can't stand, right?" (*...Jake nodded while facing the night...*) Kevin asked, "Do you have a current will?"

"Yes."

"Are you in it?"

"Yes."

"Is it lucrative?"

"Very... for both of us and the children."

"You don't need it to be lucrative for Kiernan, just for you."

"What?"

"That's how you turn the tables on her. Seize your opportunity. Remember what I always say..."

(*...shaking his head, gazing forward...*) "Don't say it, or I'll punch you again."

"But it's true; if you ain't getting—you know what? I'll give you a better phrase (*...pausing to think...*) *um*, Be Pro Bro!" He continued, "Fuck these women, bro! Fuck Shannoah! Fuck Kiernan! Be Pro Bro! Strike before she does. You get the millions. You get the house. You get the kids. You get to retire early, too. Be Pro Bro!"

Kevin gave him a minute to think on it.

Weeping-ripe at the mere suggestion, the temerity of murder, its misogynistic bent gussied up by a catchphrase: Be Pro Bro. Jake believed Kevin had a vicious talent for not only selling expensive cars to poor folk who couldn't afford them but for crafting convincing ideas for susceptible people who ought never surrender their brains to him. Nevertheless, poor folk bought Kevin's expensive cars, which made him a rich man. Over the years, Jake had acquiesced to Kevin's convincing ideas, which turned Kevin into a strongman.

Compelled to ask the question less so now, because his ailing wisdom at least encouraged that he shouldn't, Jake deliberated internally; literally, with Kevin breathing down his neck from behind. In the minds of both husbands with wives lingered that phrase—Be Pro Bro... Be Pro Bro... Be Pro Bro—firmly inculcated. Jake dropped his gaze from the night toward the nightshade-covered blooming heads of black-eyed Susans. A crickety bed of them. A yellow-orange boundary of them, which encircled the brick octagonal foundation of the gazebo. He couldn't discern why these wildflowers caught his eye, yet they did. A beautiful moment's distraction from the unavoidable question Jake had to ask to be certain of where he and Kevin stood anymore. Jake swallowed hard and asked, "What is it that you want me to do with Kiernan?"

Without pause or pity or doubt, Kevin said, "Kill her."

"I can't."

"I know, so I'll do it."

(*...A long pause amplified the chirping crickets abound...*)

Jake ungripped the gazebo railing, unhooked Kevin's fingers from his sweatpants waistband, and whirled himself around to face Kevin directly—no more talking at night or at flower beds. Bruised and battered; less swollen now, but Jake's wounds gleamed a darker purple than before. Kevin gazed upon Jake's pitiful face, as ugly and violent as a Jackson Pollock painting, but nowhere as precious. Jake appeared as someone whom no one wanted, yet through the years, only Kevin had an eye to better frame his potential. Sadly, Jake pictured himself in that same context, and therein availed Opportunity.

Jake considered Kevin's offer and suggested, "What about your problem, the pregnant woman?"

"Ah!" pressed Kevin with levity in his pitch. He asked, "A quid pro quo?"

"No, no, I—"

Kevin's pointer finger raised toward Jake's lips. Kevin insisted, "Shhh! No elaboration needed. Here, I'll make it easy for you. You take out my trash, I'll take out yours."

Before Jake could answer, Kevin slammed his open mouth onto Jake's and latched on—more head-butt than kiss, more anger than love, more for greater opportunity than what was intolerable, more "I got you" than "you got me." Jake merely appreciated the affection in any way he could get it from Kevin.

Opportunities...

Just before Kevin pulled back from the kiss of his initiation, Jake reached down, having sight-touched Kevin's erection in his sweatpants. It appeared bowed, rock-hard, ready for a second turn. Jake shirked from thinking about it anymore. It was ridiculous on its face. A crazy idea. What about the kids at the end of the day? Then Kevin kissed Jake's neck tenderly, briefly, and soothingly. The husbands with wives locked onto each other's squinty gazes, unblinking, inside the gazebo's gauzy-white lightness...

...To Kevin's Quid Pro Quo Pro Bro, as it pertained to their *Taking Out the Trash, and to Intolerability as Virtue*, Jake soundlessly mouthed the words: "Let's do it."

CHAPTER 27

WHEN THEIR END BEGAN

(FLASHBACK): April 10th
(... Two days before Neesha caught Jake & Kevin in the gazebo...)
(...almost an hour before meeting Shannoah Blakely for the first time in the Showroom...)
Moran Motors New & Used Cars (Manager's Office)
Downtown Burlington, VT
[12:40 p.m.]

Miranda Espenhoff, Kevin's secretary, used to sell new and used cars as well as—or faster than—Moran's best car salespeople (*...or women...*), including the owner, at the Showroom location in Burlington. It served to reason why Kevin reassigned Miranda from Sales to the front office as his personal secretary. At the end of the day, Kevin held true professionally to his two C's: [Competition and [C]ommission]. Miranda was too much competition and was stealing Kevin's commissions, so she had to go... from sales, not the dealership entirely. She was an asset.

On this afternoon, Kevin's asset had come through for him by far on a different venture: Zoom calling...

"You press this... click on... (*searching with Kevin's mousepad...*) that," instructed Miranda over Kevin's shoulder at his desk in the Manager's Office. Kevin asked, "But it will then connect to Norway... or wherever?"

"Yes, of course." Miranda frowned, perplexed at him. She encouraged, "It doesn't matter where your call is going, as long as the other guy downloads the app. You both should be able to connect, see each other on screen, and talk. I can't believe you are just learning all of this now for the first time, Boss."

"Call me a dinosaur, I guess."

Miranda set up the Zoom call for Kevin to reach a guy in Norway. She was curious about the contact but didn't ask any questions. Are we opening a dealership in Norway? she wondered. She said, "Press that key when you see the guy's ready in Norway. He should just pop up, but if you get stuck or lose him, I'll be right outside at my desk, okay?"

"Okay."

"I'm ordering lunch. Do you need anything?"

"Nope, I'm good."

"Can you handle this?" asked Miranda as she turned to leave the office.

"I'll be fine, thanks again."

Miranda shut Kevin's office door, and he turned his attention toward his laptop.

Using the mousepad, Kevin pressed his Control Key-F2 after he saw a Norwegian emerge on his screen...

Moran Motors New & Used Cars
Burlington, Vermont

Clarion Connections Suites
Frogner, Norway

A pale, balding, blue-eyed, plumped-face Scandinavian man, apparently in his late forties, maybe early fifties (*...no eyebrows... or were they as pale-white as himself?*), cracked a mirthless, very-toothy white smile as he waved once at Kevin. Kevin realized that his Zoom connection had become audile after he heard the Norwegian say, "Hello, American!"

"My name is Kevin Moran. Can you see me okay? What's your name there?"

Kevin shouted as if FaceTiming had been akin to communicating with soup cans and a string extended between the two of them.

Perfect English squeezed out of the Norwegian's thick accent. He assured, "I hear you just fine. My name is Gustafen Østerhölm of Frogner, Norway. It's a little outside Oslo, Norway. Do you know where that is?"

"Um... I know where Oslo is on a map. Frogner? No idea."

"You Americans talk funny English. Not proper like The Brits, but at least not as bad as The Aussies."

"I don't know whether that is a compliment or not, there, Gus, but I'll take it."

"Gus? What's that?"

Kevin frowned incredulously, then answered, "What? Gus, that's your name, right?"

"No-no. No Gus. No one ever called me that."

"No one has thought to before me? I find that hard to believe."

"Nope, no one."

"I guess we, funny Americans, just presume to shorten names to make conversation friendly."

"Right."

Kevin liked telephones better at this point in the conversation. He didn't take kindly to the Norwegian's contorted face in disapproval of his name being abbreviated. Welcome to Zoom, he thought; a brand new world. Kevin pressed, "Let's get right to it... um... Gustafen. I saw your Facebook European Marketplace ad. You're selling something I want very much. That, um, dagger you got off the set of that TV series *Vikings* that just started broadcasting."

"Yes. Yes... I understand. Have it here."

"None of this stuff you sell off these movie sets is hot, is it?"

"No-no, not hot. You can touch it."

Kevin chortled, swiped his mouth clear of his smile because he didn't want to offend Gus any more than he had already done during the Zoom call, but it became pertinent to brush up on Gus's American English slang terms. In the States, the slang "hot" can pertain to heat itself or weather, but it could be taken as "stolen" as it pertained to this dagger Gus was selling online.

"Oh, no-no-no-no!" exclaimed Gustafen. "It's legit."

"Okay, Gustafen. Let's see—"

He cut off Kevin. "What is this now you say? Gustafen?"

"Um, yeah... What now?"

"No, it's GUSTAH... GUSTAH-FAN... FAN, not fen. Not Goos-tah-fen. You say that too much now. Not the way you say it."

"You are really keen on your name being pronounced correctly, huh? Okay? I want the twelve-inch dagger... wait a sec... um, GUSTAH-FAN. Do you still have it, the twelve-inch one?"

"Yes, yes, but what is inch?"

"Oh, Sweet Jesus!" sighed Kevin exasperatedly. He said dismissively, "Never mind that. The dagger from the

Vikings series. You worked on that set, right? Your ad said so."

"Yes, yes. I acquired it on-set in Ireland where we filmed."

"Now, when you say acquired it..."

"Oh no, I mean to say that when the character completed the scene with the prop and production was done with it overall, I am allowed to have it. Now I wish to sell it, seeing the series is so popular globally."

"Okay, I just wanted to make sure, there. May I see it?"

"Sure, yes. I'll be right back," replied Gustafen. He launched up from his hotel room chair and fled off-screen. Kevin shook his head wearily outside of Gustafen's presence; not an easy call. Moments later, Gustafen emerged on screen with a cherry wood box. It resembled in texture, color, and shape a mini-coffin. The length and width of a shoebox, polished to a high sheen, Gustafen opened it carefully. Its lid squealed when reared back upon its thin brass hinges.

The upturned lid eclipsed Gustafen's hands well dug in and half of his face. On the other side of the globe, Kevin leaned forward in his office chair, his nose nearly touching his laptop screen. Desperate for a closer look. Gustafen pulled out a dark-purple velvety sack with golden corded drawstrings with tassel-ends, which appeared tied around the mouth of the expensive-looking sack.

"Unwrap it," said Kevin. "Come on, I need to see it."

Gustafen untied the golden corded drawstrings, broadened the mouth of the velvet sack, and took out the dagger. Its black leathered hilt preceded the twelve-inch stainless steel blade, which refracted the Norwegian twilight coming in from Gustafen's hotel room window off-screen.

"Sweet," remarked Kevin.

"You like?" asked Gustafen, smiling back at Kevin.

"I want," said Kevin.

"Let's talk price," said Gustafen as he repackaged the twelve-inch dagger as it first appeared to Kevin. He laid it back into its wood box before setting it aside off-screen. Gustafen said, "I'm obliged to tell you—*I feel*—the dagger is cursed."

"What?" blurted Kevin, laughing. He insisted, "Stop there, Gustafen. You don't need to sell me on it. I like it very much. That's good enough for me without the voodoo. It's what I've been looking for, and it appears to be *as advertised*, so..."

"It sat on the sets at the Shrine of Odin itself. A lot of accidents happened to crew members at the shrine during filming. It's important that you know this. People got hurt just doing their job around that shrine, so this artifact came from that place."

"Cool, dude, how much?" asked Kevin dismissively.

"You pay in Euros, right?"

"I guess I can go to my bank and do that, but I was thinking more along the lines of Pay—"

Gustafen chuckled, saying, "*Oh sure, PayPal...* PayPal... So simple, but still in Euros."

"Okay, in Euros, fine. Another question, since this is a gift for a friend."

"Sure."

"Engravings. Can you do that?"

"Sure, I can have it engraved for you. I have the equipment to do it at my home, not here in the hotel room."

"How much... in Euros?"

"On top of the dagger itself, not much extra. Given the exchange rate—*American Dollar into Euros... approximately $1.31*—say 360 €? What do you want the engravement to state?"

"Putting my friend's name on it sounds too cliché. You know anything about Chinese—"

Gustafen cut Kevin off, saying, "No! No Chinese characters!" He rubbed his hands over his balding head as if close to apoplexy. He scowled and said, "Not Chinese characters on a Norse blade! That's oil and water or fire and ice."

"Fine, Gustafen. My friend is of Serbian descent. He was raised Orthodox Christian, but he's not particularly religious. I don't even think he believes in God. He knows parts of the Bible, though, in Latin."

"So, in Latin, yes?"

"Yes, let's go with Latin."

"Okay, hold a second, please, Kevin."

Gustafen reached below the flat wood surface, which

appeared to be a desk, and pulled up a second laptop. It was closed. Kevin's screenshot of Gustafen shifted from right to left, as though he had been pushed aside to make room on the desk for the second laptop. Gustafen activated it, waited for his poor Wi-Fi to connect, and when it had done so, he started to type. Kevin watched the Norwegian's saccadic gaze study his second PC screen. He muttered, "...Latin phrases..."

Eventually, he included Kevin in the search. The search for the right phrase for this engraving of the twelve-inch stainless steel blade. Out of forty-three misses in Latin phrases, it was the forty-fourth one that made Kevin say, "Yes! Stop! That one. Yes! What does it mean?" Kevin felt in his gut that the forty-fourth Latin phrase was, indeed, the one, because Jake's age was 44. Ostensibly... fate. Kevin watched Gustafen yank a pink sheet of Post-It Note from its pad, apparently displeased as he wrote down the Latin phrase Kevin selected.

"What's wrong?" asked Kevin.

"I told you this blade is cursed, and what you selected in Latin just proves it. You—"

"What does the phrase mean, Gustafen?"

"You don't want it to mean this for a friend."

"What does 'Mimet or-/-REE' mean?"

"You Americans. If it's not English, you won't say it."

"Pronounce it, so I'll know, Gustafen. It didn't take me long to get your name right."

Gustafen sighed, then he pronounced the Latin phrase for Kevin. "It's 'Memento mori'... mee-MEN-toh... I tell you, you don't want to buy this, like this meaning."

"What does it mean?"

"From Latin into English, it means *'Remember, you must die.'* See, I tell you, you don't want this for a friend," worried Gustafen as he stared discernibly at Kevin on the Zoom call. However, the Norwegian noticed, too, a knowing smirk from this American customer. A coldness to him, if not someone who had ulterior motives with this dagger, which was a chilling sense confirmed when Kevin said flatly, *"I'll take it."*

CHAPTER 28

QUID PRO QUO PRO BRO (SHANNOAH BLAKELY REVISITED)

The Plan: Kevin will contact Shannoah, floating this quid pro quo: Leave Vermont and never return, whether or not an abortion is had, but if the abortion is not had, it must not be disclosed to the child who the father is. In return, Shannoah will receive $100,000 every year for five years. A second vehicle will be afforded freely to Shannoah—the 2013 Matte-hunter green Jeep Wrangler EV—which was her second choice to the grey Saab coupe she liked. After Shannoah accepts the deal, Jake, not Kevin, will show up at Lookout Point, pulling a switcheroo, deny Shannoah both her first installment of the money and the new vehicle, and dispose of her instead.

†

For the plan as specified to work, Shannoah would first have to agree to take the first installment of the money and the electric Jeep, but at the location of Lookout Point in Barton.

(FLASHBACK): August 8th
Standing Stallion Casino & Suites (Staff Break-room)
Evanston, VT
[1:15 p.m.]

(*...Shannoah's cell phone rings...*)

Shannoah answered sourly, "Hello?"

"You sound down," acknowledged Kevin. (*...contempt hidden masterfully in his tone...*) "Is everything alright?"

Shannoah responded, "Just thinking about your offer, lying down in bed."

Deception sold as a lie with pecuniary interests, she appeared seated upon a metal folding chair at a breakroom table at her job in the casino. She was alone at the moment.

Kevin assured her, "I think that this is the best offer for all parties concerned, Shannoah. I'm sorry that I woke you."

Her misandry scarcely restrained in her tone, she blurted, "You're not sorry. You just want me out of the way. I don't want to have an abortion, Kevin."

"Then don't have one."

"But I don't want to leave Vermont."

"You must if you accept my offer."

"You shouldn't connect the two if shh—"

Kevin cut in, saying, "Not wanting to leave Vermont? Is that because you'd rather have a double-date dinner with the wife and me at Violets On The Vine? I hear that you plan on bringing the boyfriend who knocked you up? Who is he, exactly?"

"I don't have time for games, Kevin."

"But it seems like you do, Shannoah. You started the games. Is the kid mine or not?"

"Of course the kid is yours. I haven't been with anyone else. Listen, I don't want to argue with you. This morning sickness is kicking my ass."

"Of course it is."

A long pause elapsed...

Shannoah's impatience transmitted through the call and in her response. "Are you sure you have *that much money?*"

"I do."

A non-response reverberated loudly; reminiscent of one in contemplation or in doubt or in freefall. Ever the car salesman, Kevin utilized silence amid any sale's pitch—leaving the buyer alone with their concealed thoughts and feelings—to scare the buyer into making the deal for fear of losing some of what it offered, or making the deal in fear of losing it altogether. Rich or poor, man or woman, college-educated or not, the tactic of using silence as a cudgel to make minds submit to his proposals never failed him.

Finally, Shannoah responded, "I'll take the offer."

"Then meet me at Lookout Point at 1 p.m. I'll be in your new vehicle. I'll have the first installment payment with me, okay?"

"Are you sure that you can do this?"

"Yes. Are you sure that you can do this?"

"I am."

"Meet me there."

"Okay."

"Okay, bye."

"Bye," replied Kevin, smiling without mirth as he ended the call. He switched from using his cell phone for outgoing calls to texting and reached out to Jake.

Kevin Moran Texted [9:41 a.m.]:
"It's a go. Be there at 1 p.m. The new vehicle has the keys in it. It's parked in my driveway."

Jake Montgomery Texted [10:13 a.m.]:
"Got it."

Kevin Moran Texted [10:14 a.m.]:
"Don't you want Memento Moir?"

Jake Montgomery Texted [10:16 a.m.]:
"WTF?"

Kevin Moran Texted [10:19 a.m.]:
"The name of the "thing" for making hearts in gazebos."

Jake Montgomery Texted [10:22 a.m.]:
"No, I've got a better idea. Trust me."

Kevin Moran Texted [10:32 a.m.]:
"Wait! What's the marker going to be so that I can take out the trash at the same spot?"

Jake Montgomery Texted [10:36 a.m.]:
"Using my sneaker's laces... Black. They have an insignia of a red viper on them. I'll tie them to the railing. The spot."

Kevin Moran Texted [10:38 a.m.]:
"Say no more."

[10:43 a.m.] Meanwhile...

The Montgomery Townhome

Jake's concealed thoughts with a new twist on Kevin's

idea afoot: (*...jealous wife shoots and kills husband's pregnant girlfriend...*) In other words, frame Kiernan.

Jake had risen from their bed on his side of things by the bedroom door, ajar. He closed it soundlessly. Meanwhile, Kiernan showered in their bedroom's bathroom. Summer and Chase were still asleep in their bedroom. Jake made his move. His new idea. He ambulated slyly around the footboard of their made bed to reach below the box-spring mattress on Kiernan's side of things. He slid out from under it, upon wood flooring and duskiness, into the morning light, a gun case. Kiernan's gun case. It appeared unlocked; partially opened. He placed her lightweight, industrial-strength contraption right-side up upon the bed. He opened it. (*...his gaze whipped toward the bathroom door just a few feet away...*) Spooked, because he thought he heard the showerhead shut off, but it gushed on with a steady hiss. Jake resumed his weapon's theft. He plucked out her bullets, individually encased within form-fitted black foam pockets, and situated there appeared the .22 Remington Thunderbolt. He stuffed her pistol and ammo inside his pockets. He closed her gun case. He returned it to the spot beneath their bed on Kiernan's side of things, and then he bolted.

Kiernan was in the shower at the time, but the day before, she had abandoned her Gas Card upon the kitchen countertop by the refrigerator; like almost every stay-at-home mom distracted after having settled squabbling kids incidentally, or putting away a week's worth of groceries in a hurry, or simply a by-product of Mom-brain, unfortunately, a busy woman will lose things from time to time; moreover, a mom rarely anticipates theft by her own in her home, and yet it happens.

Shit happens.

What also *happens,* especially if one lives with a liar and thief in the home, is that one can lose or have stolen trust along with the relationship; lose or have stolen togetherness along with a firearm; lose or have stolen the love along with a Gas Card, even lose or have stolen sight of oneself on the way out of the front door, because Jake made certain that he said no more like Kevin's text cautioned, and that no one heard him leave on sneakered feet.

(Hours later...)
Crystal Lake State Park, Lookout Point,
Barton, VT
[1:01 p.m.]

The time on the dashboard showed Jake was late by one minute.

Parked an inch from the Lookout Point railing—one of two vehicles (*...in the other sat Shannoah Blakely...*) two gravelly vacant parking spaces apart—Jake pulled the key out of the ignition of a brand-new Range Rover

Jeep EV colored hunter-green with an automatic retractable hard-top roof colored black; all the bells and whistles included and price-tagged just south of $75,000. Instantly, Shannoah spotted her prize pull in alongside her Grey Saab moments ago, and she muttered, "I like."

Kevin was right, thought Jake in the other vehicle from Shannoah's, nary a witness around the lunch hour.

Jake got out of the jeep (*...Shannoah's attentions turned his way...seeing it wasn't Kevin...*) in all black and black-gloved in a black hoodie with something heavy sinking its forward-facing muff pocket. The hood of the black hoodie appeared cinched ominously closed around the face, making it appear crinkled and squished to the point of its male features being undiscernible. Its black drawstrings were yanked tight and tied in a bow under the tall white man's jawline, Shannoah realized. The tall white man donned black high-tops, and his hoodie appeared wet in spots where men usually sweat heavily; around the neck and chest area and armpits; soaked right through. It was a hazy, sunny day; not a cloud in the sky, and about 80°F.

Why wear all black like that? thought Shannoah. No sufferer of fools, Shannoah's Syracuse street-smarts kicked in; red flags flailing all over in her mind once the tall white man flexed his fingers in those black leather gloves before taking his first steps over toward her parked Saab. Her tracking gaze, a leer, from right to left, into her interior rearview mirror, seeing this dark figure ambulate his way around the trunk of her car, (*...she* *quickly locked all of the car doors...)* as he made a sharp turn toward her driver's side, picked up pace, and the black-gloved white man with a distorted face squished by the hood of his black hoodie reached for the handle of her driver's side door and discovered what Shannoah made certain of...

It was locked.

Terrified, trembling uncontrollably, Shannoah glanced up through her driver's side window, and when the ominous figure dressed in black shifted slightly to block the sun's glare through the driver's side window rolled-up, she recognized a pistol at point-blank range trained on her.

SHOTS FIRED!!! (*...two of them...*)

Her driver's side window shattered entirely. The first bullet pierced through her hand, exited out of the back of it, and lodged itself into her glove compartment door opposite her. The second bullet got her in the neck; just missing her jugular. Blood splatter appeared propulsive and pervading and plashing. Through the driver's side window, reduced to an open mouth with jagged loose teeth of glass more at the bottom than up at the top, Shannoah screamed, "I'M PREGNANT, YOU ASSHOLE!"

From Shannoah's mortified perspective, the tall white man in all black and black-gloved was a savage, but no fool...*Kevin's hitman.*

The tall white man dressed in all black and black-gloved, she sensed, snatched her by her blondish blood-slickened hair, yanked her up and out of the driver's side window frame (*...glass teeth scraped the length of her body on the way out...*), kicking and screaming, spitting blood and barefooted, and a bullet in her. Shannoah clung to the formidable forearm of the tall white man in all black and black-gloved in her last-ditch effort to leverage herself better to kick him where every man crumbles; this man did not. She spotted below his waistline the Smoking Gun, as it were, that got her twice already—the pistol's hammer under his thumb had been cocked to shoot again.

Given the raw adrenaline coursing through Jake, (*... the tall White man in all-black and black- gloved to Shannoah...*), he managed her entire existence as effortlessly light as a rag doll but not yet as lifeless. By the length of her hair, shredding extensions. Just a foot-shy off the gravel, barefooted Shannoah cursed and spat and screamed. Jake never heard her, neverminded that and never responded. Methodically, Jake reared up his wife's .22, angled it closely underneath Shannoah's chin and shot her.

The coup de grâce.

The fire out in her eyes. He released her soiled hair. Gravity reduced her to a thud, aground. She landed awkwardly. Half-against her car door, half-against the gravelly parking space paralleled to her car. What was left of her head drooping. A bloodied face. A bled-out

neck wound. Her pate blown out and concaved. Her limbs bent at odd-angled positions, which no living person could master; only the dead. A deplorable death in cold blood.

Jake dragged her lifeless body toward the railing of Lookout Point. Only 14 feet away from her grey Saab, once over the concrete parking speed-bump wedged under her front tires. He bent down halfway at the waist, bent halfway at the knees, and grabbed Shannoah's arms as limp as ropes to pull her seated upright against her driver's side front car wheel. He let go quickly before gravity dipped her forward at the waist. A good catch under her armpits at the crooks of his arms. He ably launched her over his left shoulder. She appeared draped over him like a rolled up throw rug, just not as heavy.

A beautiful view: The northernmost point of the Appalachia Mountain Chain sunsoaked, but wholly disacknowledged. Jake slouched over with Shannoah on his back. Her backside sunwards, but... *toward Lookout Point railing*. He inched up to it; the railing. He teetered hisself forward, and then let her go. Taking out the trash that was Kevin's. Shannoah fell toward sundrenched depths, some 850 feet, into bone-smashing limestone talus.... that nobody heard. Immediately, Jake extracted from his black hoody's muff-pocket Kiernan's .22 Remington Thunderbolt, and he threw it over the railing too. A human body, an inanimate object, one and the same to him anymore. He took a knee in the gravel, untied his left sneaker, stripped out its sneaker lace from the laces-holes, rose up and roped the black sneaker lace quadrupled times over the railing serving as a marker for Kevin later.

His part of the quid pro quo pro bro...*done.*

Jake walked over to Shannoah's Saab, reached into his pocket, pulled out Kiernan's Gas Card and tossed it in the bloodiest part of the interior: the driver's side seat. He thought to hisself, the police will find that soon enough... along with her gun. Without looking back, without looking worried and without witnesses looking, Jake fled the scene vis-à-vis the brand-new jeep that brought him.

But it must be said...

Shannoah Blakely, casino card-dealer at The Reservation who'd like to stack the deck, was also a former prostitute who still had a few tricks up her sleeve, which she just wouldn't retire. Like, telling guys that they got her pregnant, though she hit menopause 4 years ago. Her side-hustle; theoretically, marking the cards, as it pertained to the kind of suit she had extorted for money. Your mere Three-of-Clubs kind of Nine-to-Fiver met by chance in a nightclub; doable for $10,000, or an Ace-of-Spade kind of millionaire Car Dealership Owner targeted in his showroom; definitely could catch half a million-*Oh, The Opportunities...* Shannoah valued money over morality as if with immortality until Kevin's plans punctuated ruthlessly that he was nobody's Joker.

CHAPTER 29

QUID PRO QUO PRO BRO (KIERNAN MONTGOMERY REVISITED)

The Plan: *Take Summer and Chase to the movies, serving as an alibi. Text to confirm all but "the principal" is at the movies. Text to alarm "the principal" that one of the children has taken ill at the movies and all will be returning home. This text will keep "the principal" in place at the home, waiting. Instead of Jake returning to the home with the kids—the switcheroo—* ***The Trash Collector*** *will emerge.* ***The Trash Collector****, in-the-know, will have the townhome Home Alarm System passcode to disable it and a duplicate house key for unfettered access inside to make the trash collection. The Three Agreements: no spilling or processing of the trash in the house, take out the trash where the spot has a marker for dumping, and wait for* ***The Trash Collector's*** *next text.*

(FLASHBACK): August 9th
The Montgomery Townhome
[8:18 p.m.]

Jake scurried about the living room, dining room, and kitchen looking for his car keys. He had begun to retrace his last steps. Summer had taken her sweet time getting ready in the kids' hallway bathroom. Ostensibly, it occurred every five minutes, her shouts of "Almost ready!" as she changed outfits or restyled her hair. Chase, for some inexplicable reason, stomped around the living room wood flooring in Jake's Vipers, though six sizes too large for his feet (*...the left foot's black sneaker lace missing...*), with his scrawny arms in short sleeves stiffened out in front of himself, claiming he was Frankenstein, growling.

"Take those off, would yah? Get ready!" yelled Jake at Chase while frantically searching for his car keys in the kitchen.

"Found them," he told himself.

Car keys now in hand, a twirl on his pointer finger reared up as he sauntered into the living room and made the announcement, "LISTEN UP! HERE ARE YOUR OPTIONS FOR MOVIE NIGHT! 'MAN OF STEEL,' 'THE HUNGER GAMES: CATCHING FIRE,' 'DESPICABLE ME 2,' AND 'IRON MAN 3!' I JUST WANNA SAY THAT I HEARD GREAT REVIEWS

ABOUT MAN OF STEEL! I HEARD IT'S REALLY, REALLY GOOD!"

From down the hall, while in front of the bathroom mirror, Summer was heard distantly yelling her choice: "I WANNA SEE 'MAN OF STEEL!'"

Jake glanced down at a disgruntled Chase, waiting for his movie selection. Chase, backed against the sectional armrest in Jake's Vipers with his arms crossed, responded, "Of course, Summer picked the same movie that you like. I want to see Despicable Me 2." Jake frowned, not pleased with Chase's unsubtle yet passive-aggressive complaint. It revisited the unrelenting household narrative that there's Summer-favoritism going around. Jake didn't have time to address this issue directly, and he didn't want to stoke Kiernan's ire, who would most certainly come to Chase's defense if she had overheard such a discussion with Chase... her son. A noisome belief that harkened back to Jake's previous complaint regarding Chase.

"Bro!" he said, pointing down at his Vipers on Chase's feet. "Didn't I tell you to take those off? Take off my Vipers now, and put them in the closet where you got 'em!"

Chase obeyed while Jake walked off, muttering, *"Gotta tell Kiernan we're ready to go."*

Meanwhile, Chase worked from his left to his right side when removing Jake's Vipers from his sock feet. The left-footed Viper on Chase fit looser than a flip-flop sandal—no laces—he simply stepped out of the sneaker and kicked it to the side. The right-footed Viper, however, cinched a bit closer to Chase's ankle, not tightly at all but well enough to compel him to take a knee and untie the laces. While working to unfasten the taut bow knot upon the topmost part, he noticed the point of the sneaker was besmirched with red dots. Chase inspected those red dots—circular flecks, truly—on the black leather. Chase deduced, as far as a 10-year-old mind could with a sciential frame of reference, that the red dots were splashed paint flecks that had long since dried. Perhaps Dad was painting in the garage, he presumed. To the scratch, the red dots jumped off the black leather. Chase had misidentified the red dots as paint, however.

Because what 10-year-old child thinks that red dots on their father's footwear would be blood?

The right-footed Viper's black sneaker lace, at its tying ends beyond the lace holes, displayed a red-thread embossed slithering snake meshed into its black fibers. Its tongue extended as snakes are commonly and commercially depicted. The color contrast—the cardinal-red snake against the black narrow field of a sneaker lace—was visually striking to Chase. The image stayed emblazoned upon Chase's mind.

Vipers put away in the foyer closet, Chase stood at the front door clutching the brass doorknob, dressed in grey and white Spring Athletic Gear-Casual with his kid-sized high-tops donned; Air Jordans in matching grey and white tones. Summer emerged from the hallway bathroom wearing a pair of form-fitting dark blue jeans, noticeably bra-less in a flowing white V-neck T-shirt tucked in, and a pair of red flats. She carried a matching red windbreaker in the crook of her arm in case the movie theater's air conditioning got too cold. Chase, miffed, now heard Summer yelling for their father to "Come on already..."

At the end of the hall, Jake tipped his head into their bedroom. Kiernan appeared seated on her side of the bed in jeans and a white T-shirt untucked that was Jake's. It swam on her. Her chestnut-brown hair was yanked back in a ponytail, slickened-wet as though she had just come out of the shower. Jake spied on her from behind for some time—seconds, not minutes—not knowing what she was doing sitting so still; meditating, staring out the bedroom window, or writing something? Probably writing something, he thought. And he was right. From his vantage point, shielded by her back, was Kiernan's diary cracked open on her lap, her writing grip pushing her pen along after her earlier statement...

...I lost anyways... I lost a friend....

Then and since...*Jake has never taken the children to the movies, yet he will tonight. I'm afraid to be alone...*

(...paused her pen after the wood flooring crackled beneath Jake's step at their bedroom's threshold...)

He noticed her flinch and thought he should speak, *"Kiernan?"*

She refused to turn around, but shut her diary slowly upon her lap and asked, "What?"

"The kids and I are about to leave for the movies now."

"Fine."

"You want me to stop and get you anything?"

"No."

"Can you at least face me and give me a proper goodbye?"

She declined his suggestion, but not in words. Jake's desire wasn't for a proper farewell, she thought. Jake wanted Kiernan's grace to absolve him of his guilt attributed to his deceit related to his lies; thus, another moment converted into the written word. Her next and would-be last diary entry: the nine reasons why we lie.

Summer and Chase, distantly, were heard laughing, reduced behind jangling keys, and then the front door slammed. A series of sounds in departure—Kiernan deduced her family had gone for the night to the movies, including Jake. She was alone. The house, silent. Well-lit by lamp-light and recessed lighting, yet somehow a darkness lingered; something she couldn't put her finger on. She felt afraid.

Was it Daliah's curse of death upon her?

The fear was real, though indistinct and rudderless, and dug-in. She placed her diary on the bed temporarily. Then, she lowered herself to the wood flooring on her side of the bed and glanced under the bed for her gun. Her face turned but an inch from the wood flooring as she looked underneath the box-spring mattress. It was dark, but she saw her gun case and pulled it out from underneath the bed. It felt lighter than usual as she lifted it. She placed it on the made bed. While on her knees, bedside, she opened the gun case...

"What the fuck!" she exclaimed, "Where is it?"

Kiernan turned their bedroom upside down looking for her pistol; nothing. She abandoned the empty gun case on the made bed but snatched up her diary. She fled to their bedroom's bathroom on her side of things, placed her diary on the wood flooring beside her, and frantically lifted the pink carpet mat that concealed her secret hiding space below the sink's pine wood cabinetry. Two wood flooring panels appeared intact, but they were uncorked. The only fault with the townhome when she bought it. She got down on her knees, used her fingernails—both hands—to get into the crevices of these removable wood panels. Side-by-side they lay. She lifted each of them one at a time and set the wood panels aside, angled upwards against the sink cabinetry. She turned back to what was readily perceived as a dusky, drafty, rectangular pit, two shoeboxes long and wide. She peered into it, and 15 of 16 of her brown leather-covered diaries appeared as two stacks, six-high. Fifteen of sixteen diaries for all the years she's been married, and the 16th diary by her leg on the floor was scooped up and placed with the rest of them. This was the hiding spot disclosed to Nessha, her babysitter, and sworn to secrecy to protect and only tell Chase about when he turns 18, eight years from now. It's also the hiding space where she hoped she misplaced her pistol.

No pistol, however.

SABOTAGE! (...it had to be Jake, she thought accusatorily....) Sheer terror coursed through her, lagging behind her fury, and eclipsing her desire for revenge. She returned the wood flooring panels to their proper state and covered her secret hiding spot with the pink bathroom mat; the worst best lock to keep things securely undiscoverable, again, if you are not in-the-know. Kiernan fled to her cell phone on her bedside nightstand on her side of things. She activated it and started typing with fervor...

Kiernan Montgomery Texted [8:46 p.m.]:
"Where's my handgun, Jake? Come home now!"

Kiernan paced beside the bed, awaiting Jake's text reply...

[8:48 p.m.]

The Montgomery Townhome

Back deck...

Kevin donned a black hoodie cinched closed around his face, black trousers, and black leather gloves. Only his black footwear was his. The outfit tonight was as Jake had donned to take out the trash yesterday. It still smelled like Jake *(...a little B.O. stunted by a lot of cheap woodsy-sweet cologne...)*, Kevin thought. He worked quietly under the cloak of nightshade. The Singh cul-de-sac, the quietest and sleepiest part of The Links gated community, was a sweet spot for burglars, which the gated community had yet to encounter. Kevin anticipated little-to-no witnesses, despite shimmery-lighted occupied homes at his back, but he didn't rest on those laurels. He moved swiftly, punching in The Montgomery Townhome Home Alarm System's passcode on their back deck's outside keypad hidden long ago under a faux clay flowerpot, now pushed aside on the deck floor.

Crouched down, he finger-jabbed the glowing buttons...

010671. After the Home Alarm System had been disarmed, its keypad's illumination changed from an apple-red color to a shamrock-green. It appeared to be a go, as he breached the townhome through the curtainless glass deck door. It slid upon a silvery track from left to right, and he pulled the dark-colored wood handle without hitches, squeals, or scrapes. Kevin stepped into the unlit part of the dining room. Beyond that, an archway, and the living room. Dim-lighted, all; not completely dark. The milieu smelled of potpourri indoors. Soundlessly, Kevin ambulated through the air-conditioned space, moving from one adjacent room to the next. At every turn of a corner or wood flooring creak, his confidence increased with adrenaline. Everything seemed to be going according to plan.

Kevin Moran Texted [8:59 p.m.]:
"I'm inside. Off-line til done."

Jake Montgomery Texted [9:01 p.m.]:
"Shit-load of texts coming in from the principal right now. Aware something's missing. Hurry!"

Kevin thought to himself, ***Good to know.***

He pocketed his cell phone for the night and continued up the hallway. Meanwhile, Kiernan, seated on her side of the bed, decided to put on a pair of white footy socks and track sneakers in anticipation of Jake's arrival with the kids. Since he had displayed physical violence in front of the children in the past, she thought it best to be shod than not. Additionally, she considered that Jake had stolen her firearm, which presented a threat with this would-be homecoming. She anticipated both scenarios: he could come home meekly like a lamb on a farm, or he could lash out like a lion in the wild. Either way, she was determined to project the mood of a different animal: formidable. She glanced down at her cell phone with the intent to send her fourteenth text to Jake. Unlike the others, this one was typed angrily, clearly, and concisely; then she pressed SEND.

Kevin Montgomery Texted [9:04 p.m.]:
"I want a divorce."

She waited for Jake's next reply, but it came within a minute. She read it, but in print, he sounded like she had never heard him before. His statement, both vague and clear—just six words—told her precisely what she wanted to hear. Nevertheless, she feared what it meant going forward...

Jake Montgomery Texted [9:05 p.m.]:
"Already in the works, dear. Buh-bye."

Unbeknownst to Kiernan, while her sights were focused on her cell phone screen, well-distracted by Jake's curt honesty and what it meant for the children, she had become deaf to her present home surroundings. Her wood flooring, often the home's initial and natural alarm system, indeed cautioned in advance that someone else had entered the home. She simply did not hear it. Kevin eased up behind her. The wood flooring creaked again, but with her marriage falling apart, she needed it to make clear... *someone's behind you, poised with a chloroform-soaked rag, intending to headlock you, clamp it down upon your mouth and nose until you've been rendered unconscious...*

Because that's precisely what Kevin did to Kiernan.

Crystal Lake State Park, Lookout Point
Barton, VT
[11:21 p.m.]

The night was pitch-black, crickety, and ghostly desolate. The hush came from the breeze through the dense evergreen forest all around Lookout Point. Likened to evergreen walls that stretched for thousands of miles left to right in Douglas Firs, Spruces, and White Pines without a ceiling save for a sea of galaxies and grey matter overhead. A celestial roof that dwarfed the significance of human existence throughout the park with a chill in the air.

A dead chill.

Off to the side of a densely bucolic country road, Kevin pulled over to his right. The new Jeep EV wobbled onto a gravelly berm that transitioned into unmarked parking spaces where no other car existed. Under a slow roll forward on all-wheel drive, the sound of popcorn popping emanated, but it was crushing stones and dried earth under Goodyear's upon an earthen terrace. A lip jutted out no more than 60 feet, though Lookout Point's area for parking had enough space for 8 or 10 sedans or SUVs. Tonight only one car parked up close to the half-hemispheric railing of Lookout Point...*Kevin's.*

He turned off the ignition and left the key inside. He left his headlights on to see his way. It was that dark. His headlights shone upon the railing, the marker in a black sneaker lace tied to it with slag, and yonder at an elevation where human sight lost all dimension into blackness some 800 feet high or more horizonward. Kevin pushed a button on the center console, which popped the trunk. He stepped out into the chilly summer night; a stiff breeze north-to-south slapped his face, alee, a few times. He closed the driver's side door behind himself. He walked alongside the Jeep EV toward the trunk, now ajar, and peered into it. Kiernan's head craned up from below, but her mouth was gagged by a dishrag, and her hands and ankles were bound by zip ties. Behind herself, she had long since removed her cell phone from her back pocket, activated it, and tried to call blindly anyone but failed. She had dropped the cell phone in the trunk, and it landed behind her on its floor, but she had no idea where it lay anymore. She hoped Kevin wouldn't spot it from his vantage point.

Kevin unclenched his black hoodie's drawstrings and pulled the hoodie from over his head. He removed his black leather gloves, pocketed them in his hoodie's muff pocket, and said, "Don't think I don't know where your cell phone is." He reached down behind her where she lay on her side and grabbed it. He split it apart, pulled out its SIM card, chucked it behind himself, then crushed and twisted the cell phone. He threw it over the roof of the Jeep, and the mangled device dropped some 800 feet down from Lookout Point. Kevin warned, "Now, when I pull you out of there, I don't want any problems from you, Kiernan. Understand?"

Kiernan nodded while gagged, curled up where she lay.

Kevin reached down into the trunk of the Jeep EV, pulled her up onto her sneakered feet to a stance in the trunk, and as he attempted to lift her over the front wall of the trunk, Kiernan kneed him in the chin. Kevin launched backward, holding his jaw, spat blood off to the side of himself, and blurted, "You son-of-a-bitch!"

Kiernan struggled with her ankles bound to leap over the front wall of the trunk, but it clipped her toe, and she tipped over it and face-planted the gravel below. An awkward, brutal fall, which made her groan with tears—not tears from pain, but embarrassment. Kevin laughed at her, but her adrenaline shielded her from any pain at this second hour into the abduction. Kevin mocked, "That's what you get. I was trying to get you out of there nicely. Now come over here!"

"MMFFUCKER....MMMMFFUCK!" Kiernan blasted through the dishrag over her mouth. As he dragged Kiernan by the backs of her arms from the back of the Jeep EV to the front side of it, Kevin chortled and said, "I can't make you out, sweetness. I have to hear this!"

He propped her up, seated in the gravel, back against the hubcap of the front left tire and nearest to the railing. Kevin crouched down to be at eye level with Kiernan, reached down his sweatpant leg, hiked it up, unsheathed Memento Moir, brought it toward her gag (Kiernan flinched), and he whined, "Ahh! Come here! I ain't gonna stab you with it."

He was true. He used the point of the dagger to drag down the gag from Kiernan's mouth to lay around her neck, and Kiernan hocked up spit in his face. Kevin smiled. He raised his free hand, swiped Kiernan's spit from his chin, and licked his palm clean of it. Sinisterly, he said, "Yum, you taste good, girly!"

"You think you're going to get away with this, Kevin? You won't! You're stupid for doing this! I am loved, asshole!"

"You're not loved by Daliah, I'll tell you that much. She wouldn't tell me what you said at your little Happy Hour invite, but I can take a logical guess. Jay..."

Kiernan interrupted, "I heard Shannoah Blakely is pregnant, fucker! You cheated on Daliah!"

"Oh, Little Rich Bitch got me! So what! You know Shannoah Blakely... woo-who! It's funny that you bring up her name because you are about to join her down there. Just over that railing, there."

Kiernan, stricken perplexed, whipped her attention toward the nearby railing. It dawned on her that Shannoah was killed, all of this—her abduction included—was planned, and her husband Jake was involved. Like only a woman can with her tongue against a man, Kiernan excoriated Kevin, saying, "You don't scare me. All those years behind my back fucking my husband! Yeah, I know about that one too. You're a coward! You failed as a man! That's why you can't get Daliah pregnant!"

Kevin rebutted sardonically, "I, at least, got one woman pregnant, but does it hurt knowing that Jake preferred my cock over your pussy?"

"FUCK YOU!" she screamed, lunging forward well-bound, "FUCK YOU, KEVIN!"

He laughed in her face, then mused, "The truth is the worst, isn't it? That's why lies are better. They are politer."

"You are both pathological. YOU LIARS!... YOU CHEATS!... YOU SNAKES!"

It happened so fast, Kevin's next move. His right step pushed gravel below just a smidge. That was the tell. Kiernan caught it, but she was bound at her wrists and ankles, and she was seated aground with her back pinned against the front wheel of a jeep. Kevin was crouched down right in front of her. Where could she go or maneuver or duck when the dagger—all twelve inches of it—plunged into her?

It happened so fast... Kiernan groaned and crumbled forward at the point of insertion. No scream or cry or words, but air left her like a slashed tire. A sibilance followed by her dribble from the mouth. Kevin watched her like a specimen struggling in a petri dish under a microscope. He enjoyed the science of murder. A deflated look of shock emerged upon her. Instantly, she thought of her children and Daliah's hope for her demise. The searing pain had come in as the adrenaline through her subsided. A thin silvery thread of slobber dripped from the corners of her mouth onto the black leathery hilt of the dagger. The blade still in her, he did not apply more pressure or a forward thrust or a sinister twist.

It all happened so fast... Slumped back against the jeep's front wheel hubcap with her wrists bound like her ankles, she sensed the wound was fatal. She told herself not to struggle against her binds, because it would only zap what remained of her life force. She wanted every second of her life force, even in her slow demise. She was that much of a fighter, a mother, and a sister. She loved living for all of them. Under the whitish glow of the warming headlights, which repealed the blackest night, Kevin glanced down at his blade inside of Kiernan and teased, "*Memento Moir*, sweetheart."

Through the blade's hilt, Kevin sensed Kiernan's

insides as though his fingertips handled them. He found them comparable to gutting a bow-spring mattress: her rib cage, the metal springs; her internal organs, the cotton fillers; and her spinal cord, the nicked wood crossbeam support. Kevin watched Kiernan wind down like a spinning top losing momentum upon its point to keep on spinning. Death called for Kiernan, as she thought she heard wolves howling or was it the wind through the forest all around, or was it her delusions due to losing so much blood. She couldn't discern which, focus anymore, or think clearly. However, she managed to have a question, which her rage sustained. A question that stumped every adult whenever a child asked it; a question with only one syllabic beat, unremitting in its delivery if asked more than once or twice; a question that only God can answer. Nevertheless, she put this single-worded question to Kevin. The universal question Kiernan squeezed out in a dying whimper; she asked, "Why?"

"Does it matter at this point?" asked Kevin with his mien cocked to the side, looking down at her. He added, "What's done is dead."

Kiernan fell limp after that response, which Kevin misperceived as her death, finally. The spectacle over, he moved quickly. He dragged Kiernan by hooking his grips under her armpits. He propped her up against the railing, just below Jake's black sneaker lace tied around it, and then crouched down to hoist her up. He grabbed her by her waist, launched upwards, and he almost lost his grip because she wriggled with having seizures. He shifted her body from his left side to his right over-shoulder, mostly to get her floppy arms out of his face and off to the side by his ear. Slumped forwardly, he carried her toward the railing. Paused. He faced blackness. Not as a void but a mirror. The night alongside his self; like stars above, his soul within, a remnant of the past light-years away. Back to Earth. He could sense Kiernan's fading heartbeat against his shoulder and throughout the coarse fibers of his black hoodie, shoulder-high. And without regress or regale or regret, he tossed her—still alive—over the railing.

Hundreds of feet, this drop. Talus, incontrovertibly, the endpoint, but her end akin to evaporation. Murder, apparently, soundless.

Kevin retreated from the railing to the Jeep EV, opened its driver's side door, teetered himself inside without getting in all the way, and reached over the plump black leather seats to claim his cell phone from the glove compartment. He activated it. Its screen had shone iridescently against his deadpanned countenance as he typed a text to Jake's attention...

Kevin Moran Texted [12:05 a.m.]:
"It's done."

He tossed the cell phone onto the passenger seat and followed it inside the Jeep EV. He closed the driver's side door behind himself and sat there pensively. He caught his reflection in the interior rearview mirror, which amused him along with what he had done. What he had planned had worked. He couldn't stop grinning. He reached down toward his pant leg, hiked it up, retrieved Memento Mori from his calf sheath, and brought it up chin-high to his sights. The nightshade; starlight-bright, was his reading light. But the dagger's stainless steel, even within the dark interior of the Jeep EV, shimmered with something of its own light, making the black-metallic ink engraftment most startling...

Memento Mori
(Remember, You Must Die)

He comprehended the sentiment in Latin both ways: his Promises Kept (as it related to Kiernan), and that curse Gustafen spoke of (as it related to himself)—a premonition. Either way, what was done appeared done, and he surmised what shall be shall indeed be. He returned Memento Mori to his calf sheath, rolled down his pant leg to conceal it, and reached up to start the ignition of the Jeep EV. It hummed quietly. He reversed the gearshift, kept the radio turned off, glanced behind himself as he backed up the Jeep EV away from Lookout Point's railing—having forgotten about Jake's black shoelace wrapped around its metal—and peeled off.

A cloud of beige arid dirt and marbled pebbles sprayed up, kicked up by his rear tires' rotation, and settled over trailing droplets of Kiernan's blood toward the railing.

CHAPTER 30

MEMENTO MORI (23 TIMES)

(FLASHBACK): August 10

The Montgomery Townhome

[8:34 a.m.]

Kevin Moran Texted [8:35 a.m.]:
"I'm not home yet. Still wearing same outfit. Drive your car. I still have the jeep. In Barton at Pine Crest Motel in Room 204."

Jake Montgomery Texted [8:42 a.m.]:
"Gotta get a babysitter. Single-Dad now. Be there when I can."

[9:36 a.m.] Meanwhile... an hour later.

Neesha knocked urgently on the red-painted front door of the Montgomery townhome. She appeared in a panic. Jake's call had made her that way; moreover, it wasn't like him to arrange her babysitting dates and times. Having not heard from Mrs. Montgomery for some time, she contemplated that it only made things doubly uneasy.

On the other side of that front door, Summer and Chase cried together aloud, frustrated over the whereabouts of their mother not yet disclosed. They had gone out for a family movie night, returned, and had seen no trace of her since. That was all they knew from last night to this morning. They wanted their mom back, not soon but now. The knock on the front door sounded hopeful to them. *Maybe she had lost her keys... maybe she had stayed overnight at Daliah Moran's estate...* they imagined. They followed closely behind their father as he advanced toward the front door. Sniffling. Whimpers. Summer and Chase swiped at their eyes to clear the tears from their flushed cheeks. Jake knew who was at the front door before he opened it but didn't have the heart to disabuse his children of their hopes... to kill their mother, yes, just not their hopes.

Jake repelled the front door and put on a face. Summer and Chase craned their heads from behind their father and around his arms to see who was at the door, and Neesha's eyes lit up from beyond the door frame. Not seeing Jake, she exclaimed, "What's the matter?! Is everything alright?!"

Summer backed away as Jake said, "Oh, please come in, Neesha... please."

Jake reached out to give Neesha a half-hug and corral her inside over the straw welcome mat. Odd, she thought. Chase ran around his father and cradled Neesha waist-high. He released her immediately. Neesha glanced down at Chase and asked, "What happened to your mom? Where is she?"

Chase had no answer, but Summer did. "I DON'T NEED A BABYSITTER!" she cried. "I WANT MY MOTHER!" Her scream cut through them all. Jake whirled around to face Summer standing at the edge of the foyer; he pleaded, "Please, Summer, just—"

Neesha looked at Jake suspiciously as he said, "I have to make some calls. Look for her. No one knows where she is. We came back from the movies last night, and we haven't seen or heard from her since. I can't seem to reach her because she's not answering her cell phone."

"Her cell phone? Gone? Really?"

He recognized Neesha believed none of it, but he didn't have time to waste or a lie on the fly or a backup plan if rejected. He pressed, "Listen, I need you to—"

Jake reached behind himself, pulled out his brown leather wallet, and flipped it open to reveal a parted mouth lined with cash bills. Many of them, thought Neesha. Jake sifted through his cash bills, seeking the right denomination to pay Neesha. He plucked out three bills from his wallet and handed them to Neesha, who remarked incredulously, "$300! Mrs. Montgomery pays me $50 an hour. You want me to watch the kids for 6 hours? Mr. Montgomery, I—"

"*No, please take it.* I won't be gone for 6 hours, just take it. Watch them till about..." He glanced down at his wristwatch and confirmed, "Noon or so? 1 o'clock, the latest."

Misoriented with her leer of distrust and the shaking of her head, Neesha quietly voiced, "Okay."

Summer and Chase weren't a job to her, but great kids. No trouble at all, she thought. Likewise, Mrs. Montgomery was more than a generous employer, but a friend. Neesha agreed to babysit for Jake out of respect for her friend *(...wherever she was...)* not for the snake, per se.

"Thank you!" said Jake, with relief in his tone, hurry in his step, and clothes for Kevin in the foyer closet. Neesha glanced behind herself, having peeped Jake remove the red Nike duffle bag from the bottom of the closet. Not closing the dark wood closet door, he stopped his momentum halfway. Holding the red Nike duffle bag, he appeared to glance down (*...seeing his Vipers, wondering if Kevin needed footwear...*) in the closet for something more from Neesha's vantage point. She couldn't discern what it was, but whatever it was, she thought, he decided against it. Thereafter, Jake, with the bloated red Nike duffle bag in hand, bolted out of the front door. He didn't look back. He didn't say farewell. He didn't take his cell phone with him.

It sat upright inside its charging base atop the foyer's oak wood and frosted glass-top credenza. Neesha's mind tingled with possibilities if she could get her hands on Mr. Montgomery's cell phone and sift through its data. It nagged at her, just sitting there, available to her by the front door. *Fuck it*, she thought. She bolted for it; halfway there, the front door doorknob turned, and Jake's reach back inside the house reclaimed his cell phone.

Damn it, thought Neesha; *God damn it.* Frustrated, she stomped down upon the wood flooring once. A missed opportunity, yes, but she shuddered at the thought of being caught with it, given that he had returned home for it. She reversed course from the foyer toward the living room and beyond to see about Summer and Chase in their room. Their grief was more important than that snake, she decided.

(FLASHBACK): August 10
Near Crystal Lake State Park
Pine Crest Motel
Barton, VT
[11:15 a.m.]

Jake knocked four times sharply upon the chintzy

composite-wood door, just below the peephole of Room 204. In his periphery, off to the right of himself, a shift indoors. The room's window curtain shifted more than once; again. The third time, he caught Kevin's finger hook the curtain back so that he could spy past it and see who stood at his room door upon the sun-soaked balcony this morning. Jake leaned toward the room door and said, "Open the door, Kevin. It's me."

Kevin obeyed.

The door to Room 204 opened as though no human being had been standing there. That's because he skulked behind it. Jake stepped inside, then Kevin shut the room door quickly. Jake whirled around, and there was Kevin, naked but for a white towel wrapped around his waist, beaded wet, his hair soaked flat against his forehead and dripping. His back against the door, he explained, "I just got out of the shower. Did you bring me some clothes?"

Kevin glanced down at the red Nike duffle bag in Jake's right hand as he asked that question, and Jake handed it to him. Kevin said, "Thanks for this." He walked off past Jake en route back toward the bathroom opposite the room's front door. He pointed, "I had to get those things off me."

Jake's attention had been drawn to the alley and nightstand between the two full-size beds. On the brown carpeted floor lay the black clothes, neatly folded in a well-squared stack and wrapped in clear plastic—the kind often provided by a dry cleaner. This provoked Jake to ask, "Did you have them cleaned?" From the dusky bathroom, with its door ajar, Kevin yelled, "Hell no! Like, I had time for that. Can you imagine me walking into a place of business with The Killing Clothes on? That would be insane. No, I just bagged them."

Where did Kevin get the plastic bag after midnight? Why was he preserving these incriminating clothes in plastic? Why not just get rid of them? And why was that dagger lying in plain view on the nightstand? all Jake's thought.

"Why didn't you go home?" asked Jake, still uncomfortable with sitting down anywhere inside Room 204. He stood between the foot of one full-size bed, the one closest to the room door, and the long dresser with a huge black flat screen TV standing upon its otherwise clean surface. Kevin didn't answer him, so he asked again.

Kevin reentered the common area shirtless, wearing blue jeans and dark green dress socks, and faced Jake. He responded, "Why, so I can face a barrage of interrogating questions from Daliah? Like, why are you coming in so late? Had I gone home straight from Lookout Point, I would've gotten there at 2 in the morning. So I would've gotten questions like, where were you? Why are you wearing all-black? Those clothes are a little too big for you, are they Jake's? They don't smell like you? The wife has a keen nose. She's really into scents. It's weird but...nevermind."

Jake nodded. It sounded reasonable; his suspicions of betrayal waned. Kevin peeled off again back to the bathroom. This time, he closed the bathroom door. They shouted through from their opposite vantage points. Kevin yelled (...distant sounds of urinating in a toilet commenced...), "So how are the kids taking it?"

"Not well. Crying all day."

"Aww! That sucks. Babysitter?"

"Yeah, I'm covered for a few hours, but I gotta get back. I'm glad you got this room, though."

"It's not too bad, (*...flushed toilet permeates through the bathroom door... running of sink water follows...*) I mean, a modest place, right?"

"Yeah, I think so. A little getaway."

The bathroom door swung open, and Kevin stepped out... "WHOA! Dude! What the fuck!" Jake appeared supine in bed, naked, left-handedly stroking his erection to near-firmness. With his free hand, he beckoned Kevin to come closer. Kevin shook his head in disbelief but thought there was no better time to confront Jake about their relationship going forward. Though Jake's marital problems had been murderously resolved, Daliah was still alive, and Kevin loved her very much. He didn't plan on divorcing her, leaving her for Jake, or having assignations in the future.

Kevin sighed and said, "Come on. Let's talk."

Jake stopped stroking himself, sat up with his bare back resting on the wood headboard, and Kevin walked through the alley between the beds and sat beside Jake, his back to him. Jake's carefree nudity was off-putting. Jake asked, "What's wrong? You don't wanna?"

"*Um...*" Kevin paused, searching for delicate words, but found none. He replied, "No. I don't want to have sex with you."

"Now or never?"

"Jake? I—(*...Jake scoffs in disgust...*)"

Kevin snapped, "Are you gonna fucking listen to me, or do you think you know everything I'm going to say before I say it? Tell me now! I'll shut up, then."

"Continue, Kevin."

"Listen, I thought about it, okay. After I left Lookout Point last night and got the room here... I thought about it. What would it be like to go all the way with it? But we were at this place before in college, if you don't remember. I'll remind you. You had girlfriends. I did too. We've been star-crossed, it seems, for some time. It's just our thing, and I think that's what makes us—not the going all the way. I think there's much truth in that saying about Absence...Hearts Grow Fonder...and whatnot. My wife, after I got your text, you know, we were in bed. She cried herself to sleep. She really wants children. She's saying she wants to talk to some doctors about fertility clinics or even surrogacy. I mean, I guess I want that too. I want a son like you have one, Jake. Daliah, no, she's not a high-class model, but she's a good woman. Sweet to me, always. I kinda owe her this. I'm her husband. We talked about surrogacy after making love, and—"

Shaking his head in disgust and disapproval, Jake cut in, "What, with friends like these..."

Kevin had been caught in a lie but was slow to recognize it. Jake's remark, though vague, underscored the fact, and he waited to reveal the truth. Kevin glanced behind him briefly, frowning in confusion at Jake, who, aside from being unabashedly naked on his motel bed, appeared fidgety.

Jake stroked back his long, jet-black hair away from his brilliant blue eyes and his sullen countenance. To Kevin, Jake seemed enraged, though he still couldn't bring himself to look at him fully in the nude. Kevin, staring down at the brown motel room carpet in the alley between the beds, asked, "Did I say something wrong?"

The lie was now on the verge of being exposed.

With a cross-examiner's disquisition, condescension, and moralization, Jake asked, "When did you have sex with Daliah, or...um...made love to her as you put it?"

Kevin frowned, (*...thinking...it was a long time ago...*), then he answered, "I believe it was the night before or after, or both. We are trying to have a baby."

"Before and after we had sex in the gazebo, you're saying?"

"Um, yeah...I guess."

"Even though you promised that you wouldn't?"

Kevin paused. The trap-question had indeed ensnared him. He stammered, still avoiding eye contact, "It was, like, four months ago, bro! Listen, Jake, I—"

"No-no, no-no... Kevin! NO! You promised me after sex in the gazebo, no more sex with women, which includes Daliah."

Kevin's face flushed a deep red with anger as he looked down at the carpet again, as if Jake hadn't been in the same room or on the same bed with the same lies. He asserted, "You made me make that messed-up promise while we were doing it! No one is in their right mind to decide anything but to cum during sex! Damn, bro, that was back in April. FOUR MONTHS AGO!!! You expected me not to have sex with my wife ever? You think I'd go without touching a woman for four months if I'd kept that ridiculous promise? Are you delusional? Come on, bro. You're not being rational right now."

"I stopped having sex with Kiernan."

"Yeah, but Jake, you hated Kiernan! I don't hate Daliah. You used to tell me how hard it was for you to even get it up with her sometimes. I don't have that problem with women, not even with Daliah, Jake! I think this conversation speaks to an unspoken issue between us..."

"*Oh, yeah!* I think it's been spoken, but go ahead. What's that?"

Jake's question was rhetorical. He knew where Kevin's opinions were heading. Unbeknownst to Kevin, he played into it, saying, "I'm really not gay like you. I—"

"Shut the hell up! This is like Penn State Rec Hall locker room all over again. Telling some guys on the rugby team you're not gay, but you had a freaking boner in the showers with us, bro! That's when I found out you were!"

"I think I'm, like, bi-curious or something?"

"What, with these stupid terms. Bi-curious? That's just gay-lite! You're not bi-curious, you're... you're... capricious."

"Daliah's my wife, Jake. I owe her this."

Jake shook his head, fuming, and raised his gaze slowly, staring with piercing rage at the back of Kevin's head. Next to the room's digital alarm clock lay the twelve-inch dagger—Memento Mori. Jake noticed its blade, not for the engravement but for the dried blotches of blood. His rage, initially controlled, now boiled over, and his question came out as a whisper to Kevin.

Jake asked, "What did she say?"

"Who, Daliah?"

"No. Kiernan."

"When?"

"When... or before you took out the trash."

"Why?"

"Tell me."

"Just some nonsense," Kevin said dismissively, mocking her voice, "She asked me, 'Well, why are you doing this?'"

"Did you tell her why?"

"Hell, no."

"Tell me."

"Tell you what?"

"Tell me why you did it."

"You don't know?"

"I really don't anymore. Why were you so eager to kill my wife?"

"Eager? That's crude."

"And killing my wife isn't?"

"Your wife? Don't."

"Don't, what?"

"Don't act like you care about her now. Your wife? You hated every minute with that woman. Besides, she was going to ruin you, and you know it. She'd call you out for being a faggot in divorce court, whenever it got there."

"*So you did it for gay rights?*"

"Don't be glib, bro! Listen, Jake, if you hadn't gotten your hands on that money, you wouldn't be able to do the things I thought you wanted in the future."

"So you were thinking of me?"

"Of course!"

"And not yourself? Really?"

"Yes, really."

"So when you say, 'if I didn't get my hands on that money...' Her money... Money that I used to steal from her and give to you after college, so you could avoid taking out loans to buy your first dealership in Burnham and—"

Kevin cut him off. "Come on, bro, why are you re-living the past?"

"Because if I get the money as a beneficiary from the will, then what? You would want some of that money, right? I would expect."

Kevin glanced back at Jake briefly, just to check his seriousness, and acknowledged what appeared to be sincerity. He returned to talking to that nebulous space between the beds while he answered Jake. He asked, "If you weren't naked for me to see that you didn't have one on, I'd swear you were wearing a wire right now, to get me to confess sitting here. But, um, so your intimating...*inferring*...rather... that you'll give me a cut of that inheritance?"

"Only if you leave Daliah, and every other woman behind."

Kevin contemplated Jake's version of a quid pro quo bro. Jake watched Kevin's deliberation, observing the gears shifting, adjusting, and calculating in Kevin's mind. Jake's latest quid pro quo was merely a hypothetical litmus test: Would Kevin abandon his marriage to Daliah, abandoning any hope of making babies with her to secure a partial inheritance from Jake? Or would Kevin remain committed to his marriage, pursue IVF with Daliah, and hope Jake settled for a future of secret assignations in motel rooms?

Jake's wait was short. He received his answer from Kevin, not in words but in action. Kevin rose from the side of the bed and turned to face Jake, who was seated naked with his legs crossed and his hands squeezed between his thighs. Kevin, seductively removing Jake's brown-green flannel shirt and letting Jake's too-large jeans drop to his feet, was poised to kneel beside Jake.

Jake shook his head dismissively and said just above a whisper, "Kevin... stop. Wrong answer."

Kevin halted, taken aback and blushing nude. He asked, "What?" His tone was more arrogant than confused, as if to say, isn't this what you wanted? Before Kevin could speak or move again, Jake sprang up onto his knees, snatched the twelve-inch dagger from the nightstand, and, with the blade angled down, stabbed Kevin dead-center between his nipples.

Impaled.

Kevin stumbled forward. Jake caught him, his arms wrapped around Kevin's shoulders. The dagger's hilt poked Jake's throat and slid down his body until it lodged in his chest as Kevin slid down beneath the beds. Jake hoisted Kevin up once, but the air escaped him, leaving only a plangent hiss of a dying breath. Jake turned Kevin's body around, sitting him upright facing the closed-curtained window, and clamped his legs around Kevin's naked hips to hold him in place.

Like a ventriloquist with his dummy, Jake reached for the dagger and yanked it out of Kevin's sternum. Kevin began convulsing, frothing at the mouth, and wall-eyed. Jake hugged him from behind one last time as Kevin slumped forward, his stab wound gushing blood. Jake's eyes closed with his cheek pressed against Kevin's back. He felt nauseous, bile brimming at the back of his throat, lightheaded but heavy-hearted. His descent into madness narrowed his senses to one lethal act: *murder.*

Jake's legs constricted around Kevin's lower half.

Over the course of 23 years of star-crossed love, he stabbed Kevin 23 times...*and confessed.*

"Because I was a fool!" Memento Mori plunged into Kevin's navel, then Jake extracted it. "Because I was gullible!" Memento Mori pierced the pit of Kevin's throat, then pulled out. "Because I let you manipulate me!" Memento Mori stabbed Kevin's left flank, then withdrew. "Because you controlled me!" Memento Mori plunged into Kevin's lower abdomen, then pulled out. "Because I let you ruin my family!" Memento Mori struck Kevin's right flank, then pulled out. "Because of your ego!" Memento Mori stabbed Kevin's upper abdomen and diaphragm, then extracted. "Because I'm broken-hearted!" Memento Mori pierced Kevin's liver, then pulled out. "Because of all my hopes!" Memento Mori slashed Kevin's stomach, then withdrew. "Because you kidnapped my future!" Memento Mori tore into Kevin's right pectoral muscle, then pulled out. "Because I sacrificed for you!" Memento Mori shattered Kevin's abdomen, disemboweling him, then extracted. "Because of the money I stole from her for you!" Memento Mori tore into Kevin's left pectoral muscle, then pulled out. "Because of hiding me!" Memento Mori traveled through Kevin's abdomen, piercing through veins, torn tissue, and muscle to the spine cord, then extracted.

"Because of all the lies!" Memento Mori slipped into Kevin's upper thigh, then withdrew.

Confessing, Jake said, "Because of my fear of losing you to women!" He stabbed Memento Mori into Kevin's pelvic area, his tired arm straining. He arched his back, swallowed hard, and cried, "Because you felt afraid of being gay!" Memento Mori drove into Kevin's collarbone, tearing off a strip of flesh like snagged plastic. He flicked the skin off the blade, letting it land on the lampshade between the beds. He continued, "Because you rejected me!"... (stab)... "Over!"... (stab)... "Over!"... (stab)... "And over again!"

Jake kept count—three more transgressions for years of resentment—through a wail, "Because of jealousy!" He reared back and thrust Memento Mori into Kevin's right shoulder. "Because of shame!" Memento Mori pierced Kevin's hollowed-out body, clipping bone but not flesh, then withdrew. "Because..." he wept, wiping sweat from his forehead against Kevin's lifeless head, "...If You Ain't Gettin' What You Should Get, You Getting Got!" Memento Mori jabbed into Kevin's vacant body cavity again, but the tip of the steel struck the spinal cord, snapping the blade in half. Jake was left with only the hilt and about four inches of jagged steel. The point of the blade was lost out of sight, a Hollywood prop that failed him.

The dagger's edge lay discarded within Kevin's body, among a pool of foul-smelling excrement, bile, stomach lining, tissue, and blood. Jake pushed Kevin's lifeless body away in disgust, letting it drop onto the carpeted alley between the beds. He stood in a sludge of blood, guts, excrement, and urine. The mess was lukewarm yet chilling. He was more worried about the black killing outfit wrapped in plastic, which might get saturated by the remains. Jake quickly bent down to save the black outfit and his shoes tucked under the bed. The clothes were blackened with excrement and bile, streaked with blood, and reeked of death. He wrung them out as best he could and got dressed at the foot of the bed, putting on one damp pant leg and one drippy shirt sleeve at a time. None of it was buttoned or zipped. He grabbed his red Nike duffle bag, shoes, car keys, and scrambled to exit Motel Room 204.

Squinting against the broad daylight, Jake opened the motel room door to a velvety warm, sunny day, perfumed by the evergreen forest of Crystal Lake State Park just up the country road. The motel's treeless parking lot stretched out before him, with Jake's black SUV parked front and center. A few other cars were present but none near his SUV. No witnesses saw him exit with soiled clothes unzipped and unbuttoned, carrying a black outfit in a clear plastic bag, barefooted and blood-splattered. He didn't care if he got caught at this point. Kevin was dead, and Jake wanted to be dead too.

He knew his life was over...*and accepted it.*

Jake raised his car key remote, unlocked his SUV, tossed the items into the backseat, and got in. He backed out of the parking lot and headed southbound on the country road. From Pine Crest Motel in Barton to Leeds —35 miles south—he approached a desolate location just outside Burlington. As the evergreen forest melted away, he saw a self-service Car Wash station called Soapy Selfies, with little to no patronage. He turned off the country road and drove up the ramp for Car Stall #2, leaving Stalls One and Three vacant.

Jake unlocked his vehicle's doors and stepped out, using the driver's side door for cover from any potential onlookers (no one saw). He stripped off his soiled clothes and shoes, tossing them against the wall beneath the hoses. Nude, he reached into his SUV's middle console for the ashtray filled with coins, extracting five dollars worth of quarters. Behind him, attached to the pale green-painted cinder block wall, was the Soapy Selfies Car Wash machine—a metal boxy contraption that operated the hoses coiled on either side of it. The coin slot requested quarters. Jake inserted all of his coins, and the machine's engine hummed to life. The hoses in Car Stall #2 began vibrating with water pressure. The pale-red hose, meant for shampooing vehicles, was hot to the touch, while the royal blue hose was for cold rinses, again intended for vehicles.

Jake started with the shampoo hose. He lifted it from its hook, aimed it at his shaven chest, and pressed the metal lever. The hot, foamy suds blasted him with a hiss. The thick, bubblegum-scented foam coated him thoroughly. He dropped the hose and scrubbed his scalp and skin with his fingernails, trying to remove the blood and guts. Tea-colored streaks of Kevin's remains trickled down his hairy legs and between his toes. The muck flowed down a pit in the concrete floor of Car Stall #2 and was swallowed by the drain beneath Jake's black SUV—an aftermath of murder with no love lost for what used to be a friend.

With soccer ball-sized clumps of suds on his shoulders, head, and back, Jake reached for the royal blue hose for a cold rinse. He gasped at the initial shock and shivered as the suds melted away. The cool air, tinged with pre-Autumn's freshness, made him feel exposed. He dropped the hose, bent down to retrieve his shoes, left untied, and picked up his soiled clothes, now balled up. He retreated to the SUV, collected the black killing outfit folded in clear plastic from the backseats, and headed down the asphalt drive-in ramp.

On the way, he noticed a hunter green dumpster berm-side. Without clothes or shame, but shod, Jake walked to the dumpster and discarded the balled-up clothes inside. For the first time, a witness saw him.

Seated inside Soapy Selfies' main building behind the customer service counter, the owner, Steve Altimara—a grey-haired old man in a dingy white collar shirt—had later identified Jake. Steve saw a man with longish black hair, wet-looking on his face, and bright light-colored eyes (*though he couldn't specify the color from a distance*). The man stood about 6'3" to 6'5" and was seen dumping something into the dumpster before returning naked but for boots to Car Wash Stall #2. He then got into his black SUV and drove off.

Steve, too afraid to stop Jake's actions—captured on store cameras—mustered just enough courage to recall these details and Jake's Vermont license plate numbers to law enforcement.

Law enforcement thanked him.

Jake was arrested days later. Kevin's body was discovered in Room 204 by housekeeping, who alerted the police. The police then contacted next of kin, starting with Daliah Moran. That summer, Chase learned of their mother's disappearance and their father's incarceration. Aunt Gracey stepped in to support The Montgomery family, picking up the pieces. The web of lies was irreparably torn down, unable to ensnare anyone further.

To date, *The Past as Prologue.* The State Supreme Court of Vermont granted Jake a new trial. He is now out on bail, living in The Montgomery Townhome again with Chase.

A free man.

. . . Summer, 2023

CHAPTER 31
"1+1=3"

(PRESENT-DAY): September 5th
(... One week after bailing-out Jake from County Jail...)
Crystal Lake State Park, Lookout Point
Barton, VT
[10:10 a.m.]

The morning was sharply sunny, with the clearest azure-blue skies and a nibbling-cold breeze pushing from west to east. It was a bright, crisp northeastern Vermont day. The air was evergreen-scented with a hint of burnt chicory. Summer had been sensed as dying early this year after the early August floods, or perhaps it was the Appalachian acclivity of Lookout Point—850 feet down from its railing to talus.

Chase winced as he glanced down from the Lookout Point railing, bracing himself. He was gratified to see teams of law enforcement below—*the elite of the elite* in the alphabet agencies: D.H.S., A.T.F., and the F.B.I.—an army of ants from his vantage point. They were busy in dark-blue collared windbreakers or white hazmat jumpsuits, sifting through dirt and rock at the ground zero of the gruesome crime scene discovery. Even though, for days now, the human remains—said to be female, not male—had been collected and air-lifted to a renowned forensics lab in Boston for further analysis, Chase already knew the results. Sense over science, one of the victims was his mom. Lookout Point, he believed, was the last place where his mother had lived and died.

He had to be there.

The antithesis of that same foreboding sense—where he had to be elsewhere—related to his father in the house since bailing him out of county jail. Even though Chase did the deed for the love of his Big Sister, Summer, he believed that if he had stayed one more hour in that house with his father going forward, he was going to kill him. Not that the man was a nuisance at home at all. Quite the contrary, Jake acted fatherly, fondly, or fixedly. Subsequently, Chase regarded all of that as fallacy. He just didn't trust him. Jake's decade-long state prison stint found no adjuvant post-release in Chase, only his scrutiny, skepticism, and suspicions.

The creaking of the wood flooring on socked feet was heavy-footed: meals together at the dining room table, bearing his small talk, which failed to pierce the ballooning sense of unease between father and son reunited. Not to exclude the most offensive of all dynamics, Jake's latest idea that Chase's Montgomery Home might profit as an Airbnb given the father's infamy—as though Kiernan's ghost, which wafted throughout every room in the home, could be reduced to a siren song worth the cost of admission. Just recounting the goings-on in the span of one week with this free man, thought Chase, *was enough to kill him.*

In glaring white sunlight, Chase caught himself over the Lookout Point railing crying wistfully. These tears were predictable yet unlooked-for and annoying. When they came, Big Sis told him many times just to call her.

So he did.

Chase held his phone up just below his chin, put Summer on speaker call since he was alone at Lookout Point—all the activity 850 feet below—and waited for her to pick up the call. She obliged him, not answering commonly with hello, but with, "What got you going this time, Lil' Brother?"

"(...*sniffles*...) Frickin', Jake."

"What'd he do now? (...*she hears construction going on in the distance*...)"

"He doesn't have to do anything. It's his existence. I put cameras in every room of the house so that I can watch him on my phone whenever I'm not there."

"Oh geez, Chase! A little much, huh?"

"No, not at all."

"Where are you right now?"

"At the Point."

"Why? Oh my God! Why?"

"I just can't be in that house with Jake. I feel Mom's presence strong here for some reason. I can't explain it."

"Chase, why aren't you at class?"

"I'll be there... I will. The semester just started. I'm not hurting myself in any way."

"(*...Summer sighs...*) It's really loud where you are, Chase."

"Yeah, I know. It's reassuring."

"Reassuring? How?"

"Means all those people down there are working hard to get us the truth. They aren't giving up. Using every kind of crane, dump truck, shovel... you name it. It's out here. They will find out the truth."

"I hope so, Lil' Brother... I hope so... Hey?"

"Hey, what?"

"Have you contacted Neesha?"

"No, why? It's been years since I've heard you bring her up."

"Well, she called, that's why."

"Saying what? How is she? Where is she?"

"Well, she appears to be doing great. She goes to the same university as you—"

He cut her off, surprised, saying, "University of Vermont? Really? I'm sure she has better grades than I do."

"Yes, well, she's a wee late on her obligation to you."

"What obligation?"

"Chase, Mom's will. You getting her diaries at 18 or when you graduated high school, whichever came first."

"I remember."

"Well, she hasn't. That's why she called me. Neesha said that she's been studying abroad for the past three years—in Norway, in Stockholm, Sweden—working on her doctorate. She promised to contact you if only she had your phone number or email. I gave her your phone number because I never remember your email address. She said she'll text you with the location of the diaries so that you can reclaim them as Mom wanted."

"Wow! Mom's diaries."

"It's what we always wanted, huh?"

"Yes, definitely. That will be nice to have... to read."

"Now that I think about it, maybe not."

Chase paced the length of the railing, tapping it along the way, and replied, "Why wouldn't it be nice to have them?"

"Just imagine, Chase. You're reading Mom's every thought, and Jake comes in the room and says something as arbitrary as 'Get your feet off the table.'"

"Oh-oh-oh! Don't get me riled up, Sis."

"See, I told you. Maybe not a good idea."

"What, you want me to send them to you?"

"No, Chase. Mom wanted you to have them."

"Sis, it's okay. We can share them. It's no big deal. We can share them."

"Really? That's sweet, because she might have some Mom-stuff in there I can use for you know who..."

"Is she there right now?"

"Oh, yes. Don't want to get her started by saying her name."

"How's my little niece, Sienna?"

"A lovely, beautiful terror."

"Now you understand what Mom went through with you, Karma?"

"Fully... wholly... sadly. Hey, why don't you ever ask about Darren? He asks about you all the time, Chase. He's actually been meaning to ask you out for beers with some of his fishing buddies."

"Oh, really?"

"Yep. He is your brother-in-law. It wouldn't hurt to get to know him. Spend time with him, especially on those days that Dad becomes a little too much to bear. Just hang out with Darren. Go fishing. Shoot some skeet with him."

"He shoots."

"Um, yeah? My husband's a good shot, too."

"Okay... *Okay*... Some day."

Chase continued to pace the length of the railing, warm to the touch from the sunlight overhead. He glanced down at the crime scene from time to time, and each of those times Summer sensed through the call his silence as mourning aloud. She asked, "Why are you torturing yourself there? We don't even know if those human remains are Mom and that other lady. It's going to be months before those forensics results come back.

They just took our DNA blood and plasma samples yesterday, Chase."

"I know... I know."

(*Chase's left hand clipped something as he paced, and it snagged his attention...*)

Summer continued, "Just leave, Chase. Go to class. And—"

"Hold on a second, Sis."

Summer took a beat. She thought Chase was rude but answered, "Okay."

(*Chase's cell phone dropped to Summer's ear...*)

"Hello? Chase? Are you there?"

Chase returned to what appeared to be an all-too-familiar black shoelace tied around the railing, with the front bumper of his silver Dodge Ram EV coup parked less than a foot away in the gravelly unmarked parking space.

"Chase!" yelled Summer from Chase's cell phone in the gravel. "Chase! You answer me right now!"

"MOTHERFUCKER! MOTHERFUCKER!" screamed Chase into Summer's ear.

"What is it! WHAT'S GOING ON!" she cried over the speaker call. "CHASE?"

Summer heard a scraping sound before she heard Chase sobbing uncontrollably into the speaker call, which made her cry too. No explanation was given. She begged, "What? Chase, you can tell me. Please just tell me. What just happened there? What's going on?"

Chase, as though his voice had been wound up from

a whimper to an angry wail, screamed, "We... got... HIM! WE FINALLY!... GOT... HIM!" Then he took several breaths, loudly sobbing. He said softly, "He did it, Summer. He fucking did it!"

"What are you talking about? Who got who? Who did what?"

Chase appeared bent at the waist, staring at it. If it were an actual snake, it would have bitten him. The Viper's black sneaker-lace with the embossed slithering red snake, which had been emblazoned on his mind since he was ten years old.

Summer cried and begged Chase to say something. She heard him breathing and sobbing. She asked, "Are you going to answer me?"

(*The call disconnected...*)

Meanwhile... (500 feet up a walker's path trail from Lookout Point's gravelly parking lot...)

Royse's Log Cabins & Campgrounds

State Police Mobile Outpost, Cabin (3)

[10:25 a.m.]

Four knocks in rapid succession upon the Missing Person's Unit Chief Detective's office cabin door. Seated at his desk, he glanced up into the sunlit space from typing on his laptop and noticed his corporal standing in wait to be acknowledged through the door's labeled glass window and said, "Come in."

Corporal Palomino Gutiérrez, Tech Specialist. A fit,

young officer; 5'10", light-complexioned Latino, originally from Reno; a green-eyed, perpetual worrier of a countenance with slick-backed black hair held in a ponytail, greying brightly on the sides, and he heavily egressed cologne. His Unit Chief Detective continued typing. Gutiérrez entered plainclothed in khakis, a dark-blue collared shirt opened at the top, tieless, and a holstered Glock on his right hip while holding a manila-colored file in his left hand as thick as a Bible. He plopped himself down on the folding chair situated in front of his Unit Chief's cluttered glass-top desk and asked, (*...sighing...*) "You got a minute?"

Unit Chief Detective Jamal Rivers stopped typing, rolled his dark-brown eyes with impatience, glanced over the razor-thin horizon of his laptop screen, and watched his corporal push his file across the desk over his papers. Rivers asked, "I guess you want me to stop what I'm doing to see about what you're doing? It can't be good seeing that sour-puss on your face."

Rivers opened the file, gleaned only 3 out of 364 pages of it, but listened to his corporal talk about it more.

"Sir?" responded the corporal, getting right into his assignment. (*Rivers leaned back in his reclining office chair.*) "We're talking precisely 1,329 witness sightings of Mrs. Montgomery this year, but that doesn't always translate into 1,329 living people, so we've done our due diligence on this end. All over this tip, our missing person, Mrs. Montgomery, being in Singapore, living it up, right?

Well, it has been disproven by our counterparts in the F.B.I. Three field agents were sent to Singapore. The building alleged as our missing person coming out of is not owned by Agri-Care but Red Maple Technologies. A thing we already confirmed from the court transcripts of the defeated lawsuit filed by the U.S. Department of the Interior and Commerce, not to mention what details we got from our missing person's sister, Gracey Kluger. So there's that. Then, our field agents got back to us about that 1,329 score of witness sightings versus actual people. They researched the IP addresses for each one, and they found that many of them, if not all but two, were bots. The two that weren't bots, we flagged."

"Where are the two actual living people located?" asked Detective Rivers.

"Belgrade, Serbia and Burlington, Vermont."

"What? A hit here, locally! Who?"

"Daliah Moran, sir."

"No way! Daliah?"

"Well, I'll get to her in a minute because the bigger fish is in Belgrade, Serbia. Our field agents found this guy..." Corporal Gutiérrez reached over the front of the desk toward the split-open file in his Unit Chief Detective's hands. He turned a few pages forward for him, then tapped the top of the black-and-white mini-photograph: a 3x6 glossy of a bruiser of a man. Cauliflower-eared, swarthy complected, and with a thick five o'clock shadow painted over a squared jaw. Dark-brown eyes with more of a tint pitch-black. A scowl on him, not a smile for the camera, which led Rivers to believe that he was scrutinizing a mugshot. His corporal continued, "That's Yuri Montegomovic."

Rivers said, "You've got my attention now."

"Look a few more pages ahead, and you'll see a plastic pouch with a flash drive inside."

"I see it. Take it out?"

"Yes, please. Put it in your laptop. Bring up File C-2. The field agents stored some information for us there. Take a look. These field agents graphed out how the preliminary operation worked online. It's pretty simple how they got it down for us to see, instead of typing up an entire report about it."

The Unit Chief Detective heeded those instructions. His laptop lighted to File C-2 being displayed on Rivers' screen. Corporal Gutiérrez watched his Unit Chief Detective's saccadic gaze, but he appeared flustered, not looking up. However, Rivers asked, "Okay, I'm looking at a chart of some kind... This is amazing."

"The funny thing is, I don't think Daliah Moran had a clue what Yuri was doing with the content she had supplied him, any more than Jake knew that he had a European ally overseas working to influence global public opinion about his murder case. I mean, just look at it go viral."

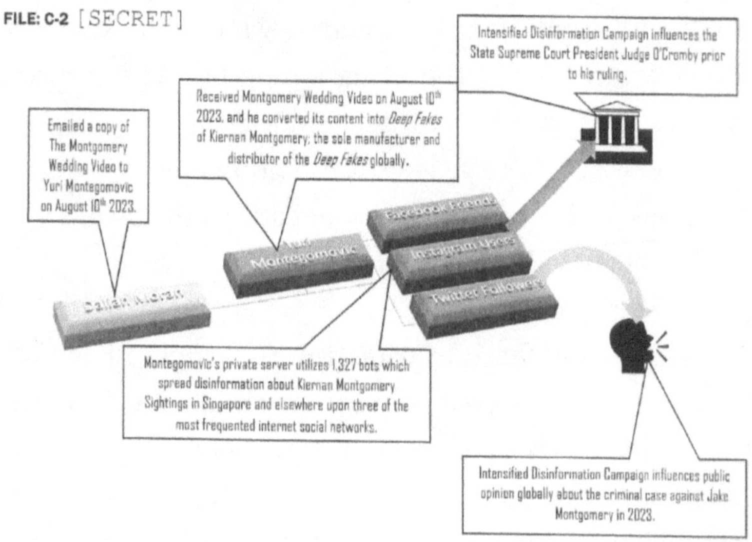

Corporal Gutiérrez explained, "Our guy lifted from that wedding video all that he needed to advance Kiernan Montgomery as reincarnated in virtual space. He used CGI-applied technologies, 3-D textile composites, and simple graphic designs on auto-drive, getting his unregistered server to mass-produce her real-life appearance, then sat back and watched the world's reactions as if he were playing a video game. He lifted her voice pattern and tone off the wedding video too... And—"

Rivers interrupted, "Summer Montgomery believed all of it. Every bit of it."

"So many thousands of people got suckered, not just her. Don't believe everything on Facebook is the less-learned here, sir. This guy, Yuri, was innovative and dedicated. It's frightening what he had done here. It's also criminal. Once he discovered how to CGI-off the wedding gown that Kiernan Montgomery had on, it was open season for what all he could do next. He could not be hacked. He used Green Screen technology to make Hong Kong cityscape look like Singapore to the masses. Keep in mind: he got that wedding video on August 10th, 2023, and in three days he managed to change public and court opinion. At that State Supreme Court Hearing, the judge remanded the Jake Montgomery Post-Conviction case to the lower court, and it was O'Cromby who had it pre-arranged to conduct the Sentencing Phase in his court per some rarely used State Rule procedure. That's why he was bailed after his ruling immediately. Jake Montgomery bailed out a week later by his son Chase."

"Frickin' O'Cromby, man! Mr. Know-It-All knows nothing about modern-day technology and how it can lie just like people, if not better or worse."

The corporal added, "In C-3 is where there's another document stamped SECRET. Next page, sir." Rivers turned the page wedged between the file cover.

"Montegomovic was also a part of that Russian disinformation campaign which used FSB hackers to attack our federal system of voting across 22 states in a failed attempt to flip votes for Trump and against Biden in the 2020 Presidential Election. He produced Deep Fakes of Minneapolis Police saying George Floyd died like a fish out of water. It went viral, and that's when the

Minneapolis Police Department was razed, remember? He's known for this shit!"

"This is explosive stuff, Palomino."

"And yet there's more."

"I'm afraid to ask."

"You don't have to. I'll tell you. Jake Montgomery and Yuri Montegomovic are related."

"(*...sighing...*) This is too much. How? By marriage?"

"No, sir, actually, by blood. Hit the audio key. That's the F1 key, sir. This file uses the function keys to maneuver through it."

"Okay... Hold on a second there (he presses the F1 key...)"

[THE RECORDING OF YURI MONTEGOMOVÏC]

"...I submitted my DNA sample to that ancestral platform 23 & Me, and the results came back that I had a blood relative from my maternal side who lived in North America. I went online, did a cursory search, and found out that my Americanized surname was Montgomery. The criminal case with that surname popped up quickly as I searched more, because back then, I think it was 2013-2014, it was the cause célèbre.

...I saw a pic of the man... He had similar facial features as us... I looked into him on my side of the ocean... My family, in small part, immigrated from Yugoslavia to the U.S. like a lot of Serbian Jews during World War II... My great-great Aunt Mischa on my mother's side made it to the U.S. by way of New York City

as a 13-year-old refugee... That's where our bloodlines intersect, as they say... When I learned that the Jake-guy in America had the same middle name as my father, Sergyi—I knew he was family for sure... Not that I doubted the ancestral test or anything like that... I couldn't reach him directly to make sure of it because he was in prison at the time, and the U.S. jails are different from those in Europe...

...We can talk to our people even when they are behind bars in Serbia... Not as strict as in the States... During my searches, though, is when I met Daliah.... We talked well together... We talked about having kids... I don't have any and she wanted some... That turned into talking about my family, and when I brought up the ancestral test and a possible American relative named Jake Montgomery... Well, um, she wasn't too pleased... She thought that I was playing some kind of game with her like the Nigerians she learned about who extorted vulnerable women via the internet... But I didn't want money from her... She didn't believe me... She cut off all contact.... Then I got an email from her... It had a lot of gigabytes... But I feared it might be a virus or spam that would hurt my server, so I didn't open it right away... I trusted later that she wouldn't do that to me, and I opened the email... I didn't understand why she sent it to me at first, but then I recognized those similar family features in a man in a tuxedo dancing with his bride at a wedding reception of some kind... It was that Jake-guy, but across the video feed—frame to frame—was pasted the word...

"LIAR"

...I found out a way to delete the word without losing the visuals... It was tricky, though... Now I had the material to produce what I needed to help this Jake-guy, because his crime was unbelievable to me... The U.S. lies on a lot of people and world leaders, so I couldn't let you Americans lie on my family name, Montegomovic... He was my cousin... I don't care how much you Americans changed the way of saying it in your native tongue, so that's when I got the idea, knowing the case, that I could use the wedding video to make the images of Jake's wife appear anywhere in the world... Make it seem like she wasn't dead, so I made the Deep Fakes, and they worked... Can't say she's a missing person, right? If she's seen coming out of an office building, a bank, or a gym... I thought I could free my new cousin from your wicked prison system... And it worked.... I got internet traffic going on the topic... I got a man off from murder charges in the U.S. I got a lot of internet cred... My Facebook friends, Twitter followers, and on Instagram... But... I do what I can, right?"

(F.B.I. Field Agents Leonar and Cole interjected the suspect with a battery of questions:)

"Son, you never met Jake Montgomery personally or directly?"

-Answer: 'No.'

"Had you known of Shannoah Blakely in the U.S.?"

-Answer: 'No.'

"Well, sir, she's a part of the criminal case you said that you had known involved your new cousin. You didn't know that fact?"

-Answer: 'No. I just concentrated on him and the Deep Fakes of his wife. I only had graphs of their images which I lifted from the wedding video. Making sure they got in circulation. No other people.'

"Do you know where Kiernan Montgomery is?"

-Answer: 'No.'

"Do you know where Shannoah Blakely is?"

-Answer: 'No.'

"Have you ever met Daliah Moran in person?"

-Answer: 'No.'

"Has she ever paid you to create the Deep Fakes or asked you to make them?"

-Answer: 'No. All my idea.'

"Were these Russian servers that you operated?"

-Answer: 'Not servers, just a server, and no. The server was mine, but it was stolen from the Russians in Kaliningrad.'

(...Rivers pressed a key on his keyboard which cut the feed of this federal interrogation...)"

"That's all we need," said Rivers. "Tell you what, though, the guy doesn't give two shits! He's definitely proud of his efforts. Honest as fuck in the way that he sounds about it all."

"A bit off-putting if you ask me, but we must circle back to Daliah Moran, sir. Her fingerprint and contribution to this disinformation campaign can't be overlooked, underestimated, or diminished. She engaged in criminal conduct explicitly. When the F.B.I. field agents compared and tracked IP addresses, segregated the two actives from the thousands of bots, they didn't get a hit on Daliah's cell phone, but on Kevin Moran's. She used his cell phone with regard to Shannoah Blakely's... hacking it to make it appear as Blakely was still alive."

"So, Daliah Moran acted out because, we presume, she found out about the affair between her husband and Blakely, not Jake Montgomery and Blakely as we initially thought?"

"Yes, sir. Fair to say. She had one angle and this Montegomovic guy had his angle. I think we can link her to criminal activity. I'm not big on correlations, but I'll wager news of the affair is why she sold her husband's car dealership business in 2018. Daliah has skin in the game."

"So, I'm not about to ask the judge for a warrant on, basically, what amounts to cyber bullying by proxy. We can't argue conspiracy with cyber bullying because we can't confirm that Ms. Moran told Yuri Montegomovic to do what he did with Kiernan Montgomery's wedding video in making the Deep Fakes or whatnot. This case is just weird and winding."

"I know."

"So, no. We are not arresting Daliah Moran. I've been doing this for years. Daliah Moran is harmless. She's got her millions, but she's alone being bitter online. Let her have that, so long as she doesn't get too crazy with it. We'll keep her on the radar. We will."

"Whatever you say, sir."

"Our teams are still working down there. Let them work," explained Rivers as he closed out the F.B.I. Field Officers Casefile on The Montgomery Case and extracted his corporal's flash drive from the side of his laptop. He handed it to him across his desk, then ordered, "Email Deputy Attorney General Grant LaPlant to let him know that you're sending him discovery which will put a massive hole in Jake Montgomery's criminal defense at his new trial coming up. He'll be back in prison soon enough."

"Yes, sir."

(*...A couple of knocks at the door part-way ajar...*)

Rivers and Gutiérrez whipped their attention toward the office door, and Rivers responded, "Yes, Officer Vess. How may I help you?"

"Have someone out here who wants to talk with you specifically."

Rivers squinted with curiosity before he asked, "It's not my wife, is it?"

"Oh, no, sir. It's Chase Montgomery, sir."

Gutiérrez and Rivers looked at each other with astonishment, shaking their heads, and Gutiérrez chirped, "The timing this guy has..."

Unit Chief Detective Jamal Rivers, with Corporal Palomino Gutiérrez seated beside him, had since invited Chase Montgomery to take a seat in the metal folding chair across from them in front of the messy glass-top office desk, which the Unit Chief apologized for.

"No problem," replied Chase with bloodshot

tanzanite-blue eyes, weeping-ripe and clearly distraught. Rivers asked, "May we help you, sir?"

Chase didn't know how to answer that question without sounding pissed, but he told himself before walking up the trail not to make allies in the fight your enemy, so he responded, "Do you care that I need to have this case solved?"

The Corporal cut in on his Unit Chief, "Of course, son. We all want to solve this case as quickly as possible."

Rivers asked, "Do you think we are failing you, Mr. Montgomery?"

Again, Chase fumed at the question, but he had taken the route of explaining things rather than excoriating them. He admitted, "On the night Jake took Summer and me to the movies is when he killed Shannoah Blakely. I—"

"WHOA! WHOA!...son," shouted Corporal Gutiérrez with hands outstretched. "Are you making a statement or a confession? What are we doing here?"

Chase said flatly, "I'm doing your job."

Rivers chortled and told his Corporal, "Record him."

While Gutiérrez scrambled for his cell phone out of his khakis back pocket and activated it, Chase continued, "I was ten at the time. Summer, my eldest sister, was 13. I was playing around wearing Jake's high-tops. Sneakers called Vipers. They are red and black; I believe size thirteens. (... Gutiérrez, now recording, places his cell phone out in front atop a stack of papers on the desk...) Back then, the sneakers lace was missing from the left-footed Viper, I believe. I remember seeing red dots all over the tops of the Vipers. I thought it was paint because there were so many of them. I know it was blood. Most likely Shannoah Blakely's blood because my mother did not go missing until the next day. I've learned through that State Supreme Court decision that Shannoah Blakely and Kevin Moran were rumored to have had an affair, or maybe the affair was with Jake; either one is culpable for her death, because I believe one took Shannoah, and the other took my mother. I also believe that it happened here at Lookout Point. I believe this was planned, killing these two women in advance, and I know that to be true because of what I found today."

Rivers had his arms crossed, studying Chase's cold demeanor, seated there, but he had a compelling delivery which begged the question, "What did you find today?"

"Do you remember those sneakers I told you about? The ones where—"

Rivers cut him off, "Yes, go on."

"That black sneaker-lace that was missing then, ten years ago, is what I found today, because it's..." He turned beet-red in the face and started shouting, "FUCKING WRAPPED AROUND THE RAILING AT LOOKOUT POINT FOR TEN, GODDAMN, YEARS, AND NONE OF YOU FOUND IT!"

"Calm down, son," said Gutiérrez.

"Don't tell me to calm down."

Rivers interjected, "We'll take a look at it, Chase.

But, listen, this case has been complicated. We are waiting for the results of the two human remains that are female. Things are not quite adding up for—"

"NO!" blasted Chase. He rose to his sneaker-feet before the front of the desk; taller than both cops, and he yelled, "Things DO add up! You want me to add it up for you?" He raised his right hand, using his fingers to count off the ways. He said, "ONE... Kevin Moran was murdered by Jake, plus ONE... Shannoah Blakely was murdered by Jake, and we all know that my mother ain't no fucking missing person! So, One plus One Equals Three... DEAD!"

Rivers shot back, "You brought in no evidence to substantiate anything you are saying. We will check out the railing at The Point, but everything you've—" (...cell phone buzzes loudly as though a text had come in...all men check themselves...) Gutiérrez knew it wasn't his cell phone; it was recording the interview at the top of the Unit Chief's cluttered desk. Rivers came to the same conclusion, but only after his attention was snagged by hearing Chase say, "Shit!"

"What?" asked Rivers as he tried to read Chase's eyes as he read the text on his cell phone. Chase said, "I have to go."

Had Unit Chief Detective Rivers read the text Chase received, he would've stopped their conversation too...

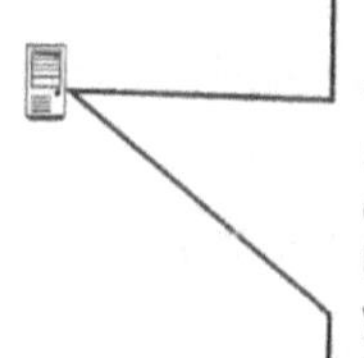

12:13 p.m., Neesha McGovern

Though I'm belated in my obligation, much apologies. Per your mother's final wish, she's instructed me to inform you that her 16 diaries are located beneath two wood floor boards that lie in front of her bathroom sink in her bedroom's bathroom. She told me to tell you what I witnessed on the eve that your father choked your mother and fled. He later had a sexual encounter with Kevin Moran in the gazebo we grew up by in the neighborhood, which I witnessed while walking my cat Mojo that night. She told me to tell you that she had written all about them and more in her diaries. As an aside, I recently learned that your father got out of prison, and he is living with you. Frankly, this information surprised me. Protect those diaries, Chase. It's what your mother would've wanted. I hope you find peace with this information and discovery.

"Chase?" called the Unit Chief, whose Corporal stood by flummoxed and fiddling with his cell phone he had turned off. Chase, with his hand resting on the office doorknob, poised to turn it, glanced back at the cops and said, "I can't debate this with you. I must go. I must."

Corporal Gutiérrez replied, "My boss is in the middle of interviewing—" *(...Chase bolted out of the office, drawing attention from other cops on the way out...)*

The Corporal, astonished, felt his arm grabbed suddenly because his Unit Chief knew he'd run for Chase. He said, "Let him go."

"What if he was going to admit to the murders?"

"Nah, he wasn't going to do that. He knows who did it," said Rivers. He took a seat, flipped open his laptop, and said, "He'll be back."

The Corporal glanced down at his Unit Chief, dumbfounded, and argued, "I think we're making a mistake. We should've detained him, sir."

The Unit Chief's cell phone vibrated. He got a text. He read it. His Corporal turned to him and asked, "What is it?"

Rivers, pitch-too shocked, answered, "A.T.F. and D.H.S. found something. Damn it! We should've detained him! Come on. We're wanted at ground-zero."

Meanwhile...

(...Lookout Point gravelly parking lot...)

Chase, out of breath, had run to his Dodge Ram EV Coup, reached the driver's side door handle he had unlocked by his car key remote a few paces back. He hurried, got in the vehicle, put his car key in the ignition, brought his car to a purr, and held onto his cell phone while managing the steering wheel. He worried for those diaries. Since Jake inherited the townhome, he had made his parents' old bedroom (which he called Mom's Room) his own. Jake was made to sleep where he and Summer used to sleep as kids. The small bedroom with a Sycamore Tree against its window. Though he never saw Jake wander back down to the end of the hall as if Mom's bedroom was still his, the chill down his spine made him worry. Chase had good instincts, not to mention he never trusted his father. Then he remembered as he put the car in reverse...

HOME CAMERAS!

He stomped the brakes.

His cell phone already on, he swiped it to reach his security features. He brought up his Home Surveillance Account and immediately got an interior view of his kitchen camera's Live Feed. He bracketed his cell phone screen with both hands. The glaring midday sun bleached his view of things in his home. His sights trained down intently, he went room-by-room. Ten more cameras to check:

The dining room... *clear.*

The outside deck and Jacuzzi... *clear.*

The front stoop and garden... *clear.*

Mom's old office... *clear.*

The living room and hallway... *clear.*

The two-car garage (left open)... *clear.*

The basement recreation room... *clear.*

The basement laundry room... *clear.*

Jake's new bedroom... clear. (*...where the fuck is he, then? thought Chase...)*

Mom's bedroom as Chase likes to call it... room camera blocked by something whitish!

"That motherfucker!" blurted Chase. He dropped his cell phone to the rubber car floor mats, kicked his coup into gear, spun out of the Lookout Point parking lot, and drove hell-for-leather. Cursing profusely... "SHIT! SHIT! FUCKER! YOU FUCKER!" His heart in his throat, squinty-eyed against the sun through his windshield, and gripping the steering like a throat he wanted to choke.

And no one to stop him.

CHAPTER 32
THE UNIVERSE WORKS

(…Almost two hours lapsed…)
The Montgomery Townhome
[1:46 p.m.]

1:48 p.m., STATE POLICE OF VERMONT Texted:

At Lookout Point, the A.T.F. and F.B.I. field teams and Forensics unearthed a .22 caliber Remington Thunderbolt pistol, which A.T.F. has confirmed as once registered to your mother in 2013. I followed-up as pledged to you, regarding what you discovered on the railing at Lookout Point, and we have cordoned off that section of the railing for further analysis on that black shoelace; in other words, it will be removed and bagged into evidence. If you have the footwear to which it belongs, please turn them in to police immediately. We need to speak with your father at this point. I need you to stay away from him, and I need you to report to any police station within a mile of your current location after reading this text. THIS IS A DIRECT ORDER; defy it and you will be arrested.

Chase seethed after he had read that text. Moreover, after a near-45-minute drive and a double and triple check of his cell phone, which revealed his mobile surveillance appeared obstructed by something whitish, he turned it off. He had to get inside. He placed his cell phone in his glove compartment and got out of his parked car in front of his neighbor's estate, not his townhome. The reason: Mom's bedroom windows faced the cul-de-sac. A peek through Mom's bedroom venetian blinds would give Jake the heads-up that Chase got home sooner rather than later, given where his car had been parked.

Chase scampered across the neighbor's front lawn, sidled up close to their estate's red-brick wall, which connected to the white siding of The Montgomery tutor townhome. He ran past his red-painted front door and stoop, up the inclined driveway to his opened two-door garage. The garage doors had been yanked up since he left for The Point earlier that morning. To Chase, this was a good sign. It meant that his interior Home Alarm System remained disengaged. Again, Chase did not want his father to have a preemptive warning of his whereabouts in close proximity. Chase sought an ambush.

Only two rooms in The Montgomery Townhome didn't have surveillance cameras: the bathrooms. The one in the hallway, which Chase and Summer used as kids, and their Mom's bedroom. Jake slept in the bedroom that was once his children's, and it was situated across from the hallway bathroom. A direct line, in fact. Jake was not captured on any of the motion-activated surveillance cameras indoors, which meant that he currently occupied the hallway bathroom or was up to no good in Mom's bedroom bathroom, where Neesha said the diaries were hidden for a decade.

Chase entered his kitchen through the doorway that connected the galley kitchen to the garage. He shut that door quietly behind himself, stepped onto the backs of his laceless sneakers to remove them, and, while on sock feet, advanced gingerly toward the cupboard below the kitchen sink. It was there where he stored his loaded 9mm Glock in a gun case behind the house cleaning materials. Carefully moving aside plastic spray bottles and aluminum aerosol cans to extract his gun case from the cupboard, he did so nearly soundlessly. He placed the locked gun case on the countertop in front of him, beside the kitchen sink, entered the passcode, which triggered a beep, and its top lid unlocked. He removed his 9mm Glock and its safety. There appeared to be a full clip inside—a thing he'd made certain of every time after target practice at Gunther's or since Jake moved back home.

If you stay ready, you don't have to get ready, as they say...

The only noise that emanated from the kitchen was the cocking of the 9mm Glock, which made him wince after he had done it. The three successive clicks and shifts that sprung the first bullet's preparatory elevation into position within the chamber were loud as fuck! On white sock feet, Chase appeared suspiciously eagle-eyed of the spacious milieu of his home, tweaked in his view with uncertainty around every corner. His sightline curved and snapped back from side to side, forwards and back at the immediate milieu and all of its angles during his advance.

(*...Shh! He told himself after the first creak emanated from the wood flooring...*) The vacant, dusky foyer at his back, he emerged through the kitchen's archway. The sun-drenched, white-furnished living room space was undisturbed ahead of his sock-feet creep. He glanced beyond and to the left of himself; nothing abnormal. He had seen through the second archway, situated off in the distance where the dining room appeared tucked behind a wall, and no one was visible. Chase crept with his knees half-bent, a crab-walk advance. His back to the walls. His glare unblinking. His firearm out in front, double-clutched. He listened for voices over his Mom's in his head, movements over his own in pursuit, or anything over his heart in his throat. Nothing.

No upstairs level to consider and downstairs—the basement—never mind. He had bathrooms to clear. He crossed the living room's threshold into the main hallway lined with bedroom and bathroom doors. With his back flattened against the opposite wall from those bedroom and bathroom doors amid his advance, he listened. The quiet was insufferable. The air too still. Nonetheless, Chase neared his childhood bedroom's door. Now Jake's bedroom. Its space appeared wide-open. A beam of sunlight from within it outmost gleamed like a spotlight upon the wood flooring in the hallway ahead of his sock feet. Backed against the wall, near the bathroom door frame, firearm forward, Chase peeked into Jake's bedroom: bed made, sunny curtained window, and nothing on the wood flooring. No Jake. Everything normal... clear. He whirled himself around, firearm out in front, and pointed it into the bathroom. Pristine and dusky. Poised to shoot anything that moved, but the yellow-colored shower curtain appeared already pushed back to reveal an empty claw-foot porcelain-white tub. Just a sink. No Jake... clear.

One room left at the end of the hall: Mom's bedroom.

Chase peeked past that bedroom's doorframe. (*...CREEEEAAAKKK!*) Chase thought Jake, if around, definitely heard that one. No Jake, however. Not a peep, but for Chase himself. His movements. He glanced up furtively at the bedroom's camera stationed ceilingward in the far corner over the bedroom windows curtained. A white terrycloth bath towel hung over its lens; the obstruction... with intent. Suddenly, Chase heard movement, however faint, and it wasn't caused by him. Chase's head pounded with blood and anger and adrenaline. He sweated heavily from his temples, down his back, and in his palms. He swallowed hard. It felt slick and slippery, the handle of his 9mm, as he worked his way around the foot of the unmade bed.

Creaky wood flooring told on him like a snitch along the way...

Chase reared up his firearm at eye level and forward toward his target's back... now in sight. Jake appeared seated upright on the wood flooring of the bedroom bathroom, fully clothed in blue jeans, a white collared polo shirt, and sneaker-feet. His legs appeared split wide apart. Something lay strewn between them, but what? His shaven-bald head craned down as if he were focused on something below on the floor or in his hands, but whatever it was, it appeared obscured from Chase's side of things amid his advance from behind Jake, which compelled Chase to say (...and presume correctly...), "Put it down. Leave those diaries alone."

Caught but unstirred and still reading one of them, Jake replied, "Damn wood floors, huh?"

"Stand up, Jake. The police are on their way. Seems as though you left something behind on the railing at Lookout Point... a black shoelace, perhaps?"

Jake's glance lifted from the diary cracked open in his hands, smiled devilishly (...*recalling the black sneaker lace and when he tied it to the railing a decade ago*...), and chirped, "It's not what you know, it's what you can prove, son."

"Face me," ordered Chase. Jake defied the order; instead, he returned his sights below toward the page in the diary he had stopped reading after he heard Chase's first steps into the bedroom. Jake told Chase, "Listen to what your mother wrote about me... Here, she said...

...We had just cooked up some pancakes together in the kitchen for the children. I pulled him away while they ate on the island seated on

barstools. I desired a quickie... I dragged him to our bedroom, and he couldn't get it up. It was my test, however, to see if he could perform after a month of no sex. I had planned this ambush of sorts... Since Chase was born, it has been 9 months and 12 days that Jake has not said he loved me; and, 7 years, because I knew he had spent the morning at the gym with Kevin... I could smell he had been with Kevin. That he savored Kevin so deeply that he refused to wash his body clean of him before making contact with me at home. Kevin's cologne lingered strongly, like a skunk that had preemptively sprayed me, knowing I'd come toward that which was his, albeit not mine... My husband is gay, and I never felt so entirely ineffective as a woman, as incomplete as a wife, or as impotent in my efforts to change him. ... Every time that I kiss him now, I am deprived of that which Kevin enjoys so richly... (*...sighing...*) She was a hell of a writer, your mom was. Wrote too much from the looks of this bathroom. It's a mess, huh? 16 of these things, huh?"

"Get up!" chirped Chase.

"Okay, but knowing that you've been waiting for this day. Training for it, so said my lawyer, Mr. Evans. You must have your gun pointed at me, (...rising to his laced sneaker-feet; joints crackling, having aged faster in prison...), and right now, (...he turns, standing in the bathroom, to face Chase standing in the bedroom...) WHOA!"

"Shut up! The police are on their way!"

Jake stared at Chase's 9mm Glock and said, "I never had one pointed at me before." He asked, "So what exactly are the police coming for? Reading your mother's diaries out of school?" He smiled; Chase didn't.

"Point."

"They are coming because you killed Mom, and you disposed of her pistol over Lookout Point."

"Do you, um, (*...cleared his throat dripping with sarcasm...*) know what corpus delecti is, son? Perhaps Rules of Evidence? Maybe, probable cause?"

"Stop talking."

"*Hmmm.* I'm a free man now, Chase," chirped Jake, adding, "We've been through this."

Chase charged forward with his 9mm Glock leading the way into the narrow confines of the pink-painted bathroom, and what stopped Chase's momentum was Jake's corrugated forehead. The point of the semi-automatic pistol pressed up against it, and Jake's blue-eyed attention yanked up toward it. Jake said, "Son, I thought you said that the police were coming? You're going to kill me, aren't you? The police aren't coming at all, and you are staring at me right now like you can taste it. VENGEANCE! I know the feeling. The thing is, son, you are not a killer. It's a little too real when what you want to shoot isn't a paper target at shooting ranges but an actual person in your home... your father in your home."

"You... shut up! Shut up, right now!"

"Put it down, son. You're not a killer."

"You're right; I'm not like you."

"Exactly, you're not like me. Nothing like me, right? You don't know what it is like to exist in a world that forces you to be what you are not. I wasn't an insurance salesman, but I had to do something so that I didn't look like your mother was my million-dollar meal ticket. I had to sell that image. I wasn't straight, but I had to conform to society's straight-laced demands of me to appear not as gay. I had to pretend to enjoy being inside my wife while thinking of my best friend to make you and Summer, or face jeopardy as a husband. These are feats of strength, not cowardice, because while your mother may have felt robbed, I too was robbed of what I am. We both lost. The Universe works! I was groomed to conceal my thoughts and feelings from others by a society who believed that their thoughts and feelings were a God-given right to denigrate mine. The Universe works! A book they deem holy but it's made up. A church they flock to in search of God, but God doesn't exist, yet that book and their church congregate and make a society of liars out of themselves; them shame me for being like them: being manipulative like them: hurting others like them.

"The Universe Works!" Jake raised his voice a couple of pitches and pressed his forehead harder against the point of Chase's pistol, yelling, "I'M MORE STRAIGHT THAN ALL OF THEM, BECAUSE I KNOW LIFE'S A CROOKED GAME WHILE THOSE FOOLS INDOCTRINATE OTHERS THAT THEY CAN BE SAVED FROM IT!"

"Jake?"

"What, Chase?"

"Who killed Mom?"

"Kevin."

Chase glumly gasped. It wasn't the answer he'd expected. He asked, "How did Kevin do it?"

"Threw her off Lookout Point. I believe he stabbed her first."

"Believe? You weren't there?"

"No."

"How do you know he stabbed her then?"

"I saw Memento Mori on the nightstand with what I believed to be her blood on it, and he didn't deny it."

"What's Memento Mori, some kind—"

Jake cut him off. "The name Kevin gave his dagger. Initially to be a gift to me. It's Latin. I can't remember what it means."

"Where's the dagger?"

"I don't know. Cops got it most likely. I left it there."

"So, at Lookout Point, those bodies—"

"Your mother and a woman named Shannoah Blakely."

"Who was Shannoah Blakely to you?"

"No one."

"Then why'd you kill her?"

"Because it was part of the deal. Kevin would kill your mother, which I didn't have the balls to do, and I'd kill Shannoah Blakely."

"Why did Kevin want Blakely dead?"

"Because he cheated on Daliah and got her pregnant."

"Why'd he want Mom dead?"

"Because he hated women who stood up to him, especially since I never did."

"Why'd you kill Kevin?"

"Like he'd say, *'If You Ain't Getting What You Should Get, You're Getting Got.'*"

"So, he didn't want you."

"*Shut up, son.* You don't know what you are saying."

Chase nodded, biting his lip, pleased he annoyed his father. He said, "You're such a fool."

Jake's eyes welled up with tears, though none fell. His lip quavered, yet no sniveling. Chase reared back the point of his pistol, and Jake stared at Chase in retreat with a blushed circle embedded at the center of his forehead. Chase kept the 9mm Glock trained on Jake and demanded, "Step out of the bathroom."

Jake obeyed his son.

"Stop there."

Jake obeyed again. The men faced off on Mom's side of the bedroom. They stood between the made queen-sized bed and the sunlit-glowing bedroom windows. Chase realized that he had more questions...

"Does Daliah know the truth like Mom did?"

"Not that I am aware of."

"Did you ever tell Summer the truth during those prison visits?"

"Of course not. I was trying to win in court, or maybe I'm a coward. I just couldn't tell Summer what I've told you now. I'm—"

"The only reason why you are telling me the truth, Jake, as you see it, is because you hate me. You are not coming clean in earnest. You seek to punish me with the truth you're telling me. And, no... you are not a coward."

"What?"

"You see, I've asked you these questions and received answers I don't believe. Some I do, but that's what your lying has done to this family and others. Made us wonder when or if you're lying; what or how you're thinking, as you conceal your thoughts and feelings that any other normal family gives up to its members without struggle. You not only murdered people, you also murdered trust. You are not some victim of this world, Jake. You will leave it, though, having made victims in it. With all of your opportunities, you still cheated. With your body built to take pain—given your past having received great amounts of it—you decided to give pain to others rather than relieve them of it. I'm not some dumb kid, Jake. I was never fooled by you. I knew precisely who you were the whole time. It's why I never called you Dad, because you aren't one.

The sick deal you conjured up with Kevin to rid

yourselves of vows exchanged, promises made, or things decided upon, you couldn't be more fearless."

"*Come again?*"

"You are not a coward because you were fearless, Jake... at ruining lives."

Chase placed his pointer finger inside the trigger guard for the first time. He appeared poised to pull the trigger from Jake's side of the pistol, and he waved frantically. Jake begged, "Wait, son! Wait! Listen to me—"

"It's time, Jake. The lies stop now. The Universe Works, right?"

"Listen, no! Listen!" cried Jake pitifully (*...no tears cadent...*). He stammered, "I'm just... I'm just..."

Here's the proofread and punctuated text:

"You're just, what? There's nothing more to say, and you've said too much."

Chase was ready to shoot.

Jake pleaded for his life. "Listen! Your mom was right. Your dad's a liar... but—"

"No, no!" interrupted Chase. "Mom WAS wrong. She was totally wrong. Neesha was right about you... You're *a snake!*"

Chase shot his father four times in the head and neck at point-blank range. He stepped over his dead body into the blood and salvaged his mother's 16 diaries from the bathroom floor. He would later load his Dodge Ram coupe with them, drive to the Student Lounge at the University of Vermont, text Neesha to come get the diaries, and give her a new set of instructions to follow. She obliged Chase but let him know that the police were looking for him. Chase said, "I know." After hugs, he left her seated with his mom's 16 diaries.

Killing his father wasn't the end of restoring The Montgomery family name; in fact, it was just the beginning...

Chase had a plan.

CHAPTER 33

MEET THE MONTGOMERY'S (REVISITED)

God-awful rains on I-89 leaving Burlington.

Had there been a Doppler Radar detection days earlier of a hurricane up the East Coast that downgraded into a tropical storm northbound, the unrelenting intensity of the rainstorm—its rolling thunder and low-roving black cumuli—would make sense. Such a torrential downpour this time of year over Vermont was as odd as having a two-procession funeral, each with only one vehicle, and a week apart. Darren accompanied Neesha, who wanted to pay her respects last week, and this week he was in tow with Summer and their daughter Sienna. Summer, too distraught to attend the planned funeral service last week, had steeled herself to enter the eye of the storm of her grief today. She had something to say, something to prove, and something to offer.

Rains be damned!

Trundles of meek thunder off in the distance, even the teeth of sleet aborning. A biting dip in temperature. The rainstorm, the downpour, a monsoon, a crackling hiss! Its swirling winds capable of crushing umbrellas instantly, whipping off clothes violently, drenching people, places, and things entirely. The city of Burlington, twenty minutes out, got swallowed quickly by the dense, herculean fog whose thick, rolling soup's advance appeared like the long reach of God, trying to grab their car from behind in the rear-view mirror to Darren. Visibility was low to none behind him and in front. I-89 was a rivulet.

"Slow down, honey," Summer said, her tone a pinch worried, and Darren responded kindly, "Of course, dear."

Never argue in the car on the way to a cemetery.

Sienna, strapped into her car seat in the back, was asleep; far too young to fear the dangers of driving through flooded roads, to experience the gravity of grief from death, or to appreciate family too few to call them *some.*

This drive had been the second tour to pay respects, as it had been done the first time. Summer's inconsolable anguish rendered her incapable of going to the funeral when it was originally scheduled last week. But for Aunt Gracey having taken the red-eye down from Fairbanks, there was no way the funeral, as originally scheduled, was going to be postponed or canceled just for Summer to get over herself. So last week, Darren led the remaining mourners, Aunt Gracey and Neesha, to the cemetery. Since then, Summer had found her strength. Darren, ever patient with her, loaded up the car—rainstorm be damned—and brought Sienna along in tow to do it all over again. This return visit to the cemetery was for Summer, who had something to say, something to prove, and something to offer.

Meanwhile...
Center Cemeteries
Burnham, VT
[1:45 p.m.]

The black iron gates' entrance fixed apart beckoned Darren down the cemetery's south end. A narrow, heavily forested, muddy service road cut through lush green lawns speckled with headstones of various faiths. The distance was long but pretty much a straight line of slick, treacherous, undulating road that his new tires found difficult to gain traction upon. Tires that either half-spun out or half-hydroplaned; subsequently, the car swerved out of control more times than he liked, despite having driven at or around 5 miles per hour. The windshield, wrinkled by rainwater, didn't help visibility. Still, Darren managed. He kept his eye on Sienna in the backseat—shifty glances through his interior rearview mirror—his little one who appeared unfazed and still dreaming; and from time to time, he extended his Dad-arm out to brace Summer from lunging toward the dashboard after he stepped on the brakes, even though she appeared securely strapped in. Holding onto her Mom's diary—Year 2013, the last in the series—over her lap. Again, Summer cautioned, "Just slow down some, honey."

Darren's patience nodded.

To die in a car wreck on a cemetery service road would be more than tragic but appropriate luck for a Montgomery family member, thought Summer. Darren squinted through his car's windshield plastered with rainwater, akin to being underneath and behind a waterfall's cascade, and whenever his windshield wiper blades side-swatted left-to-right and back in reverse, the rainfall scarcely thinned in its deluge. Nonetheless, he caught a glimpse of signage regarding their headstone's assigned row and lot. He made a left turn, pulled over, and turned off the car's ignition upon a grassy berm. Not where cars were allowed parking, but given the poor weather conditions, Darren hoped that the Center Cemetery officials wouldn't hold it against him; or, at least, they might look the other way while Summer paid her respects.

Darren faced her seated in the passenger seat. She appeared forward-focused. Her one-thousand-yard stare penetrated through the windshield of no visibility. The rainwater, the fog, a grey wall as solid as she looked deadpanned. Darren glanced down at Summer's hands crossed over her Mom's diary, likened to a woman bracing her Bible before church ceremonies. It felt like that, too—paying respects to the dead. Going to see one's mortality marked by a headstone seemed, for the surviving, a prediction of their future; daunting, this.

It had taken a minute or two for Summer to acknowledge her husband in the driver's seat—slowly coming back to Earth, as it were—but she had turned to Darren. She found his kind hazel eyes waiting for her recognition. She said, "I'm going."

"I know. No rush."

Her grin arrived late and bravely, but it failed to hold up. The tears in her eyes, not yet cadent, were meant for the dead, not Darren. He extended, "We should go with you. Let me unstrap Sienna. It will only be a second. I'll hold your umbrella while you—"

"No," interjected Summer. "Can't hold my umbrella and Sienna in all this rain. We'll all catch the flu. We don't all need to get soaked. Besides, I should've attended services last week. I should've escorted Aunt Gracey and Neesha. I shoulda—"

Darren's reach over the center console for her coat sleeve stopped her complaint, and he insisted, "Don't do that. No pity-parties, right? Aunt Gracey and Neesha both understood, even the two cops, Rivers and Gutiérrez, who paid their respects got why you couldn't make it. I got why you couldn't pick the headstones and arrange the wake and funeral and stuff, and I didn't mind a bit stepping in for it all. You must let others help sometimes. I told you that."

"I know," answered Summer meekly. She turned

from Darren to glance behind herself and through her fogged-up passenger-side window. Save for the dimpled puddles in the mud and grass aground, she noticed nothing yonder but fog, which alluded to rain in the mix of it. She whipped her gaze over her headrest and toward the backseat to check on Sienna. She told Darren quietly, "She's so peaceful. Look at her sleeping like that."

"Rainstorms do that to a lot of folks. I'm surprised we haven't heard her yet. She likes having full-on conversations while she sleeps."

The married couple smiled adoringly at their daughter: Darren over the steering wheel and through the rearview mirror, and Summer as she turned to face forward in her seat. She paused. She sighed. She remarked, "I'm stalling, aren't I?"

"I wasn't going to say that, love," replied Darren with a warm mirth to his smile. He pointed at Summer's wedding band and engagement ring on her finger and where her hands lay crossed over her lap atop her Mom's diary. He encouraged, "Together forever as family. That's what those rings promise our family, right?"

"Yes."

"You look ready to me, then."

Summer reached down toward the car floor mats on her side of things and snatched up her black umbrella. Darren detected what seemed to be tension, reservation, or fear—perhaps all three forms of worry—in his wife's countenance. Summer despised being patronized, so

Darren knew not to analyze her too much or speak on it. It was go-time! She had to do this alone. Armed with her umbrella against the storm and her Mom's diary against any loss for words, Summer tucked her Mom's diary beneath her black trench coat, popped open the passenger-side door without a glance back, and charged into the teeth of the storm and fog. She slammed the car door behind herself, and Darren watched her vanish in seconds amid the graves.

The rainstorm lashed at her, needling her face blush-red. She turned from this, wincing, drenched through. However, the diary had been held in safekeeping—well-tucked and dry underneath her black trench coat—while her other hand clutched the black umbrella. Its opened canopy quavered, embattled by the angry rainstorm. She gripped the curved handle tightly but held the umbrella's canopy more like a shield out in front of herself than overhead, weakened as the storm hit her from all sides. Thunder grumbled incessantly. The winds, though mild, were whipping. She trudged off-berm and through the muck, mud, and wet grasses in her black leather thigh-high high-heeled boots—couture and waterproof. Her blondish hairdo that had body and volume leaving the car was now flattened, soaked, and straight as straw against her face. Her lips formed a hard line against the torrential elements. Her chin dripped wet as she braved the storm. As she skulked about looking for signage and direction, the grey fog thinned by happenstance, and she noticed the lot she had sought. An alphabetized order of headstones that started with "M." She made the turn.

She glanced down furtively at the granite, marble, and limestone engraved headstones—each one ostensibly unique to the dead—and their names pulled her along: MAUPASSANT... MERWIN... MILLAY... MONK... MONTALE... MONTGOMERY.

She stopped. She glanced down. It was Mom.

While enthralled by her mortality cast in granite, an unlooked-for violent gale snatched Summer's umbrella from her grasp. It whipped her attention away from her mother's headstone as she watched the umbrella tumble into the dark open mouth of the rolling fog yonder. It vanished down the lot's alley of headstones. She turned back to her mother's headstone below. Her final resting place. A woman no longer lost but found. A woman no longer scattered among the talus of Lookout Point but sanctified at her gravesite. A small comfort amid the piercing grief.

Summer spoke clearly and lovingly, and at times as though a little girl again:

"Hi, Mom. Chase made certain that I got your diaries, but..." (crying, voice quavering) "...I wish you were here, Mommy. I miss you so much. I'm so mad." She seethed briefly, "You would've been a wonderful grandmother to Sienna. All the things you could've taught her, now robbed from her, I mourn daily. Mommy, I heard your Last Will & Testament. I'm not as eloquent as you were in that, but know that I will never know a woman braver or stronger than you. You sought to protect us. I can only hope to measure up with my daughter, with my own family now. I..." (*...sobbing..*) "...love you so much, Mommy. I'm so sorry that I was such an ungrateful brat growing up. I loved Daddy because he favored me, but I loved you because of the example you set. Being favored fades in time, especially in death, but that example you set as a sister to Aunt Gracey, as a mother to me and Chase, and as a fighter up until the end against their plans. I can only hope to measure up. I love you, *Mommy.* I'll be back with Sienna when she gets a little older..." Summer blew a kiss from her free hand.

She took a deep breath, poised to abandon her mother's headstone for another one—just two steps over to the right of herself. She glanced first before she made her way over, then glanced down at it: his white-marble headstone.

Summer worked her arms out of her trench coat sleeves but from within its buttoned-up contours. She unbuttoned her collar buttons first for gaps to peer through, then sought to hold her mother's diary behind the trench coat's lining and cracked open to the page she wanted to read to her father. Well-guarded from the inclement weather, which threatened to soak its thin pages and smudge the ink, she craned her gaze down into her trench coat. The overcast was grey, not black; dusky, not night, so she had some lightness amid the rainstorm. Summer harkened back to 2013 via this diary entry. It was Movie Night with their father, and Kiernan was home alone. Just before Kevin abducted her as Jake had planned, Summer read her mother's final words aloud...

...The eight reasons we lie: to save face, to spare feelings, to settle incoming threats, any promises unmet to offset, or to dull piercing regrets; to steal advantages from others, or to slander the truth and shore up the family... of other lies told.

Summer closed her mom's diary and tucked it away. It had gotten wet some, but not too badly. Mom's ink remained indelible. Summer shimmied her shoulders, slid her arms down into her trench coat sleeves again, all while clutching her mom's diary. She re-fastened her trench coat closed around her throat. She said, "Goodbye, Dad." Not with love, but as a parting comment in contempt.

Summer sensed herself suddenly discombobulated. She knew why. A hot ball of tension swelled in her chest, which made her empty stomach drop precipitously. The saddest dread. It was bitter but unavoidable. The funeral scheduled last week—the one Aunt Gracey, Neesha, and Darren attended—spoke of this dread to Summer. Thunder trundled overhead, mimicking the sound of a bowling ball's course down a bowling alley; though at the end of it, instead of ten pins crashing for a strike, bluish-white lightning flashed vertically across the overcast. The flickered brightness, though brief, didn't startle her; the next headstone over would...

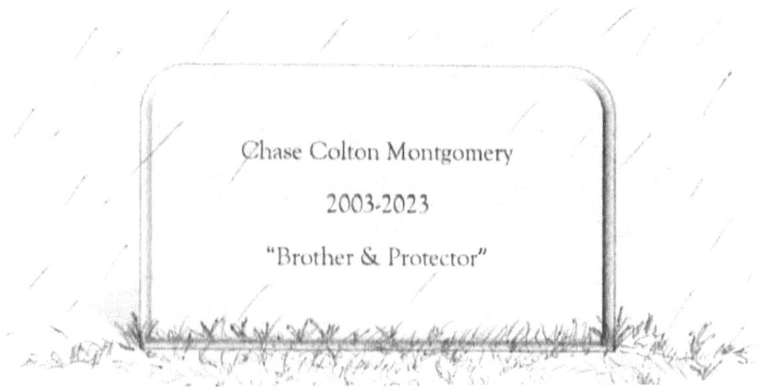

Summer lost it...

Without forethought, forbearance, or formality, she let loose a tirade: "WHY'D YOU DO IT?! YOU SON-OF-A-BITCH! I LOVED YOU THE MOST! -NOT HIM!- YOU!"

Summer collapsed to her knees in the mud, muck, and grass before Chase's headstone. Hyperventilating sobs and cadent tears in the rain, she howled with grief unleashed. She pounded the sodden earth as though Chase, six feet under, would hear her anguish, prove he had been her protector, and come back as her living brother. The fiercely funereal storm fomented the fantastical. He was family. The last Montgomery. Suddenly, she sensed her mom's diary slip from her grasp beneath her trench coat lining—threatening to touch the wet grass—and that was what brought her back with composure. The strength her mother had taught her to possess at all times; unique only to women; never in men. To do this right, not ugly; to meet this moment, not be defeated by it. Be the big sister for her little brother who killed himself... his plan.

Summer rose from the muck in the cold rains. She lowered her gaze upon Chase's headstone and spoke to him as though he had taken a seat with his back against his headstone... and listened. She imagined him that way and said, "I learned after you hung up on me that the police had found Mom's gun at Lookout Point, and you went to the cops to tell them all that you knew. Forever the protector. You always knew it was him. Um, I, um... (*...sobbing...*) learned that you've donated your inheritance to the University's Children's Hospital for Cancer Research and Treatment in Burlington and a homeless shelter for abused LGBTQ teens and minors out there in Provincetown. (*...shaking her head...*) Just imagine all else you could've done for others if not on the lam; if not for... (*...pausing to prevent from screaming...*) I can't do this! I can't do this! To, um, match your generosity, as you knew I would, I contacted Aunt Gracey and we decided to donate the Montgomery Townhome to the kids you donated to, so those kids can find refuge too, right here in Vermont. Fuck the Homeowner's Association, right? (*...sniffles...*) I learned after you got Mom's diaries out safe from under Dad, you contacted Neesha (*...lips quavering, cadent tears...*) for the last time, and then you... um... went to Lookout Point that night in your car and did it." she whined plaintively, "Why didn't you call me? You knew I would talk you out of it! We were supposed to do this together; the depression, the anxiety you felt. The PTSD.

Together, we promised since we were kids; not alone. Never would we go off alone. You went off alone! Goddamn it, Chase! I promised to make you and Dad whole again; make forgiveness for both of you from each of you, and you deprived me of the challenge, Chase! *Why?*"

Summer swiped her face streaked with tears, rain, and leaves of grass, then admitted to Chase, "I'm pregnant... *I can't do this...* I just can't."

She bolted through streams of rain, running in black thigh-high high-heeled leather boots. One hand clutched her mom's diary underneath her soaked black trench coat and through the silken pocket lining, and the other hand flailed out to her side like a propeller just before flight. Running through murky shallow puddles and sodden lawns that splashed, she made it out into the clear; away from macabre headstones and the ghosts standing at attention between them, and reached the service road. My family, she thought.

I have to get back to my family...

Finally, she came running toward the side of their parked car, teetering upon the upturned lip of the grassy berm. The rain was unceasing. She pounded upon the passenger-side window pleadingly to get inside. Winds whirled and whistled. Darren, Johnny-on-the-spot, lunged over the middle console and unlocked the car door for Summer. Rolling groans of thunder, wind, and rain let in. Sienna stirred awake and started crying. Summer darted inside, shut the car door behind herself, and threw herself over the middle console into the waiting embrace of Darren. Her loving husband consoled her as she sobbed with incoherent utterances in despair. Curled into him, Sienna's crying outburst from the backseat rivaled Summer's sobs up front. Sienna kicked the backseat with her tiny brown-leather penny loafers, her arms outstretched for affection while held back, strapped into her car seat. Darren whispered into Summer's right ear, "Come on now, Mommy. You're scaring her. Get it together."

Summer agreed.

She reluctantly tore herself from Darren's supportive embrace, put on a false face after a quick swipe of her tears, then turned and peered over the headrest toward the backseat to check on her distressed daughter. Mom told daughter, "Everything's okay, sweetie! Mommy's better now."

A half-measure as far as condolences go. Sienna's caterwaul was not convinced.

Summer wedged herself between the driver's seat and the passenger seat, maneuvering over the middle console. From the front seat toward the back seat; from the embraces of the daughter to the assurances whispered by the mother; from their tears all dried to their giggles, and from Darren's steering-wheel perspective, which he peeped through the interior rearview mirror, having seen reflected a mother and daughter who had morphed into each other's nostrum.

Darren started the car for home.

Where, in time, grief had diminished in the rearview mirror of life, as they sped away toward a future that would reveal an ultrasound snapshot of Sienna's sibling but a flickering heartbeat in utero: where, in time, the all-but-dead Montgomery surname received new life after Summer and Darren decided to hyphenate it, attribute it to Sienna, themselves, and the baby on the way—the Montgomery-Kordas—who, in all, personified forgiveness without flashbacks: where, in time, Summer's water broke after nine months but a blur, and contractions led to labor pangs only seconds apart: where, in time, Summer, on her back, legs parted, had to strain and push until Darren and the nurses and an obstetrician on the other end of things yelled, "IT'S A BOY!"

Darren's crying newborn son, greased to a high sheen by afterbirth, wrapped in a hospital-branded white terrycloth swaddling, was handed over to Summer, who was lying on the gurney, hiked up. Surrounded by blinking machines and smiley medical staff fawning over her, suddenly, Lil' Sienna—the Big Sis' now—was led in by Grand-Aunt Gracey with pink and blue balloons in hand (not knowing beforehand the baby's gender) and emerged from behind the triage curtain to have a look-see. They all watched as Summer cradled her newborn son up close to her flushed face. Quiet now, the newborn son expressed only a few coos and wiggled a bit. Darren, seated closest to Mother and son at the gurney, awaited the announcement of his newborn son's name, which he had no say in but appeared unfazed by that fact. His grace, his crown. The newborn son glanced up without focus toward his mother, who had gotten lost in his clouded Blue Jay-blue eyes. Her promise that Jake and Chase Montgomery would, one day, come together as one. She had sworn to such a yoke, and this was her Promises Kept moment.

Darren and Summer's newborn son, born 8 pounds and 7 ounces, had been given the surname Montgomery-Korda, legally, but most importantly, he was named...

...Jace.

The End

Coming soon... (*if saved from myself*)

Endling(s)

Part I: I AM NEWMAN

A Two-Part Novel/Science Fiction Series

PRELUDE

THE YEAR WAS 2034

In Barrington, Labrador, Canada, the Wynnhurst Provincial University Provost gushed over a young, ambitious American scientist who had never taught at any level in America or Canada but sought to fill a professor vacancy in their College of Sciences and Humanities. Dr. Liam Newman came with an impressive resume—highly acclaimed. He was the youngest Nobel Peace Prize winner in the field of Genetic Splicing and Biotechnology. He had worked with world-renowned Japanese scientists, namely Dr. Xia Hyoshi at Osaka University and Dr. Jinjoa Situ at Kyoto University, on advanced reproductive and synthetic genetic technologies. These close professional affiliations and successes swayed the university's Provincial Board of Governors and Trustees to take a chance on Dr. Newman. They offered him immediate tenure as a newly hired professor at the College of Sciences and Humanities, the liberty to create his own curricula for juniors, seniors, and post-graduate studies, and to lecture his own science course. Without further ado, the new core-elective course called Biotechnologies and Genetics [306] was available to students, and within one hour, the course was filled for the Fall Semester with a waiting list for the summer and beyond. Never before had a student body's collective interest been so excitedly heightened over science generally, nor had a science course—though innocuously named but with a controversial lesson plan —been offered at any other Canadian university or college, nor south of the border in the United States. And that attracted wild publicity.

Protesters all week, leading up to the first day of Fall Semester classes, swelled around the regal ivy-covered greystone frontispiece and entranceway colonnade of Harold's Hall. A sunny but cold, crisp Fall morning was electrified by vitriolic voices and incendiary picket signs in the hundreds; frothing at the mouth outside, they shouted: "Playing God! Designer Baby, Say No, Not Maybe! JOHN 3:16! Fire Professor Newman... He's Anti-Human! Go Back To Japan, American! You Are Not Canadian! BURN IN HELL Mad Scientist! Hitler's Re-Gifter! Hey-hey! Oh, No! IVG has Got To Go!" A sample of the chants, contempt, and current zeitgeist.

Meanwhile, upstairs inside Harold's Hall, specifically on the third floor, in the corner classroom Room C-105,

Dr. Newman walked in through an oakwood side door, plopped down his leather satchel upon the granite-top island, and upturned his gaze to the left, facing a classroom with stadium seating at a 120° elevated angle, accommodating three hundred and fifty-two students. He couldn't see as far as the back row, but the two men, stone-faced in black suits, who donned black ties and IBF earpieces tucked in their left ears, attempted to blend in. Students seated in close proximity saw the men as standouts—clearly non-students.

The windowless milieu was tartly fragrant with colognes and perfumes, which clashed and commingled with palpable tension. Dr. Newman sensed his heart's pace more in his throat than in his chest, but he put on a face of confidence to mask the fact that he lacked it. His first words publicly and since he was hired were a question: "Class? What does IVG abbreviate?"

Silence.

"I'm new too. First day of class jitters. No need to be afraid. Anyone just raise your hand, even if you think your answer isn't right, or if you are way up there in the back, we'll get through it together. What's IVG?"

In the third row, middle deck, fourth oakwood desk inward from the aisle of stairs, a female junior, cross-legged in blue jeans and a Wynnhurst-monikered sweatshirt, stopped gnawing on her pen top briefly as she raised her hand. It snagged the professor's attention, and he replied, "Yes, brave soul?"

Smatterings of laughter erupted.

The female junior answered, "In vitro genetics?"

"Not quite, but you are on the right track." He turned from her attention and toward the broad face of the class and announced, "IVG abbreviates the term In vitro Gametes. IVG is a process whereby scientists turn ordinary skin cells into artificial embryos for the purpose of reproducing human life. We can manipulate these artificial embryos to our whims. IVG can help anyone make babies. That means anyone: male or female, gay or straight, trans or infertile, married or not. IVG is not only formidable but the future as now. Why have a baby the traditional way when results may vary? Make a baby the sciential way for results by design."

From the back of the class, someone blurted, "SO YOU ARE PLAYING GOD!"

Boos and hisses filled the air. Attention and heads turned toward the back of the class to spot the disrupter, who remained undetected. Despite the professor's saccadic flash-read of as many students' countenances as he could for any tells, he failed to pinpoint him. Nevertheless, all eyes were laid upon him at the well of the classroom.

What to do next?

Lecture, he told himself. Unfrozen and suddenly with a sense of being overheated, he removed his earth-tone-colored tweed blazer. He swiped the top of his shaven bald head in frustration—mostly from the beads of sweat that had formed—and made his way around the black granite-top island to get up close and personal with his class, if only to assert some dominance over the active listening front row of students who awaited him to say something, anything. His muscular physique of average height appeared tightly gripped by his white-collared shirt, which was overlapped by his silky red wine-colored vest buttoned up. He slid his hands down into the steep pockets of his baggy olive-colored corduroy trousers and rocked back and forth on the balls of his feet, shod in brown leather loafers.

He took a moment to find his words; any further search for the one student who had publicly challenged him seemed futile. He sensed, in varying degrees, that they all—outside protesters and students in his class alike—believed what the disrupter had blurted. So, he decided to address all of his students seated before him as if they were the disrupter in hiding and rebutted, "I'm not playing God. I'm playing it safe!" He added, "Last year alone, according to a University of Alberta survey, 10% of new mothers died during childbirth in Canada, and that percentage appeared doubled south of the border in the U.S. Triple the percentage if the American was Latino or Asian. Quadruple that percentage if the American was Black. This same survey found that Canadian children born with Down Syndrome, Cerebral Palsy, and any of the common but terminal pediatric cancers jumped by 15% in each category, and in the

U.S., it was higher at 23% in each category. The one bright spot for Canadians was in the category of stillborn births. Down by 5%, but in the U.S., it ticked up to 23% for new mothers. Post-partum depression-related infanticides, though rare in First World nations, ticked up by 7% last year. Why all the statistics in a science class? Because scientists not only rely on them but see them as equations to solve for the betterment of society in the future. The future, as long as Earth spins upon its axis, will come to fruition, whether you accept it or shrink from it. You must meet the future..."

"*Heck!* Our hidden protester in class today—I predicted him in my future. I was eating breakfast with my wife this morning, watching the news and all the press on campus involving the first day of classes this Fall... This Fall class in particular, and I told my wife I expected to be attacked in some way, physically or verbally, in class. And I was right! I predicted the future, but I did it unafraid. I didn't shirk from it. I accepted it. I have accepted being a professor here at Wynnhurst, and there will be students or people generally who are afraid of change, the unknown, or their tomorrow. Ironically, you have been told all of your lives that no one is promised tomorrow, yet when science teaches you that tomorrow is guaranteed, it is met with your fears instead of your gratitude..."

"Your brain is a tool to be utilized for your survival, not just a sponge for your memories, religious beliefs, and headaches. Science is about using your brain for the future, so your next outburst should be," he shouted, "WHAT IS THE FUTURE?"

He smiled, waiting for such an outburst, but his class —a collective grimace—listened intently for his description of the future. He obliged them. "The future is this: you never want to suffer from the common cold or the flu again, nor succumb to diabetes, cancer, Alzheimer's, or dementia. What if we created an individual immune to sickness of all kinds? You reject the concept of gender identity: what if we created an individual who was neither male nor female but both male and female? An individual who procreated interchangeably like a man or woman and naturally? You wish to venture light-years away from Earth, but interstellar space exploration under no uncertain terms promises a death sentence for space crews: what if we created an individual who could endure weightlessness with agelessness and without mental or physical decline? You aspire to win the wars of the future, which portend nuclear holocaust for sport: what if mutually-assured destruction, which will reduce us all to Endlings, could be deemed a victory rather than a defeat? That is to say, what if we created an individual born with lungs and gills, and the two organs worked in concert to breathe oxygen and radiation from nuclear fallout? What if we classified such an individual, clearly evolved, as a *polysapien*; first in that person's name? Imagine it. That *polysapien—the Last Man Standing*, as it were, post-World War III—wouldn't you want that individual to be an

American or Canadian as opposed to Russian, Chinese, North Korean, or Iranian? Of course not, if you are indeed Russian, Chinese, North Korean, or Iranian!"

He won boisterous laughter from most of the class, then a hand appeared raised from the second row, aisle seat. Sandwiched between two female students, a male student with longish red hair, wearing a dingy white T-shirt with an emerald green image of a large marijuana leaf across his chest, lowered his hand after Dr. Newman nodded at him, seeking to know his question. The male student asked, "What are Endlings? You said something like 'reduce us to our Endlings.' What is that?"

"I ordinarily don't answer a question with a question, but what is your last name?"

"Hodge, sir."

"Do you have brothers or sisters?"

"No, sir."

"Are your parents still alive?"

"Yes, sir."

"Let's say that your parents were lost in a nuclear war, but you survived somewhere in a government-controlled bunker that sheltered you from nuclear fallout. You, being the sole survivor of the Hodges, your namesake, would be considered an Endling. The end of your family line."

The student nodded, poised to pick up his pen and write down that definition, but Dr. Newman added, "That won't be on a test. I'm just showing off my vocabulary."

Some chortled.

"But I got sidetracked." Dr. Newman's forehead furrowed slightly as he recalled his closing to the lecture and continued, "Point of fact: polysapiens are the future! Put aside your God complexes and fears propped up by moralization on God's behalf. You owe Him nothing, remember? He sacrificed His only begotten Son to save your soul, but you owe yourself a passing grade in my class, and the only way you're going to get that is to perform your labs. Yes, there will be labs, and they will involve cadavers, fetal tissue, and aquatic animals in some cases. It's all in the pursuit of knowledge, as we will be learning together. Secondly, you cannot get a passing grade if you don't buy my book, which happens to be the assigned text for the course... now grab your pens."

The class of students, in all, motioned for something by which to write whatever he cited.

"The text is titled *Genetic Splicing and Advancements in IVG Technology*, written by me and Dr. Situ. The cost of the text will set you back 235 GF's. You can find it in stock at the campus bookstore. I checked before I came in to see if the shipment of 500 books arrived for as many students as I see here in class today, so I don't want to hear that you don't have the text for this course. This won't be an easy A or B or C for that matter; you will have to study hard. With that said, I'll see you all next Thursday!"

The class surged up from their desks and applauded Dr. Newman. He nodded, half-embarrassed and half-proud. Not a bad first day of school... *or so he thought.* As the students ascended up three rows of stairs to reach the landing at the back of the classroom, all but two pushed through the pair of wooden doors. The two men in black suits, who donned black ties with earpieces in their ears, rose from their desks and walked in the opposite direction from the rest, who filed out of the room. They headed toward the professor at the well of the classroom. He hadn't glanced up yet. By the time Dr. Newman raised his head to put on his blazer, the two men in black suits stood in front of the granite-top island, expressionless.

Dr. Newman adjusted his lapels and asked, "May I help you, gentlemen? Are you students?"

"No," answered the man to the right of his partner.

"Okay? What did you need?"

"For you to stop talking," answered the man to the left of his partner.

Dr. Newman's stomach knotted up. Quizzically, he asked, "Excuse me? Who are you two? What are you doing here exactly? Because neither of you look like students, act like protestors, sound like university administrators, or dress like Labrador Mounties..."

"We're NSA," replied the man to the right of his partner, now that it had become clear to Dr. Newman that he was in the presence of American agents. Sly, the agent to the left of his partner reached for Dr. Newman's satchel, which lay on its side, unzipped, upon the island countertop between them. However, the professor's quick reflexes snatched it up by the shoulder strap. He clutched his satchel close to his chest under his arms crosswise and warned, "No! You cannot see my things. You are way too far north. Out of your jurisdiction, and in no way do you have a warrant. I can't believe this!"

"Not only is he a professor but a lawyer too... interesting," quipped the agent to the right of his partner, who then gave him The Nod. The agent to the left of his partner cut in front of him and moseyed around the island—two car lengths long—whistling. His ominous trek was slow, yet it captured Dr. Newman's full attention. He swallowed hard. His gaze flitted between the two agents: the one who stood stone-faced opposite the professor on the other side of the island, and the agent closing in now behind the island, who extracted clear plastic zip-ties from his trousers' right pocket.

Dr. Newman pleaded, "Don't do this! I will not be your next Dr. Manhattan. I am a scientist, not a warmonger. I told your Director back in March that I can't do it... that I won't finish it."

"It's called the Newman Project... Who else CAN finish it, Liam?" asked the agent who stood across from the professor.

"Find someone else. I left the intel. All of it."

"No," interjected the agent behind the island, now face-to-face with Dr. Newman. "Like you said in your lecture: 'You Must Face The Future...' Or am I paraphrasing here?"

Suddenly, the agent behind the island grabbed the

professor's left wrist, pierced the professor's pressure points with his thumbs, yanked upward his left arm, and contorted it in a way that human arms don't bend. The professor winced and hissed in agony as the agent turned him and slammed his face into the white grease board, which rendered him discombobulated, giving the agent enough seconds to slide on the zip-ties with little resistance. Pinned against the white grease board, unable to wriggle free with the agent's forearm as firm as a crossbar down on his neck, the professor turned his head to the right and spooked himself. A foot away, the other agent stood with a silvery metal case in his hand. Poised to open what appeared to be the length and width of a flask, but it wasn't that. The agent cracked it open, revealing two syringes embedded in black foam compartments. One syringe had a robin egg-blue colored solution in its vial, and the other syringe was half-filled with a water-clear solution. The agent plucked out the first syringe, set the silvery case down upon the island countertop, and reared up the syringe. The professor, spooked, whipped his head from right to left against the grease board and begged, "No! Wait! Don't!"

The agent injected the point of the needle through the professor's tweed blazer's sleeve, near-shoulder high, until he sensed he had pierced skin. Holding onto the syringe like a hilt, the agent's thumb pushed down on the plunger. The solution drained away within the clear plastic vial while the professor wriggled to no avail, pinned in place. He sensed a snaking chill travel down his left arm, reaching his fingertips. He tasted a flat cola soda flavor on his tongue, then disorientation rocked him before he fell unconscious. The agent extracted the needle at the same time that his partner caught the professor as his knees buckled. The agent returned the emptied syringe to its black foam bedding, shut the silvery case until he heard it click, and slipped the case down his blazer's inseam pocket. Meanwhile, the agent's partner had laid the unconscious professor down on the classroom floor, on his back, behind the island. Off to the side where the professor's brown leather satchel had fallen amid the struggle, the agent picked it up and placed it atop the professor's chest. The satchel's shoulder strap, the agent wrapped around the professor's neck twice over—in anticipation of moving him to that planned second location—so that if the satchel slid from his body, it would not fall to the ground but simply dangle from his neck.

At the halfway point in the mission, the agents split up as a team: one was tasked with securing the classroom and transportation, and the other had to finish processing the subject for departure, which required the NSA's latest invention in his possession. That agent, with a specialized pocket sewn into the back of his black blazer's tails, reached behind himself and pulled it out. It was an air-sealed, compressed plastic package the size of a laptop. Inside was the Black-Ops invention called the INVISO-tarp. Worth south of 7 GB's (Gold Bars), the agent carefully ripped the package open with his teeth and hands. The invention appeared translucent and was made of polyurethane plastic. Rigid as a new shower curtain liner, it could have been mistaken for one if not for its attachment: a clear plastic cord. No longer or wider than a man's belt, its plug lay atop Dr. Newman's forehead incidentally. The agent stuffed the plastic packaging down his secret pocket behind his black blazer's tails (*there shan't be any remnants of evidence left at the scene*). He flicked up the INVISO-tarp twice, which expanded its width mid-air and landed over the professor's body, like a floating bed sheet. Head-to-toe, the professor lay completely covered with slack at both ends on the floor.

The agent who had inoculated the professor had long since fled from the island. While gone, he darted up the classroom's center aisle of ascending stairs. Seven decks lined by rows of wooden desks in the hundreds in his wake. He reached the landing of the classroom's catwalk. A catwalk without a railing, where the entrance of Classroom C-105 appeared unlocked. Its pair of pinewood doors had metal crossbars to push, not knobs to turn. A foot away from the left side double door entrance, a flagpole stood with a deflated Canadian flag wrapped around it. The agent snatched it up. He rammed the flagpole's length through and over the metal crossbars, and it stayed in place; most importantly, it fused the double doors together, which would prevent anyone on the other side from entering while they continued their mission. The classroom now secured, the agent had to check for transportation.

Their getaway car.

While the agent sauntered down the center aisle of stairs to rejoin his partner behind the island waiting patiently, he tapped his IBF earpiece, raised his right hand limply toward eye-level, and spoke into his black acrylic wristband fastened on his left wrist. He asked, "Central Command... Room is secure... Our ride? Over..."

A female voice, Central Command NSA Operative (*a would-be stunning revelation to Dr. Newman, because it was his wife*), responded, "By sky. The EFV (*Electric Flying Vehicle*) sedan has been sent remotely and is parked on the rooftop. Is the satchel and the subject in custody? All fully processed? Over..."

"Yes, we have the satchel and subject in custody. He's under the tarp, not yet processed. Over..."

"You've got 10 minutes before classes let out. *Over and out...*"

The agent lowered his hand. He looked at his partner, whose IBF earpiece was on the same frequency, and said, "You heard her. Let's move."

"You've got the cell phone, sir. It's your turn. Here..." replied the agent who had initially covered the professor under the INVISO-tarp. He bent down to retrieve the plug-end of the clear plastic cord and extended it over the professor's body so his partner could take it, but his partner wasn't ready for it yet. He had just pulled out the military-grade cell phone from his black blazer's side pocket and activated it. He swiped it once to reveal an on-screen myriad of NSA top-secret apps. He tapped the one marked INVISO-1. The app opened with a blinking prompt that sought the agent's security clearance code. He entered his 9-digit number, then pressed SEND. He took the plug-end of the INVISO-tarp's clear plastic cord from his partner and plugged it into the port on the left side of his military-grade cell phone. Automatically, the INVISO-tarp came to life. Its polyurethane texture crinkled, then stiffened as flat as a board for about six seconds. Gradually, the INVISO-tarp distended around Dr. Newman as though it had melted and formed a cast. The INVISO-tarp's surface lit up like a TV screen turned on, but without a broadcast signal. Nothing but snow distortion animated the INVISO-tarp until the agent's military-grade cell phone uploaded all of the INVISO-tarp's sensory data absorbed from the subject it cloaked. Snow faded into colors; first, all blue morphed into all red; then, its blinkered final stage appeared all green. The agent's military-grade cell phone screen revealed one word: PROCESSING...

The agents backed away from Dr. Newman under the INVISO-tarp, not afraid of it but cautious of the unexpected. Though they trained extensively together on the INVISO-tarp's proper use, it was performed on a simulator at a base where mistakes were expected, not applied during a mission where mistakes could take your life; moreover, the mission's abort-time was fast approaching. They worried. Finally, the agent's military-grade cell phone screen diffused all anxiety when he read: CONNECTED...

The INVISO-tarp stopped transmitting primary colors and did what it was supposed to do: it vanished. And so had Dr. Newman. Below, nothing but the classroom's tile floor appeared between the two agents, who stared downwards, awestricken. It worked. The professor, however, wasn't physically gone. He still lay there on his back, unconscious, with his brown leather satchel perched on his chest; they just couldn't see that. The INVISO-tarp—American-made!—when activated, made anything underneath it appear invisible. Up close, a foot or less away, there was a tell that something was there on the floor, about six feet long and two feet high between the agents, but the space appeared like a hot summer day's air rising from cooked black asphalt; it crinkled. Nonetheless, the professor couldn't be seen near or far.

"Cool!" remarked the agent who re-approached the professor where his head should've been. His partner detached the INVISO-tarp's cord (now invisible) and let it drop toward the tile floor. Upon impact, he heard a faint scraping sound, so it was still there. The agent pocketed his military-grade cell phone and said, "This thing only keeps him this way for an hour. We've got about two minutes to get out of this building. We gotta move!"

"Yes, sir," muttered his partner.

They moved swiftly. Hooked at the armpits and raised at the ankles, Dr. Newman's body was lifted by the agents. Immediately, their attention turned to themselves rather than the way out or toward the subject or the risky mission, because the INVISO-tarp, as high up as toward the crooks of their arms in the blazer's sleeves under the INVISO-tarp, reflected the classroom's tile floor below. Not their physical person. Just by reaching under the INVISO-tarp to move the professor from behind the island—20 yards—toward the pinewood side door, they vanished, in part, too.

Stunning technology.

The agent who led the way, walking backward carrying the professor topmost, set him down gently because he had to check the hallway on the other side. To become spotted hunched over as though they carried something that was six feet long, but that something having been see-through like air, could've painted them publicly as pantomimes performing a skit for no audience in particular or like weirdos in black suits who lost half of their arms from their elbows down; either-or promised to attract a crowd—a sight to behold—if that hallway appeared peopled.

The agent pushed in the crossbar to the side door, opened it slowly, and craned his sights beyond its pinewood frame. Both directions, left and right, and second glance; no one. This signaled that the first day of classes was still in session on the third floor. Good, he thought. A red-illumined EXIT SIGN ceilingward down the hall to his left indicated their escape route. Underneath that signage, per Pre-Op run-throughs of Harold's Hall a month prior, confirmed that it was the floor's main staircase which led to the rooftop. The agent ducked his head back inside. With his foot holding the side door ajar, he turned to glance behind himself at his partner hunched over and wide-eyed. He warned, "It's all clear."

Still holding the invisible Dr. Newman by his ankles, his partner nodded.

They lifted Dr. Newman and made their way out of the classroom in a hurry. Sixty-four yards to the main staircase door. A vacant hall with waxed floors at high sheen. Their running steps, rubber-soled, squeaked. Some classroom and faculty office doors appeared open as they fled past them, but no stoppage or questions or dropping of the professor. The EXIT SIGN overhead. The agent in the lead, who backed into the main staircase door, pushed through its metal crossbar, and they rushed inside with the professor clumsily. They had no struggles with carrying him up until this point because the professor proved awfully heavy halfway up four flights of stairs. The agents panted. Thin threads of sweat trickled down their temples. Meanwhile, relief was in sight. Up one more flight, the last landing neared. Its focal point was a steel door with a wide yellow and black painted crossbar. Above it, at eye level, the steel door warned: EMERGENCY EXIT! DO NOT ENTER!

It was the rooftop entrance.

At this juncture, situational awareness screamed tricky. NSA field operatives' Pre-Op couldn't find nor gain access to Harold's Hall fire alarm system. The steel door's crossbar was rigged to go off; one push threatened to trigger the fire alarm siren. Of course, it would stir the morning slumber of Harold's Hall on all floors and attract attention to the agents' exit strategy. Already running past the time allotted to complete the mission, but no voice in their IBF earpieces on how to proceed given this obstacle, the agent that led the carry of Dr. Newman backed into that yellow and black painted crossbar. The steel door popped open. Autumn was cold; excessively sunny. White-blinding. The agents winced, not at the sun in their eyes, but the fire alarm in their ears. Too goddamn loud, they thought. Relentless! From staircase wood flooring to a gravelly rooftop, they stepped. A red Stalantis EFV sedan, as promised, appeared out in front of them. Centered on its tire-tread skis, it popped unlocked automatically. They hurried toward its passenger-side backseat door. The agent who led, backward-stepping with Dr. Newman in tow, reached behind himself for the car door handle and pulled. The car door opened. He climbed inside without losing his grip on Dr. Newman. His partner pushed forward and yelled, "The alarm shut off! Hurry! People must be coming!"

The agents only had seconds, not minutes, before they were sighted.

The agent at the professor's leg end pushed, as the

agent who hovered at the professor's head end pulled. The agent who pulled reached behind himself, turning the interior car door handle. It popped open, freeing him to get out on the other side of the EFV, and he avoided being sandwiched. He shut the car door afterward and fled to the driver's seat. Due to steadfast invisibility and hurry, the professor did not appear to the agents situated on his side, but he was indeed visible, which resulted in his satchel sliding from his midsection, though it stopped short of reaching the floor mats. However, it dangled beyond the seam length of the INVISO-tarp. Clear-sighted. Beyond the field of invisibility. Because the satchel was unzipped, files began to slip out of its opening—files marked CLASSIFIED. The agent at the professor's leg end, situated halfway in and halfway out of the EFV, scooped up and gathered the remaining classified files.

"Oh, shit!" he exclaimed after inspecting their clarion markings.

"Hurry!" yelled the agent driving. "Get in!"

His partner obeyed. He rushed to shut the backseat car door but noticed, to the right of himself—some 30 feet or less away—frightened folks huddled by the rooftop's emergency exit door. They stared back at the agent, confused by his presence on the roof with an EFV and fully aware he had to be the culprit who set off Harold's Hall fire alarm. The agent hurried to get into the front seat. He swept his legs indoors, then shut the passenger-side door behind himself. He turned to his partner in the driver's seat and yelled, "GET US OUT OF HERE!"

The agent driving had long since plugged in his military-grade cell phone into the EFV's center console computer and ignited it for flight. An app activated the EFV's steering wheel, gear shift, and pedals floorward, causing them to eject from behind their quick-opening compartments. The steering wheel, gear shift, and pedals adjusted their positions to the drive's height and leg lengths using heat-sensory technology embedded in the black leather driver's seat. Automatically, the driver's side sun visor slid down in front of the agent's face, and a horizontal line of quantum dots—invisible to the naked eye—inlaid within the sun visor's leather coating emitted a faint red laser beam as thin as thread that scanned the green eyes of the agent driving. The technology functioned as eye-scanners, reading the thoughts of the driver. The agent driver's thoughts ordered the EFV to spark its three jet propulsion silos situated at the undercarriage. Short bursts of fire shot from below, lifting the EFV about a foot or less from the gravelly rooftop surface, spraying rock and debris in every direction, which the students and faculty shielded their eyes from in the meantime. At the preparatory lift-off stage—hovering mode—the center console computer awaited coordinates to be given. The agent driver's thoughts ordered the EFV to raise its landing gear. His thoughts directed the EFV's navigational system to their desired destination: *Washington D.C., The Pentagon's rooftop heliport.*

The computer's delayed processing took a few excruciating seconds to clear, which felt like minutes given the crowd forming on the roof. A quick glance in the rearview mirror revealed a problem while hovering. To his count, the nine students and faculty members, some who neared their vehicle below, had one of them handling a cell phone with its camera trained on them, recording.

"Look!" he told his partner. "That red-headed kid in the marijuana leaf t-shirt—wasn't he in Newman's class earlier?"

His partner tore his attention from those classified files spread open on his lap. He glanced up through his fogged-up passenger-side window and muttered, "Yes, he was there. The curious fuck!" He added, "PUNCH IT!"

The computer cleared them for flight.

The agent driving adjusted the EFV's gear shift into VERTICAL. He released the clutch and stomped on the gas pedal. From 0 to 134 miles per hour, the EFV shot up toward the sunny blue skies over Wynnhurst. The red-headed student's sights (*...and camera shot...*) were yanked up at a 90° angle, filming only the EFV's undercarriage spitting blue fire without exhaust until all sight of them was lost. Between the bald, glaring sunlight and a myriad of other EFVs overhead buzzing distantly like a cloud of gnats stratospherically, it seemed futile to keep recording.

The red-headed student shut down his cell phone, but he rejoined the others on the rooftop, and they questioned how an EFV acquired campus clearance to park atop Harold's Hall. Ignorance being more than bliss but plausible deniability on matters of national security, a fleeing red-colored EFV sedan was all anybody saw and later reported—not the abduction of a firebrand geneticist who never lectured a class at Wynnhurst again. To the student body, Dr. Newman simply disappeared.

Therefore, the mission was a success.

Inside the agents' EFV, just five minutes from leaving Canadian airspace, an intriguing conversation between spies commenced:

"Why does he have all of these classified documents in his bag? In a classroom, for Pete's sake?" asked the agent from the passenger seat, his tone ripened with a mix of frustration, dismay, and shock. He flipped through scores of typed pages followed by various forms of photographs. The agent insisted, "Look at this stuff: 'S.E.A.L.S. (*Synthetic Eco-Elastic Anti-radiation Lycra Skin*), S.H.I.F.T. (*Sensory Hologram Interface For Teleportation*), U.S. Navy Black Sites (*Nautical coordinates and blueprints of two 70-story Big Seascrapers built within the blackest trenches of The Atlantic and Pacific Oceans*), and Nuclear Fallout-free Outdoor Bunkers (*Satellite imagery showing two American-made man-made islands capped with glass dome cities and situated off the coasts of the Falkland Islands and the U.S. Marshall Islands*). What the fuck, man! He should not have any of this. If the Chinese or Russians got their hands on this..." Shaking his head, he complained, "Why, though?"

"It doesn't matter, the why. Even senior members of Congress with the highest security clearances can't look at what you are looking at outside of a S.K.I.F.F. I'm glad we recalled him. I'm glad the Director had the balls to send agents in to close that campus bookstore and confiscate that asshole's book! Now we'll work on his publisher. And I can hear it now: First Amendment rights! First Amendment rights! But fuck our national security that makes sure we all have a First Amendment right, right! Without this asshole, Wynnhurst will have to cancel that class."

"That's a lot of refunds. 350 of them, to be precise."

"They shouldn't have hired him. He's a traitor to N.A.T.O. forces and our country."

His partner closed the classified files on his lap, stacked them neatly together, and placed them below his seat behind his heels. He stared blankly through the windshield as the front of their EFV's forward course tore apart white pillowy cumulus, akin in feature to weightless cotton balls. The agent wondered aloud, "Do you believe Newman was going to give it all up to the Canadians? I mean, that would've been stupid had he done it. They are not only a N.A.T.O. ally but our closest one. Hell, they are the ones who allowed us in to get him today."

"I don't know. Maybe he found a different foreign contact and decided to meet them in Labrador. Meeting them in Ontario or Quebec would've been risky. Of all the provinces in Canada, no one thinks of Labrador. Maybe his foreign contact selected Labrador; we don't know. Maybe being a professor at that obscure little college was a clever ruse to get and pass on our intelligence. I don't know. Maybe he found out that his wife is a mole all this time, and now he's retaliating for money, selling our secrets. Maybe he's pissed at our military objectives. He did say after class that he wouldn't be our next Oppenheimer... Dr. Manhattan... or whatever. That's a stupid thing to say. We're the good guys trying to restore world order. I can't get into the mind of a traitor, sorry."

"When Newman mentioned polysapiens in class today and that kid happened to follow up with that question about Endlings, my heart was in my throat, man."

"Too coincidental for my taste."

"I don't think that Q & A was scripted in any way. The red-head kid was curious, just like with his cell phone on that roof. But our military objectives, there, in that stupid science class, were almost disclosed... Sheesh."

"As much as Newman is dangerous, we need him. His Newman Project and all that intel he stole will help us win the war of the future. The future is unavoidable; he was dead-on to warn his class about that. It's time to wake up these liberal socialist bastards, thinking geopolitical world powers in cold wars won't get hot one day. It won't be good enough to duck under school desks when hypersonic nuclear missiles get to their targets within five minutes. Without the Newman Project and all that it encompasses, America will be defeated, and Americans will face extinction."

His partner swallowed hard at the thought. He whipped around in the passenger seat to check on the professor. A steep compression as long as the black leather backseats themselves, where a person should've been seen to make it that way, proved the INVISO-tarp still worked; not to dismiss the professor's floating brown leather satchel nearest to the floor mats, which was all the agent saw. He faced forward, his focal point the clouds yonder. Grappling with the concept of Americans becoming extinct, he told his partner driving, "I don't think he will betray us. He's an American citizen."

"He'll betray us because he's an American citizen, but not if he's made a father... *and a mother?*"

The agent in the passenger seat turned his attention toward his partner with fearful incredulity. He needed to be certain of what his partner implied and asked, "A polysapien pregnancy? Who will carry the child to term without facing prison time? Bush II's law is still on the books."

"Eons ago, Bush II and General Powell flouted the law when they ordered the invasion of Iraq."

"With that rationale, who's the surrogate?"

"Our mole. His wife."

"Shit!"

"Yep."

"The Director green-lighted the Newman Project..." he said with astonishment, "He does have balls."

The agent driving elaborated on what little he knew, which happened to be enough: "Using Newman's skin cells and his years of successful clinical trials' results, he's now the unsuspecting Dad and Mom of three viable embryos," he confirmed with whimsy in his tone. "Already planted in his wife's womb. Her body hasn't rejected them yet."

"Oh, my God."

The EFV's GPS navigational system stopped their forward momentum abruptly mid-air, and the agents glanced down as they began to descend from the sky into American restricted airspace. 300 feet... 200 feet... 100 feet... The Pentagon's rooftop heliport neared their landing gear's tire tread. Happy to be home, the agents were. Dr. Newman, though, after he had been awakened and debriefed of his new reality, was not so much in a homecoming mood. And he'd become homicidal to show them all.

"...What if we created an individual who was neither male nor female but both male and female? An individual who procreated interchangeably like a man or woman naturally... You aspire to win the wars of the future, which portend nuclear holocaust for sport: What if mutually assured destruction, which will reduce us all to Endlings, could be deemed a victory rather than a defeat? That is to say, what if we created an individual who was born with lungs and gills, and the two organs worked in concert to breathe oxygen and radiation from nuclear fallout? What if we classified such an individual, clearly evolved, as a polysapien, first in that person's name? Imagine it. The Last Man Standing, as it were, post-World War III..."

Former W.P.U. Professor, Liam Newman, Ph.D.,
Geneticist & Bio-Technician
4th September 2034

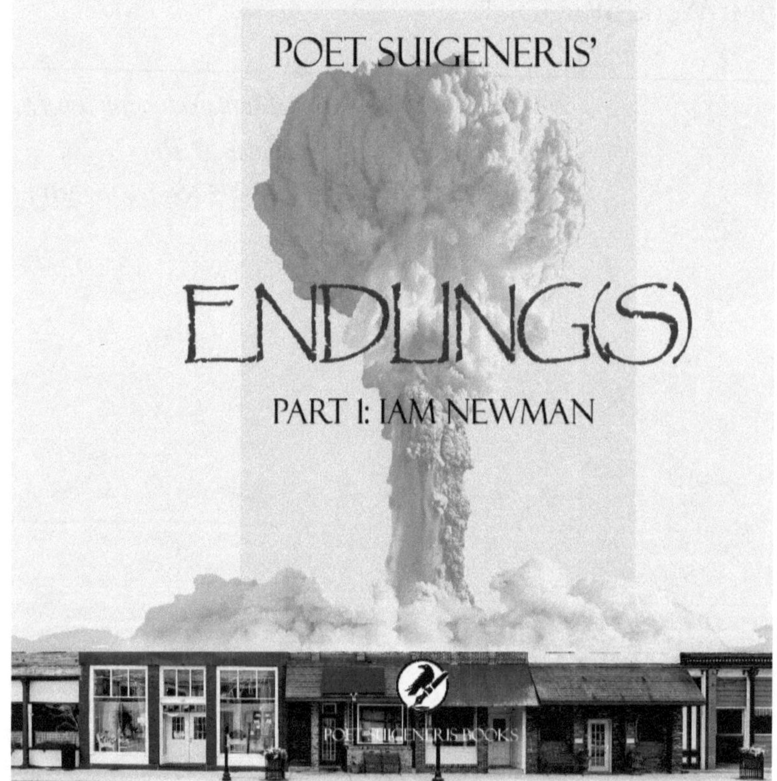
POET SUIGENERIS'
ENDLING(S)
PART I: IAM NEWMAN
POET SUIGENERIS BOOKS

THAT WAS A SNEAK PEEK AT THE NEXT BOOK FROM POET SUIGENERIS…

INTERESTED?

For more information, please make contact by direct message or email:
metapoetica2@gmail.com
www.instagram/poet. .suigeneris.com
YouTube Channel: poet suigeneris